D1561736

CARTER G. WOODSON

RACE, RHETORIC, AND MEDIA SERIES
Davis W. Houck, General Editor

CARTER G. WOODSON

History, the Black Press, and Public Relations

BURNIS R. MORRIS

UNIVERSITY PRESS OF MISSISSIPPI / JACKSON

www.upress.state.ms.us

The University Press of Mississippi is a member of the Association of
American University Presses.

First printing 2017

∞

Library of Congress Cataloging-in-Publication Data

Names: Morris, Burnis Reginald.
Title: Carter G. Woodson : history, the Black press, and public relations /
Burnis R. Morris.
Description: Jackson : University Press of Mississippi, 2017. | Series: Race,
rhetoric, and media series | Includes bibliographical references and index.
Identifiers: LCCN 2017010442 (print) | LCCN 2017011103 (ebook) | ISBN
9781496814074 (cloth : alk. paper) | ISBN 9781496814081 (epub single)
| ISBN 9781496814098 (epub institutional) | ISBN 9781496814104 (pdf
single) | ISBN 9781496814111 (pdf institutional)
Subjects: LCSH: Woodson, Carter Godwin, 1875–1950. | African American
historians—Biography. | Historians—United States—Biography. | African
Americans—Historiography.
Classification: LCC E175.5.W65 M67 2017 (print) |
LCC E175.5.W65 (ebook) | DDC 973/.0496073007202 [B] —dc23
LC record available at https://lccn.loc.gov/2017010442

British Library Cataloging-in-Publication Data available

CARTER G. WOODSON'S ENABLERS IN THE BLACK PRESS, WHO PROVIDED HIM AN UNHERALDED PLATFORM FOR TRUTH, AND ALAN B. GOULD, WHO KEPT THE MEMORY OF DR. WOODSON ALIVE IN WEST VIRGINIA

CONTENTS

ACKNOWLEDGMENTS

THE GENEROSITY OF THREE ORGANIZATIONS SUPPORTED THE RESEARCH from which this book evolved: the John Deaver Drinko Academy's selection of me as a Distinguished John Deaver Drinko Fellow; West Virginia Humanities Council, which awarded me a 2011 fellowship; and Emory University's Manuscript, Archives, and Rare Book Library, which selected me as its Carter G. Woodson Fellow in 2012.

I am also grateful to a crowded list of individual supporters led by historian Alan B. Gould, who was as helpful to me, a journalist, as I postulate journalists were to Dr. Carter G. Woodson, when the newspaper men and women of his day joined the historian's cause and generously supported preservation of black history. To the present project, Gould provided equal amounts of enthusiasm, advice, and appropriate criticism. As executive director of the Drinko Academy, Gould not only delivered the Academy's resources to my project, but for more than three decades he also played a facilitator's role in attempts to keep alive the Woodson connections to Huntington, West Virginia, when he was a dean and provost at Marshall University. He served as an early champion of the committee that preserved Woodson's likeness with a statue there in 1995.

Strong support for this project also came from members and leaders of the Association for the Study of African American Life and History, whose stewardship helped this group, which Woodson founded, reach an impressive milestone—its centennial (1915–2015) and beyond, in large measure as its demanding founder had intended.

I also acknowledge several Woodson relatives who provided insights and documentation about the Woodson family, including his great-nephew

Nelson Bickley and his wife, Ancella, as well as Adrienne Cannon, a distant cousin and African American History and Culture manuscript specialist at the Library of Congress.

Kristin Steele, my former graduate assistant, worked tirelessly on this project's behalf, and my colleagues Charles G. Bailey and Rob Rabe were uncomplaining as sounding boards. For inspiration, I also cite the support of two of my former students, Kayla Queen and Kyle Dyer, who announced their wedding plans to each other using Woodson postage stamps from the 1980s.

Kathleen Bledsoe and other members of the Special Collections staff at the Marshall University Libraries maintained a shelf in my name behind the service desk for several years, and library boss Monica Brooks invented creative ways to circumvent the many obstacles to research during an age of declining library resources.

Andrew Salinas and his colleagues at the Amistad Research Center at Tulane University were not only well prepared for my visit to their campus, but their request for a copy of the newspaper I founded for black students at Ole Miss in the 1970s made Woodson's admonishment—to black editors to preserve copies of their work—a personal issue.

Others who should be identified by name for their support include: Tewodros Abebe, Moorland-Spingarn Research Center, Howard University; Francine Archer, Special Collections and Archives, Johnston Memorial Library, Virginia State University; Emma Barnett, widow of a Woodson cousin; Randall Burkett, African American Collections, Emory University's Manuscripts, Archives, and Rare Book Library; Sylvia Cyrus, Association for the Study of African American Life and History; Beverly Cook, Vivian G. Harsh Research Collection of Afro-American History and Literature, Carter G. Woodson Regional Library in Chicago; Cicero Fain, College of Southern Maryland; Kenneth Hart, businessman, Norfolk, Virginia; Willie James Maiden, architect, Washington, DC; Carmen Manning-Miller, professor and former chair of mass communications, Lincoln University of Pennsylvania; Daryl Michael Scott, Howard University, and former president, Association for the Study of African American Life and History; Fleury Sommers, of Sommers and Associates, Houston, Texas; and my extended family at Marshall University—George Arnold, Woodrow Berry, Nathaniel DeBruin, Renee Denney, Corley Dennison III, Janet Dooley, Terry Hapney, David Harris, Frances Hensley, Dan Hollis, Andre Jones, Josh Lycans, Newatha Meyers, Gayle Ormiston, Jessica Patterson, Don Van Horn, Malcolm Walton, and Sandy York.

I would be remiss if I did not express appreciation to the University Press of Mississippi and Craig Gill, who immediately understood the importance of publishing a book about an overlooked perspective of Carter G. Woodson's work—a side of him that set the stories of black contributions on a path of acceptance by most Americans as HISTORY. I also thank copy editor Robert Burchfield for his contributions and thoroughness.

PREFACE

THE IDEA FOR THIS EXAMINATION OF DR. CARTER G. WOODSON'S USE OF the press and public relations to preserve and promote an accurate record of history evolved by happenstance from a visit to the Underground Railroad Freedom Center in Cincinnati, Ohio, on the national holiday honoring the Rev. Martin Luther King Jr., January 17, 2011. While browsing the museum's gift shop, I purchased a copy of *The Mis-Education of the Negro*, Woodson's best-known book, first published in 1933 and not read by me for several years. It remains, personally, a riveting page-turner after all these years.

The study that evolved after my exit through the gift shop reveals the details and significance of what Woodson hinted at in passing in the foreword to *Mis-Education*—which I, and probably countless other readers, did not comprehend previously. Woodson's brief statement mentioned that the book was based on ideas he had recently expressed in speeches and articles. However, he did not expressly state in that book's foreword that the articles were published in black newspapers or that the newspapers were essential to the build-up of publicity before publication of *The Mis-Education of the Negro* and were central elements in his selling the broader Modern Black History Movement. If I had thought about it at all during a previous reading, I would have presumed that as a scholar the articles to which he alluded had been published in scholarly journals.

Woodson's links to Cincinnati, surprisingly, were extensive, too. The city had figured prominently in his research. The first full-length article published in the scholarly journal he founded, the *Journal of Negro History*, in 1916, was "The Negroes of Cincinnati Prior to the Civil War." Woodson had not yet honed his press scheme and was not publicly advising journalists about how to conduct their affairs, but that article—and others published during the early years of the *Journal of Negro History*—demonstrated uses for the press in research and roles played by white-owned news publications whose files assisted historians in documenting history (simply by preserving their printed editions and making them available to the public, especially to scholars). Woodson would later advocate the same uses and roles for black publications that he had observed about the white press in his research.

Newspaper articles have long held such research value for researchers, but many African Americans and their news publications were often negligent in preserving information Woodson believed would help document their communities' past. Woodson demonstrated how reliable newspapers could be used to help everyone rediscover their history. Eighteen of the sixty-three footnotes Woodson used in the Cincinnati article, for example, involved articles in local and national publications, including the *New York Tribune*, and they helped Woodson document black people's early struggles for equal treatment and education in the Cincinnati public schools. He documented the lives and number of blacks living in Cincinnati in 1840 through examination of editions published by the *Cincinnati Daily Gazette*. Articles published in the *Philanthropist*, an abolitionist newspaper, were used by Woodson to document black achievements and their economic conditions before the Civil War (Woodson, 1916). Recognizing the important role of the black press, Woodson thus challenged black journalists to correct this major weakness—by preserving their published articles to document success of the black experience.

Woodson's press agenda and influences were further revealed after he founded the *Negro History Bulletin* in 1937. The first issue of that publication featured two well-known journalists who had been active in the early abolition movement—William Goodell, a founder of the American Anti-Slavery Society, and Cassius Clay, who moved his abolitionist newspaper from Kentucky to Cincinnati ("Persons and Achievements to Be Remembered in October," 1937). The cover story of the second issue, published in November 1937, featured Robert Gordon, an entrepreneur and former slave ("Robert Gordon a Successful Business Man," 1937) who had been mentioned in "The Negroes of Cincinnati Prior to the Civil War."

Woodson also traveled to Cincinnati, delivering an address with aspirational messages and *Mis-Education of the Negro* themes ("Notes," 1931) two years before the book's publication, and since his death the Association for the Study of African American Life and History, which Woodson established as the Association for the Study of Negro Life and History in 1915, has met twice in Cincinnati, in 1972 and 2009. It is also believed that the first national meeting of black newspaper publishers and editors was called in Cincinnati by P. B. S. Pinchback, a black publisher and former interim governor of Louisiana, in 1875 ("A History of the National Newspaper Publishing Association," 2013).

Having rediscovered these long, lost or forgotten connections, my interest in *The Mis-Education of the Negro* morphed into the analysis found in the following pages. Examined is a rarely explored area of Woodson's career as a historian, journalist, extraordinary newsmaker, and promoter. The results explain how Woodson used his relationship with the black press to build mass appeal and to bolster support for his black history campaign.

PROLOGUE

HISTORIAN CARTER G. WOODSON'S EMPLOYMENT OF THE BLACK PRESS and modern public relations techniques to preserve and popularize black history during the first half of the twentieth century is rediscovered and examined in this study. This rarely examined side of Woodson's career resurrects the lost image of a leading cultural icon who used his celebrity in multiple roles as an opinion journalist, newsmaker, and CEO/publicist of black history to honor a subject whose past was clouded by misinformation and contempt. During his era, 1915–1950, Woodson cultivated and won crucial press support for his Black History Movement. In doing so, he merged his program's interests and the interests of the black newspapers. His cause became their cause, and for present and future generations he became the Father of Negro History (Father of Black History, or Father of African American History).

Woodson paid homage to the generation of black leaders that preceded his ascension. He heard Booker T. Washington speak for the first time in Lexington, Kentucky, in 1903, when Washington was the preeminent leader of Black America. Woodson marveled at Washington's oratory and was spellbound by the prophecy included in a Washington joke about how dutifully blacks were serving whites, even in hell, as he urged blacks to become scientifically trained in order to serve whites more efficiently. The joke was perhaps a shot across the bow aimed at Washington's critics who had accused him of accommodating whites in race relations. Woodson, who said Washington feared blacks might be headed toward serfdom, was still quoting from that Lexington speech in a newspaper article three decades later, when he attributed this more solemn statement to Washington: "Little did I think at that time that I would live long enough to see myself in this veritable hell" (Woodson, 1933j).

Woodson himself provided pessimistic assessments during the early years of what would become his decades-long intervention to alter the course on which African Americans seemed headed without knowledge and appreciation of their past. He even warned a New York audience that "segregation is the next step to extermination" ("Jim Crow," 1928).

Segregation had become slavery's brutal, legal successor. Many blacks, notwithstanding the promise of citizenship rights granted by the US Constitution, simply had little to celebrate politically or economically when Woodson began his quest in 1915 to unleash black potential and self-respect—through a proper education and increased knowledge of their history by all races. For years, black achievements in history had been under siege and/or denied. The conditions in 1915 were dire for many African Americans, and the outlook was gloomy.

Thousands in Chicago during the summer of 1915, including Woodson, observed the fiftieth anniversary of emancipation. The observance at the Illinois National Exposition of Half Century of Negro Freedom and Lincoln Jubilee lasted from August 22, 1915, to September 16, 1915, but the occasion was not entirely joyous, as African Americans were being denied basic rights, and lynching and vigilante justice were rampant. During the post-Reconstruction period and under Jim Crow laws, few blacks held political offices or voted, and business and educational opportunities were restricted. The US Census estimated that illiteracy was 30 percent among blacks, six times the rate for whites, and less than half of black school-age children attended school when Woodson entered the national debate ("National Assessment of Adult Literacy," 1993).

The Great Migration of rural, southern blacks to other sections of the country had begun, with disputed results. The migration, however, would make Woodson's list of the most significant events in African American history (see Table 5.3). The *Chicago Defender* initially encouraged black migration to Chicago, but the *Defender* and the National Negro Press Association would ultimately recommend a more even distribution of the exodus, because of racial tensions and other problems created by migration ("Constructive Programme," 1927).

Black leadership also was in transition in 1915. Booker T. Washington, Woodson's hero, was in decline and would pass from the scene before the year was out. Other able black leaders would surface, but without question no single person possessed Washington's stature and broad appeal—until the rise of the Rev. Martin Luther King Jr. in the 1950s. King's leadership of the civil rights movement arguably would eclipse Washington's influence, but King's entrance was decades away, for he would not be born for another fourteen years. Few people in this period could have envisioned the possibilities of electing a black president, except Ann Dunham, future President Barack Obama's mother, who was born in 1942 and gave birth to Barack in 1961 (Bingham, 2012).

In the meantime, in 1915 an unknown Carter G. Woodson helped fill the leadership role being vacated by Booker T. Washington and introduced himself to a national audience. Woodson, who did not aspire to become a civil rights leader in the post-Washington era, carved out a new area of influence separate from protest. Woodson would use his expertise as a historian and his skills as a journalist and publicist to attack ignorance and inequality. Using historical research to correct mistakes about black history and serving as an advocate for improving education, Woodson launched a public-education program and helped change attitudes about African Americans. Not only had many whites believed blacks had contributed little in history, but many blacks held similar opinions. To achieve success, Woodson leaned heavily on one institution—the weekly newspapers, among the oldest and most powerful organizations in the black community. Because of his frequent attacks on black church leaders, whose organizations also published periodicals, Woodson could not rely solely on church publications to spread his words without filters. An alliance with the general-circulation black press, however, would enable him to affect public opinion among the masses and deliver his messages efficiently (see chapter 4).

Woodson denied being a race leader and discouraged his closest associates from wearing such a label because he felt many so-called race leaders had misled followers. He was a strong supporter of civil rights, but he advocated it separately from his research, drawing strict lines to be followed by associates who assisted him in research. Both Woodson and civil rights advocates were engaged in the same war for black rights and respect, but their campaigns differed in terms of strategies and tactics.

For his version of the war, Woodson shunned protests common among civil rights advocates. He created a public-education campaign about black history to save the black race from extinction. His antidote to racism and low self-esteem among blacks was a crusade against propagandists masquerading as historians and denying black contributions in history, which, because of errors and misinformation, deprived people of all races of an accurate record of their past. If accurate accounts of black lives were missing from history books, then all people, regardless of race, were mis-educated. Woodson's solution involved correcting the record, rediscovering black achievements, and promoting progress through knowledge. As a transformative figure, Woodson sought to change public opinion by seizing moments in newspaper headlines and staging a friendly takeover of the black press on matters of history and culture.

African Americans had been shortchanged. But, while their positions in society were restricted, their newspapers managed to serve community interests and in most cases remained loyal to their readers during these challenging times (the Woodson era, 1915–1950). A few of the newspapers made their owners wealthy and were viable economic units. Other members of the black press, including several of Woodson's relatives, had to maintain their day jobs, sometimes as educators.

The press–black history collaboration that Woodson created and led was timely in journalistic terms and fruitful for both sides. The increased concentration of blacks in urban areas and a rise in literacy and school at- tendance rates brought about increased interest in reading and improved opportunities for the larger black weekly newspapers and enabled them to support their communities and Woodson's cause. On the news and editorial side, the articles and books Woodson produced became raw materials for their weekly editions.

The influence of the black press was expanding just as Woodson was founding the Association for the Study of Negro Life and History (ASNLH) in 1915. Black newspaper efforts were fueled by the desire for African Ameri- cans to be treated as Americans, to confront racial issues, and to improve edu- cational achievement. Educating readers about their past through Woodson helped build their audiences. In the process, the papers made Woodson and his activities newsworthy events. This dynamic evolved as both sides realized the potential impact of the other: the press delivered a larger audience and brought success to Woodson's program, while providing a public-service element for the newspapers as well as substantial content for their news and editorial pages (generated by Woodson) without additional expense to their organizations or Woodson's.

The journalism and public relations aspects of Woodson's program are among the least-explored areas of his career. Discussion of this topic does not suggest that no one previously reported that Woodson wrote for news- papers and promoted history. Woodson's major biographers—Pero Dag- bovie, Jacqueline Goggin, and Sister Anthony Scally—mentioned he wrote newspaper articles and was a promoter of history. Tony Martin, in a Marcus

Garvey biography (*Race First*, 1976), cited Woodson's interest in newspaper writing and the assistance he received from time to time from journalist John E. Bruce. However, the following pages explore black newspapers as collaborators in the promotion and success of Woodson's program. These pages document Woodson serving in several capacities as a conspicuous newsmaker, journalist, and CEO/methodical publicist for black history.

Journalists and historians are not incompatible, as Woodson demonstrated—he was both. Woodson advocated a dispassionate approach to historical research, but objectivity was a relatively new concept in journalism during the early twentieth century, without question younger than Woodson (who was born in 1875). Newspapers began learning the value of limiting their news workers' opinions during the Civil War, when their correspondents transmitted stories over the telegraph, finding it was quicker and cheaper to omit opinions in news stories. The notion of objectivity and fairness began evolving between 1880 and 1900 (Emery, Emery, and Roberts, 2000).

In the public relations world, changing public opinion and behavior, a course Woodson pursued, often requires unconventional tactics, such as the wealthy John D. Rockefeller handing out dimes during harsh economic times in New York and softening his image or, more recently, public service messages showing the startling health effects of smoking. Writing books and making speeches, typical tools in a scholar's arsenal, by themselves do not move public opinion or change behavior. An issue as large and as neglected as African American history required a grand sales job, too, as this study explains.

Carter G. Woodson: History, the Black Press, and Public Relations is a case study of a pioneering historian whose ingenuity and hard work helped him attack a major problem and succeed, with unusual assistance from black newspapers, whose full attention he commanded as they made coverage of him and his work their priority. Remnants of their cooperation are visible today, with succeeding generations of media having assumed ownership of one of Woodson's greatest accomplishments, the annual celebration of black history.

This focus on the public relations aspects of Woodson's strategy and tactics in the selling of history to the masses in no way reduces his many accomplishments, for it should enhance what is already known about Woodson's dedication and commitment. The present study reexamines Woodson's outreach to the newspapers for support and depicts him as he has rarely been seen since the middle of the last century—in a combination of nonacademic roles he played for his cause. Woodson's legacies and other accomplishments,

reported by his biographers and others, remain untarnished, but the following pages provide new insights and a narrative documenting contributions
to Woodson's public-education program based on his methodical use of the
black press and public relations techniques.

The purpose of this book is to explain how Woodson, at the beginning
armed with little more than the power of his intellect and the will and determination to lead a movement, seized opportunities available through the
black newspapers—that helped make his a household name and leveraged
his celebrity—to sell and popularize history.

Many of his followers may be surprised by this characterization of Woodson as something other than a historian, and the journalism and public relations communities likewise may discover a long, lost fraternity member—a
former high-profile celebrity, erstwhile journalist, and publicist who managed to keep press attention focused for nearly thirty-five years on him and
a public-education program that changed the fabric of America. Modern
journalism and modern public relations evolved together, for it should be
noted that during most of the twentieth century, journalism and public relations were usually housed together in departments, schools, and colleges of
journalism and mass communications. Other universities have been known
to combine them in liberal arts and business colleges and with fine arts.
Woodson was a liberal arts dean at Howard University when he made his
strongest statements about the purpose of journalism education.

By the time of his death at age seventy-four in 1950, Woodson's work
in history, journalism, and public relations had already brought dramatic
changes in attitudes about African American history and culture. Generations later, his strategy should be useful to everyone concerned about finding
solutions to the great issues of the day, during any era.

ABOUT NEWSPAPERS IN THIS STUDY

This study is primarily based on an examination of archived documents,
including more than 500 articles encompassing hard-news stories, features,
columns, and editorials that newspapers published by and about Carter G.
Woodson and the Black History Movement, from 1915, when he created the
Association for the Study of Negro Life and History, through 1950. Articles
examined for the most part include those published by the following African American newspapers (with the years of their founding in parenthe-
ses): *Atlanta Daily World* (1928), *Baltimore Afro-American* (1892), *Chicago*

Defender (1905), *Cleveland Call and Post* (1934), *Louisiana Weekly* (1925, New Orleans), *Negro World* (1918–1933, New York), *New York Amsterdam News* (1922), *Norfolk Journal and Guide* (1916, Virginia), *Philadelphia Tribune* (1912), and *Pittsburgh Courier* (1911). The examination also includes the *New York Times* (1851), a white-owned, mainstream daily newspaper that published items about Woodson, sporadically, as did several other newspapers whose articles are cited. The term "mainstream" in this study refers to white daily newspapers. Among African American newspapers, only the *Atlanta Daily World* published daily during part of the period for this study (since 1932). The other papers published weekly editions, sometimes twice weekly.

Many of the newspapers and other publications were accessed through microfilm and other resources in Special Collections at Marshall University Libraries and the Library of Congress; the Amistad Research Center at Tulane University (for access to the *Louisiana Weekly*); and the Public Library of Cincinnati and Hamilton County, University of Cincinnati Library, and Moorland-Spingarn Research Center at Howard University (for access to the *Negro World*). Database services accessed include JSTOR and the ProQuest Historic African American newspaper service available through Marshall and the Library of Congress; and Readex, a division of Newsbank (accessed at Marshall).

The attrition rate for black newspapers was high. For example, of the 144 newspapers for which the Census Bureau reported data in 1944, there were 110 with general circulations. Ninety-seven of the 110 papers were founded between 1920 and 1943. Throughout this period, it was widely believed that the number of black newspapers was 200 to 300. Underreporting of the number of papers by the Census Bureau was possibly caused because many editors and publishers were either not reached by census personnel or the newspapers simply did not report their data.

The newspaper managements printing the articles selected for this study, however, were among the most stable and powerful newspapers in black publishing during this period. Four of the African American newspapers analyzed were in business when Woodson began his movement. All four were still operating when he died. The other six black newspapers used in this study were founded after Woodson's history movement began, and five of the six were still operating when Woodson passed from the scene. As a result, nine of the ten black newspapers in the present study were still publishing at the end of Woodson's life—the exception being the *Negro World*, which shuttered in 1933, after years of decline, following the legal problems of its founder, Marcus Garvey ("Negro Newspapers and Periodicals," 1944). Their stability made these newspapers dominant forces on issues affecting Black America during most of the first half of the twentieth century.

References to the black press and African American press in this study generally mean weekly newspapers—not magazines, which were usually published monthly or quarterly during Woodson's era. Many of the black magazines from this period were church organs, and they were mostly excluded from analysis in these pages, unless they were involved in Woodson's feuds with black preachers. This study primarily focuses on the shorter weekly news cycle of the general-interest newspapers to determine press support for Woodson and his movement.

HOW THIS BOOK IS ORGANIZED

Chapter 1 explains how the stage was set early in Carter G. Woodson's life for his understanding of race, the mis-education, poverty, hard work, and the role and impact of newspapers. His worldview was heavily influenced by his illiterate father. He read newspapers to his father and other illiterates he encountered in the West Virginia coalfields. His father gave him his moral bearing, and the newspapers contributed to his intellectual development and understanding of issues involving politics and economics. These experiences in Appalachia, before his world travels and move to Washington, DC, laid the foundation for the public-education program he later developed for African American history.

Chapter 2 connects newspaper history and Woodson's partnership with the black press, including his merger of the Black History Movement and interests of the black newspapers. They were suitable allies during the period of this study, 1915 to 1950, because of their support for education and other issues and the impact of black migration to urban areas, especially in northern cities, which increased the size of black newspaper markets and made them a mass medium.

Newspaper coverage of Woodson, from his graduation from high school as an unknown through his rise as one of the most significant newsmakers in the black press during his era, is retraced in chapter 3, from Appalachia to Washington, DC, and beyond. Black newspapers defined Woodson as news, making him a national hero and celebrity, assets he used in support of his cause.

As an opinion journalist, Woodson wrote hundreds of newspaper columns on a variety of subjects. Some involved personal feuds. Others involved promotion of books he was publishing through his publishing firm and his history movement through the Association for the Study of Negro Life and History. He also engaged readers on politics and an array of international issues. Chapter 4 explores the themes of the columns for their news and promotional value and provides a rare listing of all of his known newspaper bylines.

The practice of modern public relations during the early twentieth century is reviewed alongside Woodson's publicity activities in chapter 5. Details of Woodson's public-education program and PR style are revealed through his correspondence with Luther P. Jackson, a Virginia State College history professor, collaborator, and fund-raiser for Woodson's cause. Woodson's last known letter was mailed to Jackson and was dated two days before he died in Washington, DC. Woodson's command of public relations methods also is demonstrated through examination of two of his most acclaimed legacies—the *Journal of Negro History* and Negro History Week—in public relations contexts that sought and won press support.

Woodson was not the first black historian, but his research and advocacy were transformational in bringing about recognition of black history and including it within the American way of life. Chapter 6 argues that after Woodson's death, knowledge of his partnership with the press was lost, but black history became so popular (and commercial) that the week he founded to commemorate black contributions in history now takes a month. Mainstream media have taken ownership of Black History Week/Black History Month, amid claims it has been commercialized.

CARTER G. WOODSON

Chapter 1

FINDING HIS BEARINGS

THE NARRATIVE OF DR. CARTER G. WOODSON, HISTORY, THE PRESS, AND
public relations begins far from the glittering spotlight of the media and
political capitals in which he operated. It begins under humble circumstances,
an upbringing through the foundations of life given him by his father, and
lessons a young Woodson learned about the press during his apprenticeship
in the coal mines of Appalachia.

Carter's father, James Henry Woodson, a Civil War veteran, was one
of several former slaves who helped Collis P. Huntington complete the
Chesapeake and Ohio Railroad on the Ohio River, in an area that became
Huntington, West Virginia, in 1870. The elder Woodson used his skills as a
carpenter in contributing to the building of that city, and in 1874 he moved
his family back to Virginia, where his son Carter Godwin Woodson was
born on December 19, 1875, in the New Canton area of Buckingham County.
As one of nine children, Carter would eventually rise from the poverty of
the New Canton area and become the driving force behind an improbable
Black History Movement, begun fifty years after the end of the Civil War
(Woodson, 1932c, 1932h, 1944a).

When he attended school in Virginia, Woodson was an excellent student
who often completed assignments early in class, and with nothing else to do,
he sometimes became a cutup in class. On such occasions, he said he received
whippings at school, and his father greeted him with additional punishments
when he arrived home ("Carter Godwin Woodson," n.d.).

At age twelve, Woodson said, he read a story in a William McGuffey fifth-
grade reader about two boys moving in opposite directions. One boy, Charles
Bullard, studied hard, played hard, was well-liked, and achieved great success

in college and beyond. The other boy, George Jones, did not study before going out to play, was unpopular with playmates, and was unsuccessful in life. The impact of that story with deep religious and moral overtones influenced Woodson to pursue a college education and follow in the footsteps of the hero of that story. He said he wanted to become Charles Bullard ("Carter Godwin Woodson," n.d.).

Woodson identified his uneducated father as the person who gave him his bearing in life, the guiding principles by which he lived. Years later, he recalled the scarcity of material-world assets in his childhood upbringing. He said he went to bed early on Saturday nights to allow his mother to wash and iron his one set of clothing to enable him to attend Sunday school in clean clothes (Woodson, 1932h).

Often during the winter and spring, he had so little to eat that he would leave the family's table and go into the woods in search of persimmons. At other times, he said, he ate "the sour grass that grew early in spring out of the providence of God." Despite the poverty, Woodson said his father "believed that such a life was more honorable than to serve one as a menial" (Woodson, 1932h).

Woodson said he was incorrectly taught, as were many other Americans, from books that blacks were inferior and should accept the status of inferiority. Many blacks from similar circumstances were thus mis-educated, and they championed the cause of segregation in church and state, he said. But such training never corrupted Woodson's thinking because of the influence of his father, the former slave. He explained that his had been a difficult path and struggle to overcome, but he preferred his situation to that of his acquaintances in African American communities who prospered financially in jobs that supported segregation (Woodson, 1932h). Appropriately, one of the first schools named in tribute to Woodson's work while he was alive was the Carter G. Woodson High School in Hopewell, Virginia. After the Virginia schools were desegregated, Woodson High School was the first black school in the state to receive white students ("Virginia Breaks Tradition," 1963).

Woodson said he had been well-grounded in the fundamentals of education by the teachings of two of his uncles in rural Virginia schools. At an early age, he demonstrated a willingness to share what he learned with others, especially reading. He read newspapers to his illiterate father, a reading exercise repeated in countless African American homes throughout the country, in which the contents of the local newspapers—both mainstream white and black—were transferred to those who could not read (Myrdal, 1944). Woodson continued to perform this newspaper-reading ritual with his father even after he was a high-school principal (Goggin, 1993; Scally, 1985). In providing this service, Woodson developed an understanding of the value of using newspapers to inform and educate (Woodson, 1944a).

The influence of newspapers seemed to run through several generations of Woodson's family. John Riddle, an uncle identified as his first teacher in the obituary he published of him, was a schoolteacher and editor of a newspaper in Ohio ("Notes," 1942). Riddle also was a longtime justice of the peace in Buckingham County, and one of the people who came before him was the man who had sent Riddle's mother and two children, one of them Riddle, to the slave market in 1859 (Woodson, 1946b).

Woodson's first cousin Carter H. Barnett was an educator and editor of the *West Virginia Spokesman*, a newspaper published briefly in Huntington. Woodson's younger sister Bessie Woodson Yancey wrote letters to the editor of the *Herald-Advertiser* in Huntington that were published in the 1940s and 1950s, many of them topical and columnlike, in tones similar to her brother's (Morris, 2009).

The foundations for Woodson's understanding and appreciation of the American press, which he would later enlist as a powerful ally in his history-selling program, were laid in these rural Virginia and West Virginia communities between the years following Reconstruction and the close of the nineteenth century.

Woodson also had railroad and coal-mining experiences that helped him recognize and exploit the value and utility of the press in educating readers and shaping public debate. Woodson said he had a six-year apprenticeship in the coalfields and cited the sway of Oliver Jones, a black Civil War veteran who worked in the West Virginia coal mines and operated a tearoom where black miners could relax and unwind. Jones owned a large collection of books and subscribed to newspapers edited and published by black and white journalists.

Woodson said Jones was well-educated, but illiterate, having learned from others who were educated. Woodson's use of newspapers expanded through his association with Jones, who asked Woodson to read to the illiterate miners from his library and compensated him with food (Woodson, 1944a).

Calling a man who could neither read nor write well-educated was not a contradiction from Woodson's perspective. In many of his newspaper columns and especially in his book *The Mis-Education of the Negro*, Woodson expressed disappointment with blacks who had obtained college degrees and who knew little about African American people. He compared them unfavorably to people without college degrees who had not been incorrectly taught. Woodson's respect for the illiterate people he met remained high even after he achieved fame. For instance, his account of the first time he heard Booker T. Washington give a speech in 1903 remembered and complimented an "illiterate, but thinking" elderly black man seated high in the gallery who expressed his enthusiasm for Washington's oratory, even confirming the truthfulness of his assertions about the grim conditions faced by African Americans with the words "'hish yer mouf, boy!'" Woodson thought this man understood Washington's message as well as anyone there, if not more so (Woodson, 1933j). He told that story in a newspaper column thirty years later and used similar experiences to express his belief on other newspaper platforms that many people who never attended college were better educated than those who had degrees.

At Jones's tearoom, Woodson said he was affected by discussions regarding the works of Murat Halstead, an author and former Civil War correspondent, and several other well-known journalists from the late nineteenth century—Samuel Bowles of the *Springfield Republican*, Charles A. Dana of the *New York Sun*, and Whitelaw Reid of the *New York Tribune* (see Table 1.1). He said he learned much from the newspaper accounts of speeches, lectures, and essays about civil service reform, taxation, free trade, the gold standard, silver coinage, business monopolies, economics, politics, and other issues. Woodson thus used the newspapers to provide intellectual stimulation, and they became part of his educational foundation. These newspapers helped shape his worldview (Woodson, 1944a).

The readings and discussions at the tearoom also contributed to Woodson's understanding of race issues. He remembered that the discussions often involved the history of African Americans, "and my interest in penetrating the past of my people was deepened and intensified" (Woodson, 1944a).

The Woodson family returned to West Virginia, roughly two decades following their first residence there, on the recommendation of Robert Woodson, Carter's older brother. Robert had already migrated west. On a return visit with his family back in Virginia, Robert gave such a glowing report of prosperity in West Virginia that all of the Woodson children wanted to return there with him. Their mother, Anne Eliza Woodson, also a former slave, was immediately on board, but their father agreed reluctantly. Woodson did not explain his father's tentativeness, but the family moved to Huntington in 1893. Carter and Robert wrapped up jobs building the railroad from Thurmond to Loup Creek and working as coal miners at Nuttallburg * in Fayette County, West Virginia (Woodson, 1944a).

* Woodson spelled it Nutalburg in the *Negro History Bulletin*, but he probably meant Nuttallburg, named for John Nuttall, a mine owner from England.

Table 1.1: Books and Newspapers Carter G. Woodson Read at Oliver Jones's Tearoom in the 1890s

Books	Authors
The Black Phalanx: A History of the Negro Soldiers of the Wars of the United States 1775–1812, 1861–'65	Joseph T. Wilson and Dudley T. Cornish, American Publishing Company, 1888
Men of Mark: Eminent, Progressive and Rising	William J. Simmons, George M. Rewell & Co., 1887
Black Newspapers	**Editors**
The Pioneer (West Virginia)	Christopher Payne: first black delegate in the West Virginia legislature, founder and editor of the *West Virginia Enterprise*, the *Pioneer*, and *Mountain Eagle*; he was born free but was forced to serve in the Confederate Army (Rice, 2015).
The Richmond Planet (Virginia)	John Mitchell: said to be a "man who would walk into the jaws of death to serve his race" (Planet/John Mitchell Jr., Exhibit).
White Newspapers	**Editors**
Cincinnati Commercial-Gazette	Murat Halstead: author and Civil War correspondent
Cincinnati Enquirer	John R. McClean: also owner of the *Washington Post*; *Cincinnati Enquirer* known for yellow journalism
New York Sun	Charles A. Dana: editor and anti-slavery journalist
New York Tribune	Whitelaw Reid: successor to Horace Greeley as editor and owner of the *New York Tribune* and ambassador to France and Great Britain
Pittsburgh Telegraph	Not much information available about this newspaper. The *Weekly Chronicle Telegraph* was published 1884–1927
Toledo Blade	Robinson Locke: president and editor and son of David Ross Locke, a well-known copperhead journalist (Robinson Locke, n. d).
Springfield Republican	Samuel Bowles Jr.: known for fairness and covering all sides (Newspapers, 1775–1860, n. d.)
Louisville Courier-Journal	Henry Watterson: influential member of Congress, winner of the Pulitzer Prize for editorial writing in 1918

Sources: Developed from Carter G. Woodson, "My Recollections of Veterans of the Civil War" (Woodson, 1944a), and other sources cited above.

In Huntington, Woodson enrolled in 1895 at Douglass High School. He missed many classes because he was also working. He studied Virgil and Caesar on his own ("Carter Godwin Woodson," n.d.). The school, all-black, was named in honor of Frederick Douglass, a former slave, diplomat, and journalist. The Douglass School offered a two-year high school program when Woodson was a student, and he completed the course requirements in half the time, graduating in a class with one other student in 1896 (*Huntington Advertiser*, 1896). The graduation requirement was raised to four years in 1899 (Gould, 1985).

Although it did not hurt him scholastically, Woodson's sporadic school attendance before (and during his) Douglass School years was not unique among African Americans living in the South before the early twentieth century, especially those residing in farming communities, where educational opportunities were limited. Many states provided insufficient access to schools for black students after the Civil War, and no US Census report until 1920 showed a majority of blacks of school age (53.5 per 100) attending school. School attendance for African Americans living in West Virginia after the war was further suppressed by the fact that the black population was much smaller than that found in most former slaveholding states and the white leadership's insistence on keeping the races apart, which meant blacks often went without schooling if their numbers did not meet minimum population requirements for designating schools. In a report on the history of education for West Virginia's black population, written at the behest of the president of the West Virginia Collegiate Institute, Woodson described the school year as four months in West Virginia schools through the 1890s. In some cases, blacks shared school facilities with whites, but the classes were not integrated because white students would attend classes from September to Christmas, after which blacks would occupy the facilities (Woodson, 1922).

Following graduation from Douglass, Woodson pursued his goals for college when he studied briefly at Berea College in Kentucky and at Lincoln University in Pennsylvania, which is considered the first degree-granting college for African Americans ("History," n.d.), but he left college to accept a high school teaching job in Winona, in Fayette County, West Virginia. While there, he was also a Sunday school teacher and president of the board of deacons of the First Baptist Church in Winona. He also returned to Huntington as principal of Douglass (1900–1903)—having worked initially in Winona and Huntington without a teaching certificate, which he received in 1901 (Logan, 1973).

Woodson eventually received a BL degree from Berea College in 1903 (Logan, 1973), during an interracial period, before the Kentucky legislature outlawed such contact between blacks and whites in 1904. Berea was founded by abolitionists on land donated by Cassius Clay, publisher of a newspaper, the *True American*, which supported gradual emancipation. The college was closed to blacks until the 1950s ("Berea College," n.d.; "Personalities," n.d.).

Several reports show different dates about Woodson's formal education, but Logan's appears to be the most persuasive because of its documentation. In an article, he cited letters and reproduced documents verifying the dates used here. Woodson's bachelor's and master's degrees in history from the University of Chicago were awarded in 1908, and his PhD in history at Harvard was conferred in 1912, three years after he completed the required courses for the degree (Logan, 1973). W. E. B. Du Bois (in 1895) and Woodson were the first two African Americans to earn doctoral degrees in history at Harvard. He is believed to be the first child of former slaves to receive a doctorate in history from any institution (Goggin, 2014). He also studied at the Sorbonne in Paris. Woodson's advanced studies and family background enhanced his unique perspective regarding slavery and history, which would later influence other scholars to consider slavery from the slave's point of view (Goggin, 1983, 1993).

Woodson never forgot his roots. He used them as resources in his research and writings, referring often to his upbringing and reminiscing about the teachings of his father and his parents' stories about their experiences as former slaves. He rarely criticized West Virginia, parts of which had been hostile to secession and which was separated in 1863 from Virginia—one exception being his complaint in his historical study of the state's African American schools and how West Virginia leaders chose to maintain segregation (Woodson, 1922). On the other hand, he was sometimes openly dismissive of his native state, having written his dissertation, "The Disruption in Virginia," about its secession.

His sarcasm was demonstrated on the occasion when he was the main speaker at the dedication of a shrine honoring Booker T. Washington in 1932. The speech, covered by the *New York Times* and other newspapers, was delivered in Malden, near Charleston, West Virginia. The newspaper reported Woodson declaring that the state of West Virginia was lucky that Washington had settled there, and Washington was lucky in growing up in a state with more freedom than Virginia offered ("Booker Washington," 1932). In showcasing his humor, Woodson glossed over the fact that West Virginia was part of Virginia when Washington was born.

Woodson's perspective on West Virginia seemed to be shared by Kelly Miller, a Howard University professor, newspaper columnist, and occasional Woodson adversary, who embarked on a well-publicized 10,000-mile tour of America's heartland in 1920 and had similar positive words for West Virginia.

In commenting on the leg of the journey that took him through Wheeling, West Virginia, Miller observed good race relations in that city. Despite segregation, Miller noted that the schools were administered fairly for blacks and whites (Jones, 2011).

By 1915, induced by omission and mistreatment of blacks in textbooks and elsewhere, Woodson was in a position to start bringing about change—ultimately writing more than a dozen books and hundreds of articles; creating an organization, the Association for the Study of Negro Life and History, that continues to carry out his wishes; establishing the *Journal of Negro History* (1916), and a magazine designed especially for teachers and students, the *Negro History Bulletin* (1937); creating his own book publishing company, Associated Publishers; establishing Negro History Week in 1926, later becoming Black History Month in 1976. Woodson's will bequeathed $500 to a brother and sister who were alive at the time of his death, but the remainder of his estate was left to ASNLH, among the conditions being that the *Journal of Negro History* should bear his name as founder as well as his suggestions for its editorial board ("Woodson Will," 1934).

Woodson served a year as dean at Howard University, a tenure cut short by a clash with Howard's president, prompting him to accept another job as dean at West Virginia Collegiate Institute in 1920 (now West Virginia State University). He returned to Washington, DC, in 1922, having performed his last duties as an employee of a college or university, but he continued to speak out on education issues through the remainder of his life, as many of his most important contributions to education (such as Negro History Week, *The Mis-Education of the Negro*, and the *Negro History Bulletin*) would come after he left these institutions. Fluent both in Spanish and French, Woodson traveled to Europe for research purposes during the Great Depression, and he did not seem to slow down until the 1940s.

Woodson did not publish an autobiography, despite owning a publishing company. It is possible he thought as a historian it was too soon to assess his own long-term impact. However, he did show signs of wanting to be remembered for his achievements through his will, as founder of the *Journal of Negro History*. He also included discussion of his work, along with other black achievers, in publishing *The Negro in Our History* in 1922 and in various newspaper columns over the years (Woodson, 1936a). The most plausible reason for not publishing an autobiography, however, is that he did not want to write one.

Still, Woodson's attitude about jumping the gun in assessing historical impact could be found in his writings advising journalists about their practices and complaining about the press's handling of trivial matters, which, in his view, would interrupt their responsibilities to preserve black history and document achievements. He was outraged by the salacious side of newspapers that produced stories about a black congressman having lunch with a woman at the Capitol. In this sensational press environment, Woodson did not contribute much of his personal story for press scrutiny—carefully avoiding tabloid journalism, unless it suited his terms (Woodson, 1934).

To be sure, details about the history movement are available through his Library of Congress papers, newspaper columns, and the works of Dagbovie, Goggin, Scally, Scott, and other scholars. However, an autobiography or authorized biography could have avoided much of the misinformation and errors of fact about Woodson—including such basic information as when and where he attended school and when and where he worked in the coal mines. Some mistakes, no doubt, have to do with followers and people who knew Woodson well, failing to conduct due diligence. For instance, a photograph of Niagara Movement participants printed in an article about W. E. B. Du Bois in the *Negro History Bulletin* incorrectly identified Woodson, who was neither pictured in the photograph nor a participant in the group that met in Canada as a forerunner to the NAACP (Aptheker, 1969).

Even Woodson's obituary published in the *Journal of Negro History* incorrectly listed his survivors, and it was written by his immediate successor and former associate, Rayford W. Logan, who signed it using initials, as Woodson frequently did (R.W.L., 1950). Actually, Woodson's surviving sister should have been listed as Bessie Woodson Yancey, and her grandson, whose college tuition was paid by Woodson, was Nelson Bickley, Woodson's great-nephew (A. R. Bickley, correspondence to author, October 20, 2013).

An autobiography also might have cleared up what he thought of Booker T. Washington's program for educating blacks and whose work Woodson praised in his articles and public speeches, even though the system of education Woodson was proposing seemed to go well beyond Washington's advocacy of training blacks for manual labor.

The absence of a book-length personal story written by Woodson, however, should not suggest that Woodson did not tell his own story. In fact, his books, journal articles, and hundreds of newspaper columns—all taken together—comprise at least a partial autobiography, for often embedded among his commentaries about contributions of African Americans in history, preservation of records, and issues of the day are some of Woodson's most personal memories, just not the kind for tabloid interest. For example, he provided a stark view of the abject poverty in his background in an article complaining about some blacks who had lost their way (Woodson, 1932h).

Woodson maintained an image of all work and no play—his Spartan lifestyle rarely disputed—which made him a sympathetic figure in the press. Years after his death a few of his friends suggested publicly that he might have had a relaxed, private life away from the public's view. Lois Mailou Jones, whom Woodson had employed as an illustrator for books and the *Negro History Bulletin*, recalled Woodson's visit to her Paris studio in the 1930s and his invitation to dine at the legendary Maxim's restaurant, telling her it was his restaurant of choice whenever he visited Paris. Jones was surprised he knew such a place. Charles H. Thompson and his wife were similarly surprised when they encountered Woodson on a stroll on the Place de la Concorde in Paris in 1935 (Association for the Study of African American Life and History, 1990).

W. E. B. Du Bois expressed yet another view that was in partial conflict with Woodson's media image and mystique. The *Afro-American* quoted Du Bois, saying he knew Woodson for more than forty years; he had few close friends; he cared little about sports, smoking, or drinking; and he was an overeater ("What Dr. Du Bois Said," 1950). The Du Bois statement was roundly attacked and disputed by Woodson's friends in the press ("Du Bois," 1950). However, there had been concerns about Woodson's health among his friends and journalists since the 1920s (see chapter 2). Just months before Woodson's death, Edwin B. Henderson added a note to the bottom of a letter discussing promotion of publication of a revision of his sports book. He wrote Woodson: "I hope you keep up with yourself in terms of health during the coming year. You ought to live one or more decades longer with care and my good wishes" (Henderson, 1949).

Some forty years later, Willie Leanna Miles, a Woodson employee from 1943 to his death in 1950 at both his publishing company and ASNLH, wrote an essay about Woodson that was more consistent with his public persona than Du Bois's description. Miles's portrait of Woodson was that of a simple man-of-the-people, the image Woodson had cultivated in the press for nearly thirty-five years. She further remembered him as an accomplished storyteller who produced an endless supply of jokes like a chain smoker. Miles said Woodson seemed to be a lonely man who frequently dined at the Union train station and Phyllis Wheatley branch of the YWCA in Washington. The next day he would tell the staff about his "delectable meal." She said Woodson "had penetrating eyes, thin lips and a very rigid posture. He was light skinned, stood about 5 feet 8 inches tall, wore a size 10 shoe," and weighed about 175 pounds (Miles, 1991).

Adrienne Cannon's great-grandmother Sallie Woodson was the first cousin of Woodson's father. Cannon, African American History and Culture manuscript specialist at the Library of Congress, said her mother told of meeting Woodson in the late 1930s or early 1940s when he returned to New Canton and visited the home of her aunt Emma Toney during a summer family reunion.

"My mother distinctly recalled gathering around the piano in Aunt Emma's home with other family members, singing church songs and popular songs," Cannon said. "Woodson sat at the piano singing along, simply blending in. No fuss was made about him. My mother distinctly recalled Woodson as a small man with an unusually erect posture that mirrored the stiff white collar of his shirt." He encouraged her to work hard in school and follow her dream after she told him of her interest in traveling to the places she read about in *National Geographic* magazine. She became a travel agent (Adrienne Cannon, correspondence to author, September 30, 2013).

Nelson Bickley also remembered Woodson for his brief, formal visits with him and his family in Huntington. Bickley, though saddened by his great-uncle's death, was relieved when he arrived for Woodson's funeral in Washington, DC, to notice that his college grades were on his desk and had been opened, suggesting Woodson died knowing Bickley had turned his life around after a struggle (Morris, 2012).

OTHER EARLY BLACK HISTORIANS

Woodson was not the first African American historian, and he never made such a claim. His writings pay homage to William C. Nell, William Wells Brown, and George Washington Williams—nineteenth-century writers Woodson identified as the first to write African American history, despite limitations, which he described as their lack of training in scientific research (Woodson, 1928b). The inaugural issue of the *Journal of Negro History* praised the work of Booker T. Washington, describing his book *The Story of the Negro: The Rise of the Race from Slavery* as "one of the first successful efforts to give the Negro a larger place in history" ("Notes," 1916).

Others made contributions to the preservation of black history during the Woodson era, and he acknowledged many of their accomplishments.

Several of them served on ASNLH's Executive Council—including Monroe Work, a sociologist and founder of the department of records and research at Tuskegee Institute, and Woodson's associates Charles H. Wesley, John Hope Franklin, and Rayford W. Logan.

The *Journal of Negro History* paid tribute to Arturo Schomburg, whose collections are part of the Schomburg Center for Research in Black Culture at the New York Public Library. Schomburg was an assistant editor of the *Journal*, and its obituary of him said, "He was one of the most distinguished bibliophiles of his day" ("Notes," 1938). Schomburg, a cofounder of the Negro Society for Historical Research, an organization that predated ASNLH, apparently had viewed Woodson's work as that of a rival early in the launch of Woodson's program. When Woodson began publishing the *Journal of Negro History* in 1916, Schomburg reportedly responded that the Woodson group was "stealing our thunder in which we are pioneer" (Martin, 1976).

John E. Bruce, a member of the American Negro Academy and founder of the Negro Historical Society of Brooklyn, also was recognized by the *Journal of Negro History*. Bruce's obituary said he had been one of the first of the *Journal*'s subscribers and a life member of ASNLH ("Notes," 1924). Bruce also was a journalist who wrote for more than twenty newspapers and magazines, and several of his articles were used to publicize Woodson's history projects (Martin, 1976).

As the first African American to earn a doctorate in history at Harvard, W. E. B. Du Bois's work as a historian also deserves attention. He served as an occasional surrogate for Woodson during some Negro History Week events ("Notes," 1931). However, the works of Brown, Bruce, Du Bois, Schomburg, Washington, and Williams did not produce the Modern Black History Movement. Nothing they accomplished could be termed a movement before Woodson and his collaborators.

Woodson scholars tend to date the start of the Black History Movement with the creation of the Association for the Study of Negro Life and History—after he attended the Illinois National Exposition of Half Century of Negro Freedom and Lincoln Jubilee. With three associates, he founded ASNLH on September 9, 1915, in Chicago, and incorporated the organization on October 2, 1915, in Washington, DC. In Washington, he might have been the best-prepared leader among his contemporaries (Logan, 1973). Woodson's activities through the association became the engine of the Black History Movement and efforts to restore African Americans to their rightful place in the history books ("ASALH Timeline," n.d.).

The people who knew Woodson and recalled his life, as well as those who understood him from their studies, rarely mentioned his journalism and public relations methods, although they described him as a promoter. However, Woodson's use of the press and public relations methods, which the present study documents, predates the launch of his history program by several months, beginning with a *New York Times* review of his book *The Education of the Negro Prior to 1861* (1915) and public appearances in support of the book.

Chapter 2

ENLISTING THE PRESS

CARTER G. WOODSON WAS IN GOOD COMPANY AS A LEADER WHO USED the press to support a cause. Before and since Woodson, black leaders and their allies have waged battles on behalf of African Americans who used public-education methods through alliances with the mass media—sometimes testing the limits of freedom of the press in America. For example, the struggles for black rights and journalists' rights to free speech were conjoined during the abolition movement, during which Elijah Lovejoy was killed and his newspaper destroyed by a mob protesting his freedom to oppose slavery. He is considered the first American journalist to die for freedom of the press in opposing slavery, and his martyrdom became a motto for the American Anti-Slavery Society (Folkerts and Teeter, 2002).

William Lloyd Garrison and Frederick Douglass, two other giants of the nineteenth century, also employed their newspapers as tools in fighting slavery and exposing its horrors. Ida B. Wells, who lost her Memphis newspaper to a mob when she crusaded against lynching, continued her crusade for years in other newspapers. Emmett J. Scott, a journalist and former Booker T. Washington aide, was employed as a special assistant to the secretary of war to encourage black press support for World War I. The *Pittsburgh Courier* encouraged Major League Baseball to recruit black players and served as a support system for Jackie Robinson, the first black player in the Big Leagues (Togneri, 2015). *Jet Magazine*'s coverage of the Emmett Till case, including photographs of Till's mutilated body, galvanized awareness of violence against African Americans into the national conscience in the 1950s. Dan Rather, the former CBS television news anchor, said Martin Luther King Jr. pulled him aside in the 1960s with a plea for journalists to report truthfully what was happening in the civil rights movement ("Media and Civil Rights Movement," 1998).

During the early twentieth century, Woodson began putting his own stamp on history through his books, lectures, pamphlets, and the press. He educated black journalists about history and their role in it, as he appealed to their shared mission and elicited their support. The black press was counted among his earliest converts, and his close association with the press helped him reach important milestones. The newspapers' use of his information (publicity) helped make Woodson one of the major black figures of his time.

HISTORICAL PERSPECTIVES OF THE PRESS

Woodson's use of newspapers in promotions was not anathema to the industry. Historically, a wall has separated newsrooms from advertising, but most news organizations do not shy away from promotions to build circulation and readership. In 1889, the *New York World* sent Nellie Bly around the world as a promotion, and later "Yellow Journalism" was used to promote newspapers in competition, especially during the Spanish-American War (Emery, Emery, and Roberts, 2000). Even in the twenty-first century, newsrooms seem to embrace promotions for their own survival ("Future of *The New York Times*," 2015).

The concept of newspapers as agents of change, truth, information, and education, as Woodson and many members of the press advocated, is grounded in the early history of the country and the beginning of American journalism. *Public Occurrences: Both Foreign and Domestic* is widely regarded as America's first newspaper, but it was banned after its first issue in 1690 because it printed information without permission, making the *Boston News-letter* the first US newspaper to print regularly with service to its readers, beginning in 1704. Among the most celebrated journalists of the eighteenth century was John Peter Zenger, who dared to print the truth during the Colonial period and survived prosecution before truth was a recognized defense in American libel cases (Emery, Emery, and Roberts, 2000).

In their more than 300-year history, US newspapers have played active roles in the lives of their readers. The earliest American publication known to acknowledge newspapers' roles in education was Massachusetts's *Portland Eastern Herald*, which printed this statement on June 8, 1795: "Much has been said and written on the utility of newspapers, but one principal advantage that might be derived from these publications has been neglected;

we mean that of reading them in schools, and by the children in families"
(Sullivan, 2001).

Members of the nation's press tend not to be just supporters of education. They represent diverse interests. Benjamin Franklin is known in most
history books as an inventor/scientist and one of the nation's founders;
however, in journalism history books, Franklin is also known as a businessman, writer (Silas Dogood), and printer. Another of the nation's founders,
Alexander Hamilton, was secretary of the treasury and founder of the *New
York Evening Post*.

Newspapers and their key players also have often been heavily involved
in political activities. Henry J. Raymond, a founder of the *New York Times*
in 1851, was a journalist-politician who headed Abraham Lincoln's reelection
campaign and the Republican National Committee (Emery, Emery, and
Roberts, 2000). Abolitionist newspapers such as the *Liberator* and *North Star*
led the fight against slavery, and Horace Greeley, editor of the *New York Tribune* who advised President Lincoln in an editorial to confiscate property of
the Confederate states and free the slaves ("The Prayer of Twenty Millions,"
1862), was a presidential nominee in 1868. Newspaper giants Joseph Pulitzer
and William Randolph Hearst both served stints in Congress. Henry W.
Grady, an editor and part owner of the *Atlanta Constitution*, sold the nation
on ideas of a New South following the Civil War. The relationship between
newspapers and political interests that supported them was waning after
the Civil War, but two Ohio newspaper publishers, James Cox and Warren
Harding, were the major political parties' nominees for president in 1920.
Cox's running mate, Franklin D. Roosevelt, also had journalism ties as a
former editor of the *Harvard Crimson*. Most news organizations separated
from political interests in their news columns when it became profession-
ally advantageous, especially as rising revenues from advertising allowed
newspapers to be more independent of political interests overall during the
new century (Petrova, 2011).

African Americans would have to wait at least until 1827 (thirty-two
years after the *Portland Eastern Herald*'s statement) for the start of a black
publication that would inform, educate, and provide other support services.
Black newspapers were limited, initially, by slavery, discrimination, and much
higher rates of illiteracy among their core markets.

During Woodson's era, black newspaper reporters and editors usually
were not dispassionate in their presentation of the news involving him, often
displaying little objectivity in their coverage. The black newspapers in this
study cheered on Woodson, but a careful reader of the mainstream white

press during the Woodson era would notice the black press was no less objective in coverage of African American communities than their white counterparts were about coverage of a segregated America. With few exceptions, the mainstream press accepted and often defended racism; the black press aggressively fought it. In the 1950s, the American Society of Newspaper Editors got its first black member, Robert Sengstacke, the nephew who succeeded Robert Abbott as head of the *Chicago Defender*.

Newspapers obtain their freedom from the US Constitution and the American people, and the black newspapers during the period of this study appeared to be patriotic, fervently showing African Americans as American citizens and strongly supporting strict interpretations of sections of the Constitution that were supposed to ensure freedom and equality under the law for all Americans. The mainstream white press, on the other hand, rarely supported such interpretations of rights for black Americans, much like their readers. They were slow to the scene in covering the civil rights movement, too, one of the biggest stories of the century (Roberts and Kilbanoff, 2007).

Samuel E. Cornish and John B. Russwurm founded the first black newspaper, *Freedom's Journal*, in 1827 for the purpose of having black people accurately represent their own concerns—speaking for themselves, telling their own stories, providing the kind of documentation of their own lives that Woodson would begin advocating early in the next century (*Freedom's Journal*, 1827). Russwurm also was significant in the history of higher education. He has been widely identified as the first African American to graduate from an American college, Bowdoin, in 1826, an event that establishes a direct association between higher education and black newspapers.

Freedom's Journal was the first of 2,700 black newspapers identified by Pride's register of newspapers founded between 1827 and 1950 (Pride, 1950). It has been argued that *Freedom's Journal* was as much the first black magazine as the first black newspaper because its content was closer to that of magazines than newspapers. It had little current news, and its articles, one researcher observed, were the kind rarely associated with newspapers—such as "The Mutability of Human Affairs," "Memoirs of Captain Paul Cuffe," and "Ambition, or the Rise of Pope Sextus V" (Johnson, 1928).

Most of the early black newspapers had short life spans. *Freedom's Journal* disappeared after 1830, but as many as two dozen black newspapers were published before the Civil War, including the *North Star*, edited by Frederick Douglass, the statesman and abolitionist, perhaps the nineteenth century's most famous black journalist.

Besides Douglass, who was one of the men Woodson honored with the creation of Negro History Week, the other leading black proponents of fairness and equality tended also to have interests in journalism. Booker T. Washington, the educator, held part ownership and influence in several papers; W. E. B. Du Bois, an NAACP cofounder and newspaper columnist who began writing for newspapers while a high school student (Aptheker, 1969), was editor of the NAACP's *Crisis*, one of the most influential publications in civil rights and politics during the first half of the twentieth century; and Marcus Garvey, the early twentieth-century leader and founder of the Universal Negro Improvement Association, controlled the *Negro World* and other newspapers in several countries before his deportation. George Washington Williams, who wrote what many regard as the first book of African American history (*History of the Negro Race, 1619 to 1880*), also mixed politics and history as a journalist. Williams was the first black member of the Ohio House of Representatives and later served as a US diplomat.

The basic philosophy of the black press changed little since the founding of *Freedom's Journal*, it has been argued, because the goals of black journalists involve delivering messages to readers and letting the white world know that black people are humans who deserve fair treatment (Simmons, 1998). That argument withstands scrutiny only at a simplistic level of analyzing journalism and the evolution of black newspapers from the early days of their existence—when they could be defined by their opposition to slavery and discrimination, which hampered their operators' progress as both journalists and proprietors. However, the members of the black press have not been that simple to define or describe as static over time, even if one separates the editorial philosophy of their institutions from the bravery of their workers. Black newspapers did fight slavery and discrimination, but they were so much more, as many analysts have discovered.

Black editors tended to publish newspapers in the public's interest and for social betterment (Yeuell, 1928), and from their earliest days their publications were concerned with ending slavery, followed by periods of battling the remnants of slavery and supporting black Constitutional rights (Simmons, 1998). Many of the newspapers also supported uplift, vindication, and a socialization function. Woodson, too, was included among black leaders with a race-vindication theme (Franklin and Collier-Thomas, 2002).

Often these activists with journalistic enterprises commingled the fervor of their causes with their journalism. For instance, as commencement speaker at Case Western College in 1854, Douglass used his speech, "The Claims of the Negro Ethnologically Considered," to attack the *Examiner*, a white Richmond, Virginia, newspaper that printed an article using science to defend racism (Douglass, 1854). Douglass demanded truth, as would Du Bois, Woodson, and members of the black press who followed him in similar roles. Washington, holding ownership interests in the *Colored American* and *New York Age*, was accused of subsidizing various publications to silence his critics, particularly those who accused him of accommodating white racism, but he is remembered today for his devotion to black education, too (Meier, 1953). Black newspapers of the first half of the twentieth century, the period covered by this study, pursued truth, rights to education opportunities, a better life, and other public-interest issues, during a period of open hostility to African Americans.

Well into the Black History Movement, Rayford W. Logan, a Woodson protégé, argued that the black press provided better information about African Americans than was available elsewhere, but he expressed concerns about publicity, saying that the black press had glorified black athletes (Logan, 1940). The black press was said to exert "the most powerful educational influence on adult [N]egroes that can be found" (Lawson, 1945), and was regarded as special-interest and supplemental (Wilkerson, 1947), because black consumers also read mainstream white publications, which did not cover specific news of interest to blacks—consistent with other descriptions of the black press as serving primarily as news sources about events occurring in the "Negro World" (Bayton and Bell, 1951). The black press also was called the "most effective communication channel leading directly to the Negro people" and a "publicity medium" (Wilkerson, 1947). Garvey's *Negro World* argued that the black press should be allies of education and complained bitterly about sensationalism ("Variety Is the Spice of Life," 1931).

Gunnar Myrdal, in a landmark study of race in America, concluded the black press was so intertwined with and supportive of the black community it could not be bought. Myrdal added, "Practically all Negroes who can read are exposed to the influence of the Negro press at least some of the time" (Myrdal, 1944).

Fortune magazine, the business publication, took note of the role of the black press and sent Woodson advance proofs of its analysis. "Chief concern of the Negro press is Negro progress, with editorial policy covering a wide range of attitudes, Fortune finds, after examining data collected by the newspaper analyst, James S. Twohey," the letter accompanying the proofs stated (Fisher, 1945).

So influential was the reputation of the black press as an institution that many observers of this period argued that few organizers of cultural or political movements had any hopes of succeeding without its cooperation. Woodson accepted this view of a powerful press, and the newspapers accepted his understanding of history. Their embrace helped make Woodson a celebrity as he led the charge, armed with the power of his intellect, his father's guiding principles, and the will and determination to succeed.

A powerful black press holding sway over readers was presumed during the Woodson period, but the belief that the media tell their consumers what to think lost ground during the late twentieth century. Many media research studies now focus on agenda-setting, newsworthiness, framing, and other aspects of media power (McCombs and Shaw, 1993; Gitlin, 1980). Agenda-setting theory is a major focus of public relations practitioners who are concerned with influencing the media and the public. In fact, the Public Relations Society of America counsels candidates studying for its accreditation examination that the agenda-setting process is an interplay among the media, the public, and policy makers and not the linear process of early research about setting the public agenda ("Study Guide," 2010).

Recent studies continue to show black newspapers performing traditional support roles for black communities. A study of the *Chicago Defender* found it promoted a pattern of African American advocacy (Strother, 1978). A study of Hurricane Katrina coverage by the *Chicago Defender, Louisiana Weekly,* and *Amsterdam News* suggested these papers were continuing their traditional roles for uplift and advocacy (Dolan, Sonnett, and Johnson, 2009). Another study suggested black newspaper readers depend on black newspapers for health-related information and trust black newspapers for cancer information more than they trust general media (Len-Rios, Cohen, and Caburnay, 2010).

WOODSON'S ASSESSMENT OF THE PRESS

Woodson repeatedly demonstrated his keen awareness of the role of newspapers during the period of this study and no less so than on the occasions when he reviewed a history of the *New York Tribune* under editor Horace Greeley (Woodson, 1937b), or when he published obituaries of other journalists ("Robert Sengstacke Abbott," 1940; Woodson, 1950a).

He expressed admiration for the black press and identified several journalism heroes: Frederick Douglass, whom he called "the most influential editor among Negroes"; Robert Abbott, founder of the *Chicago Defender*; and John B. Russwurm and Samuel E. Cornish, founders of *Freedom's Journal*

(Woodson, 1928b). He applauded the black press for reporting African American concerns and exposing the lynching of blacks, which he reported as 2,522 killed from 1885 to 1918 (Woodson, 1922).

Woodson's praise for journalists did not often extend to the white press, whose policies mostly avoided coverage of black communities and their concerns, except during Negro History Week observances. Several black newspapers, on the other hand, won Woodson's admiration because they filled the void left by white newspapers and covered many facets of black life. "Seeing this opportunity," Woodson observed, "the Negro press displayed race wrongs, race protest, race progress, and race aspiration" (Woodson, 1922).

Woodson promoted and encouraged the black press. Praising Abbott's work in the 1920s, as the *Journal of Negro History* would state later in an obituary of him, Woodson said Abbott had made his newspaper one of the best weeklies in the world—a restatement of the *Defender's* masthead, which claimed to be "The World's Greatest Weekly," its version of the *Chicago Tribune's* self-proclamation as "The World's Greatest Newspaper" (Woodson, 1922).

Woodson reevaluated the press in the 1930s, and he still was critical of white newspapers for ignoring black news. He objected to southern blacks cooperating with white newspapers to produce "star-marked Negro editions" about black news—in segregated versions—that white readers would not see. He again praised black newspapers, saying they connect leaders within communities and play up news about black interests. "Years ago when one wanted to reach Negroes he approached their preachers," Woodson said, "but now the preachers appeal to the newspapers" (Woodson, 1969).

As an educator and student of newspapers, Woodson had strong views about journalism by the time he rose to positions of influence and sought support from the press in Washington, DC. Many of the skills required for editing two history magazines—such as appealing to reader interests, acquiring articles, and dealing with printers and deadlines—also are necessary for editing newspapers. Woodson clearly understood newspapers as businesses and their editorial models, which he discussed on numerous occasions in books and articles. In 1920 in the *Howard University Record*, he argued that "journalism is as practical as carpentry, but requires a foundation in education of the highest sort" (Woodson, 1920).

Woodson lectured journalists at black newspapers about their responsibilities for documenting the accomplishments of achievers in their communities. Their newspapers made him the people's historian—his messages delivered, often unfiltered. Black newspapers amplified the cause and served as conduits for the public-education program. Woodson's views of history and education were widely disseminated by the newspapers, and journalistic cooperation and persistence, along with Woodson's prodding, proved a winning formula.

Woodson, however, was concerned that journalism education was falling short of the ideal education he was proposing in that Howard University article on a practical education for journalists, which he authored as dean of liberal arts. Many departments and schools of journalism in the twentieth century began as academic units in schools and colleges of liberal arts. His discussion of the inadequacies in the education of journalists in that article would be sounded repeatedly in the years ahead—and not unlike the concerns about journalism education expressed by journalism educators of any period during and since the Woodson era.

At that time, conventional education was not practical or useful for journalists or most other people, he argued, saying journalism students should be treated as professional journalists at early stages of their training and that classes should not be used to reshape their minds but to equip them to function well in their chosen profession (Woodson, 1920).

Woodson's interest in journalism education did not end when his tenure in academe expired. In 1925, he helped conduct a summer high school workshop at Morgan College on the essentials of journalism and journals ("Conduct Journals," 1925). Woodson commended Fisk University for its progress in surpassing other programs in the number of courses offered on black history, literature, sociology, and religion, but he admonished Fisk for not doing more for the study of black newspapers (Woodson, 1931a).

Later, writing about how the most successful editors of black newspapers had overcome inadequate education, Woodson praised "uneducated printers who founded most [of] our newspapers which have succeeded, these men of vision have made it possible for the 'educated' Negroes to make a living in this sphere in proportion as they recover from their education and learn to deal with the Negro as he is and where he is" (Woodson, 1933a).

Woodson was arguing that uneducated blacks were better educated than educated blacks, a central theme of his writings during the 1930s. He ascribed similar qualities to the illiterates he met in the coalfields, and to his father. Literally, he meant the uneducated had not been exposed to the wrongs of conventional education.

Woodson's comments on the education of non-journalists clearly received wider publicity, but his criticism of journalism education was just as caustic.

He concluded that black journalists were not being trained to produce news in the real world of segregated America. Black journalism students were not being taught how to function in black communities, but unrealistically, he argued, they were "being taught how to edit such metropolitan dailies as the *Chicago Tribune* and the *New York Times*, which would hardly hire a Negro as a janitor" (Woodson, 1933a).

Long after Woodson's death in 1950, white-owned newspapers began hiring African Americans in significant numbers after the civil rights movement and the "Report of the National Advisory Commission on Civil Disorders" in 1968, which criticized the media for inaccurate reporting during the 1967 urban riots and for misrepresenting minorities. The report recommended encouraging minorities to enter journalism and hiring minorities as journalists ("Report of the National Advisory Commission," 1968).

Having strong views about how newspapers should operate, Woodson preached to black newspaper editors the necessity of publishing articles about accomplishments of local residents and the wisdom of preserving their newspaper files as evidence of achievements (Woodson, 1932e). He also complained about news coverage of the many black men who began careers as porters and janitors and died as porters and janitors, never having been promoted by the white people they faithfully served. Occasionally their former white bosses performed pallbearer duties at their funerals and lamented their service. "Thoughtless Negro editors," Woodson said, "instead of expressing their regret that such a life of usefulness was not rewarded by promotion, take up the refrain as some great honor bestowed upon the race" (Woodson, 1933c).

Despite expressing such criticism, Woodson found much on which to commend newspapers. He urged readers to buy books and subscriptions to black newspapers and magazines, saying, "Many of them measure up to the standards of the best in our time; and others, when encouraged properly, will rise higher and higher." Woodson said the black press was "helping to popularize our history," and he added, "Those rendering this service efficiently cannot be too highly praised. Without such a voice of the people a race cannot advance" (Woodson, 1938c).

One way newspapers could demonstrate black achievements was in the printing of obituaries, which Woodson advocated and referred to as biographical sketches. He demonstrated his preferred style for obituaries in the *Journal of Negro History* and the *Negro History Bulletin*. The obituaries he wrote and published were less like the funeral-home death notices found today in many newspapers, but were more elaborately written and researched commentaries about the deceased person's entire career, along the lines of longer articles found in such publications as the *Washington Post* and *New York Times* after the passing of a government official or well-known artist or musician, in which their lives are laid bare.

Concerned that newspapers might neglect their duties, Woodson encouraged local ASNLH affiliates to save such records as old newspapers, receipts, manumission papers, deeds, and wills, and association members were asked to "write the life histories of the 'near great' but useful Negroes of whom editors and authors take no account" ("Notes," 1928). He congratulated himself for making the decision to print the obituaries in his magazines, calling it both wise and profitable ("The Study of Negro Life and History," 1950).

Woodson wrote final thoughts on several of his relatives and leading figures from the black communities and beyond. Often he had the last word on many of the people who had supported him (Robert S. Abbott, Robert L. Vann, and Oswald Garrison Villard, for example) and those who opposed him or with whom he disagreed (Kelly Miller and Thomas Jesse Jones). His instructions to journalists and others stipulated objectivity, removing the observer's personal opinions and balancing the good with the bad in writing the obituaries, and he demonstrated how it should be done in obituaries he published with and without his signature. No byline was listed for many of the obituaries, but those printed were written in Woodson's style.

Sounding very much like a dean passing judgment on a candidate's application for promotion and tenure, Woodson wrote that Miller, a columnist and Howard professor, was "one of the important men of the entire country," yet he faulted Miller for his lack of scholarship in many of the areas in which he provided commentaries, such as his being trained as a mathematician but speaking most often in areas of sociology, in which he was not trained (Woodson, 1940a).

Of Abbott, the *Journal* recognized his strong contributions to the black press and cited the rise of his newspaper's circulation above 200,000, making him one of the richest African Americans. The obituary suggested Abbott's accomplishments were the standard by which black newspapers should be judged ("Robert Sengstacke Abbott," 1940).

The obituary of Vann, a founder and editor of the *Pittsburgh Courier*, carried fewer laudatory comments than Abbott's. It merely cited, matter-of-factly, Vann's law and business success and service in politics—including being publicity director of Calvin Coolidge's campaign for president and assistant attorney general under Franklin Roosevelt (Vann, 1941).

In writing Villard's obituary, Woodson noted Villard was the grandson of abolitionist William Lloyd Garrison and compared him unfavorably to his grandfather, the editor of the *Liberator*, largely because Villard had accumulated great wealth. Woodson, however, did praise Villard for his support of ASNLH and other causes beneficial to blacks. "To organizations thus battling for opportunity and freedom for American Negroes, he gave not only his time but a considerable portion of his means," Woodson wrote (Woodson, 1950a).

Thomas Jesse Jones's obituary was published in the same issue as Villard's, and coming toward the end of Woodson's life, serves as a test of Woodson's principle of reporting both the good and the bad of people's lives. Jones, whom Woodson had blamed for his loss of philanthropic support, also was accused of forcing his ideas on black education in America and Africa and for inflicting cruelty against those who disagreed with him. Woodson, however, credited Jones for some success, but it was an obituary filled mostly with criticism. Still it fell within the broad outlines of Woodson's requirements for obituaries because it showed both sides of Jones. The obituary stated that Jones would have achieved greater success "if he had not been so narrow-minded, short-sighted, vindictive and undermining." Woodson wrote, "Rarely would a Negro leader in the United States speak commendably of such an unscrupulous man" (Woodson, 1950a).

The significance of preserving files, not just obituaries, also was routinely demonstrated by Woodson, beginning with the first article he published in the *Journal* ("The Negroes of Cincinnati Prior to the Civil War," 1916). Many of the other articles he published then and later contained research that employed old newspaper stories, among several devices used in documentation. For example, Woodson reprinted a letter to the editor of the *New Orleans Daily States*. A reader of that newspaper informed the editor that P. B. S. Pinchback's name was not included on a list of Louisiana governors who had stayed at the Cosmopolitan Hotel. The reprinted letter demonstrated how preservation of newspaper records and other documents could be used to preserve black achievements that might be lost over time (Hart, 1917). Another example of Woodson's use of newspapers to demonstrate how they could be used in helping to document and corroborate is the reprinting of a *Boston Journal* article from an 1897 newspaper account of a black man, Salem Poor, who fought at the Battle of Bunker Hill (*Journal of Negro History*, 1916).

Preservation of newspaper articles about black achievements, as Woodson advocated after noticing many black papers were not maintaining their files, would assist historians in evaluating black achievements down the road. It also made good business sense for the newspapers to maintain and preserve their files as news-reporting tools, the needs of historians notwithstanding.

Amid rising literacy rates during the first half of the twentieth century, it also made sense for the newspapers to sign on to a public-education program based on reading. The interests of both groups—historians and journalists—were interlocked. If only white newspaper files were available to researchers, some stories of black achievements would be lost. As previously stated, many mainstream, white publications ignored their black communities, and their news personnel often reported news in racist, anti-black tones so prevalent in American society. As such, they misinformed readers about both history and the news.

Woodson urged newspaper staffs and members of the public to send files and documents to ASNLH or the Library of Congress (Woodson, 1936e), and representatives of the library were given prominent speaking roles at ASNLH meetings. In a similar vein, the editors of the *Negro World* had asked readers to send their purchased copies of the newspaper to the New York Public Library because the editors did not have enough copies to send to the public library. Woodson established a relationship with the Library of Congress for preserving documents he collected in 1928. Librarian of Congress Herbert Putnam confirmed the agreement with Woodson in a December 5, 1928, letter, in which he expressed doubts Woodson would be able to collect materials the library would deem significant involving the history and culture of "negroes." Putnam's letter spelled "Negroes" with a small n, a spelling often considered contemptuous (see Appendix).

Black newspapers embraced Woodson's prosecution of his war and public-education program goals, often acting in concert as fellow warriors helping him correct, preserve, and popularize the history of a people whose standing Woodson feared would become negligible if it were left unattended.

Woodson—despite the awkwardness of his Thomas Jesse Jones obituary—emphasized the important role newspapers had to play in reporting the truth and in a balanced style, giving the full picture about people in their communities. He was arguing this point in a column even toward the end of his life (Woodson, 1948a).

Woodson's late-life comments about the practice of journalism in that 1948 newspaper column also were consistent with the points of view reflected in at least two of his books, *The Negro in Our History* (first published in 1922, it was in its ninth edition when he died) and *Negro Makers of History* (printed in three editions in 1928, 1938, 1942). *Negro Makers of History* was adapted from the earlier *Negro in Our History* and written for elementary students, carrying a complete chapter called "Authors and Editors."

Above all, Woodson schooled journalists about their own principles of fairness and balance. He urged them to rise above their personal and professional prejudices in reporting news, for he knew newspaper obituaries and feature stories about the lives of local residents often were used by researchers in compiling data and interpreting history. Mishandled news could lead to misinformation and inaccuracies, as he already demonstrated in his writings about black history. As a result, he complained that "the annalist is not recording the worthwhile deeds of his time when he merely lauds the race to which he belongs while enlarging upon only the shortcomings of other elements of the population" (Woodson, 1948a).

NEGRO NEWSPAPER WEEK

By the late 1930s, long after joining Woodson's history movement, the black press was waging a parallel campaign on behalf of its own history. The Negro Newspaper Publishers Association (NNPA) launched an annual National Negro Newspaper Week, beginning in 1939, more than a decade after Woodson's outreach to the newspapers with commemoration of the *Freedom's Journal* centennial at an ASNLH meeting. The publishers also promoted Negro Newspaper Week in ways similar to Woodson's promotion and observance of the annual Negro History Week—through newspapers and periodicals, posters, and local speakers (Oak, 1942).

Although blacks were having difficulty breaking into radio, they succeeded in getting on-air support on national network stations for Negro Newspaper Week promotions, as Woodson was doing by the late 1930s with Negro History Week. Moss Hyles Hendrix, director of National Negro Newspaper Week for the NNPA, solicited support from local editors and national broadcasters. In one letter, C. A. Scott, editor of the *Atlanta Daily World*, was solicited to write Ambrose Caliver, senior specialist in black education in the US Office of Education, to support efforts to get "Freedom's People," an NBC show about African Americans and their war effort, to feature a segment on the black press (Hendrix, 1942). Hendrix also observed that already "Wings Over Jordan" had signed on for March 1, 1942. Woodson served as an adviser to "Freedom's People" and "Destination Freedom," another show, which featured Woodson in 1950 during Negro History Week (Durham, Betts, and

WMAQ, 2000). Caliver also participated at ASNLH conferences and made a presentation on black education that was published in the *Journal of Negro History*.

The black press was largely supportive of the nation's efforts in World War II, as it had been during World War I, but the federal government was uneasy on both occasions that a number of black newspapers might use the war in Europe as a civil rights issue at home. Among the concerns was the *Pittsburgh Courier*–led Double-V campaign—victory at home and abroad (Savage, 1999). Black soldiers and support for the war were welcomed topics, but not protests. Annual celebrations of black newspaper history, combined with the medium's support for the war, were acceptable topics.

Claude A. Barnett, founder and director of Associated Negro Press (ANP), cleverly presented such a vehicle, reminding audiences that blacks are Americans and their newspapers patriotic, in celebrating National Negro Newspaper Week and black participation in World War II on a CBS radio broadcast. "The Negro newspaper is an important arm in the effort to marshal the entire man and woman power of our nation for the prosecution of our war effort," said Barnett, according to the transcript he provided ANP subscribers. "Next to the Negro church, the Negro newspaper is the most powerful influence operating within this group of thirteen million Americans of African descent, and who constitute one-tenth of our entire population" (Barnett, 1942).

The following year, P. B. Young Sr., editor-publisher of the *Norfolk Journal and Guide*, addressed another radio audience on CBS during a National Negro Newspaper Week observance on March 6, 1943, declaring that "the Negro Press is fundamentally an advocate."

The role of advocate was detailed at the publishers' meeting by another *Journal and Guide* editor. During a panel discussion on "Community Service: The Newspaper's Relation to Civic Planning and the Future of the Community" at the NNPA's 1947 annual meeting, Albert L. Hinton, managing editor of the *Norfolk Journal and Guide*, told members, "we share the belief that it is the inescapable obligation of every newspaper worthy of the name to be the outstanding exponent, in its particular community, of a functional belief in the democratic ideology and the doctrines of our government." Hinton also said, "In order to fulfill its proper destiny, the newspaper—and particularly the Negro newspaper—must be an active and perpetual editorial champion of every cause which has as its objective the civic, educational, cultural, and religious betterment of the community of which it is a part. In no other way can it ever hope to fulfill its destiny" (Hinton, 1947).

This sentiment was repeated in 1949 by Thomas W. Young, NNPA president, during a broadcast over NBC radio about Negro Newspaper Week and a discussion among Young; B. M. McKelway, editor of the *Washington Evening Star*; and NBC moderator Charles Batters.

Responding to a question from McKelway, Thomas Young explained three functions of the black newspaper: report the news, whether good or bad, about blacks because the white press distorted and/or ignored such news; "marshal public opinion against all wrongs and injustices," especially wrongs "adversely affecting the aspirations of the Negro"; and inspire the black community to pursue higher goals "by heralding the accomplishments of Negro individuals, groups and institutions" (Young, 1949).

Young's statement of the functions of black newspapers could easily have been given by Woodson in explaining the purpose of the Black History Movement and his standards for the black press. Such sentiments were expressed, too, by Luther P. Jackson, the Woodson collaborator on publicity and fund-raising who served as chair of the history department at Virginia State College, declaring the significance of the newspapers' value to African American history, as Woodson and the black press had done in the 1920s. Jackson authored a two-part newspaper series in support of Negro Newspaper Week in 1945 with this lead paragraph, which appeared to repeat Woodson's earlier observations:

> If an individual wants to know what the Negroes of our country were doing in bygone days his best source of information by far is the Negro newspaper. If he wants to know what was happening in the past among the schools, the churches, and the lodges; or if he seeks data on the business life, political life, or social life among these people he must turn to the files of their old newspapers. (Jackson, 1945a)

Like Woodson, Jackson also was critical of previous generations of black editors who did not preserve copies of their papers. Jackson understood that many of the old editors had suffered financially and did not have facilities to store newspaper files. He softened his criticism, choosing to praise that generation on its gains in this area:

> At this writing the best we the guild of Negro historians can say to the editors in their National Negro Newspaper Week is that we are mighty grateful to the Negro press of the past and present, be-

cause their papers constitute an indispensable aid for Negro history. (Jackson, 1945a)

In part 2 of the newspaper series on February 28, Jackson cited white-owned newspapers (such as the *Chicago Tribune* and *New York Times*) for their contributions to Civil War history, while noting the correspondents were primarily white men who ignored black heroism. Jackson was optimistic black points of view would be included in historical accounts of World War II, reporting that the University of Virginia had acquired war issues of the *Norfolk Journal and Guide* and that attempts were being made to acquire copies of the *Afro-American* (Jackson, 1945b).

THE BLACK PRESS BY THE NUMBERS

Beyond their own communities, several black newspapers had considerable influence nationally. The *Defender, Afro-American*, and *Pittsburgh Courier* had national readerships, and the *Atlanta Daily World* controlled a syndicate of thirty-one newspapers. Moreover, many of the articles used by black newspapers were distributed to them by several news services (Table 2.3), such as Associated Negro Press and CNS.

Between the two world wars, black agencies provided news-gathering and distribution services, similar to wire services provided by white agencies such as Associated Press and United Press International. Their distribution of articles, to upward of 300 weeklies, included Woodson's columns and other news releases. With the *Defender* and *Courier* each claiming circulations of more than 200,000 subscribers before World War II, including their national editions, and ANP distributing articles to as many as seventy newspaper customers, the major news organizations selected for this study controlled access to what millions of black readers learned about their neighborhoods, the world, and Woodson's history movement (Tables 2.1, 2.2, and 2.3).

Woodson's history movement, 1915–1950, coincided with the peak of the black press's power and influence. Aggregate circulation of black newspapers, often understated because many of the newspapers were not represented in census data or other private data collection services, ranged from a conservative estimate of one million at the start of Woodson's public relations program to well beyond two million by the late 1940s. Census takers never reported as many black newspapers as black leaders, including Woodson and members of the Negro Newspaper Publishers Association, often cited.

For example, the black press often claimed knowledge of 250 to 300 black newspapers ("Twelfth Annual Negro Newspaper Week," 1949; "The Functions of a Minority Press in War Time," 1943). Newspaper circulation did not include readership estimates or provide the full picture or reach of the black newspapers' influence because newspapers were shared with family and other acquaintances, bringing an unknown number of additional readers. One report indicated the *Defender* was read aloud in barbershops and churches, and from person to person, with four to five readers for each paper sold during its peak circulation period (Newspapers: *The Chicago Defender*, n.d.). By such estimates, black newspaper readership during this period would have been a multiple of circulation recorded by census-takers, and the newspapers would have had as many as 4 million readers out of a black population of 13 million by the 1940s (see Tables 2.1, 2.2, and 2.3).

The black population doubled from 1890 to 1950, and both newspapers and Woodson's movement were beneficiaries of rising school attendance and

Table 2.1: Number and Circulation of Black Newspapers by Region, 1938			
Geographical Divisions	**Number Operating**	**Number Reporting**	**Total Circulation**
U.S. Total	227	145	1,322,072
New England	2	1	5,000
Middle Atlantic	33	24	375,928
E. North Central	37	16	267,399
W. North Central	16	9	71,855
S. Atlantic	57	38	257,632
E. South Central	36	22	105,907
W. South Central	31	22	142,651
Mountain	5	4	8,200
Pacific	10	9	87,500
Note: The Census Bureau reported the total number of black newspapers as 227 in 1938, but it received circulation information only from 145. Others estimated the number of black newspapers at 200 to 300.			
Source: Bureau of the Census, Department of Commerce, "Negro Newspapers and Periodicals in the United States: 1938," Statistical Bulletin No. 1, May 1939.			

Table 2.2: Number and Circulation of Black Newspapers by States with Three or More Newspapers, 1943		
State	Number	Circulation
Total Papers Reporting	144	1,613,255
Alabama	6	22,250
Arkansas	6	37,600
California	6	80,500
Colorado	4	11,200
District of Columbia	5	82,795
Florida	5	33,867
Georgia	7	32,600
Illinois	7	180,572
Kentucky	4	26,098
Louisiana	6	50,200
Michigan	5	48,506
Mississippi	8	17,208
Missouri	5	63,986
New Jersey	3	43,500
New York	7	113,193
North Carolina	3	16,564
Ohio	6	39,500
Oklahoma	4	10,381
Pennsylvania	10	286,345
Tennessee	6	141,580
Texas	11	73,453
Virginia	4	64,255
All Other States	16	137,282

Note: All black newspapers are not represented in the circulation data published by the US Census, and only states with three or more black newspapers were reported in the above table. Notably, black newspapers in the state of Maryland were not included, even though the *Afro-American* was located in Baltimore. Either there were fewer than three black newspapers in Maryland that year, or information was unavailable. An unknown number of the *Afro-American*'s subscribers, however, were probably included among those reported for the District of Columbia because the newspaper circulated in more than one city. During the Woodson era, the Negro Newspaper Publishers Association claimed at least three hundred black newspapers were publishing each week. (Negro Newspaper Publishers Association, 1943).

Source: "Negro Newspapers and Periodicals in the United States: 1943," Negro Statistical Bulletin Number 1, August 1944.

Table 2.3: Black News-Gathering Agencies, Their Locations, and Frequency of Distribution, 1943

Name	Location	Frequency
Associated Negro Press	Chicago, IL	3 Times/Week
Negro Digest News Service	Chicago, IL	Weekly
United News Co.	Chicago, IL	Weekly
Howard News Syndicate	Des Moines, IA	Weekly
White Newspaper Syndicate	Hamtramck, MI	Weekly
Continental Press	Kansas City, MO	N/A
Negro Press Bureau	Los Angeles, CA	Semi-Weekly
Pacific News Service	Los Angeles, CA	Weekly
Victory News Service	Milwaukee, WI	Weekly
Calvin's News Service	New York, NY	Bi-Weekly
Great Eastern News Corp.	New York, NY	Weekly
Independent Press Service	New York, NY	Semi-Weekly
National Negro Features	New York, NY	N/A
Negro Labor News Service	New York, NY	Irregularly
Progress News Service	Newark, NJ	Semi-Weekly
Prudential News Agency	Washington, DC	Semi-Weekly

Source: US Department of Commerce, Bureau of the Census, Washington, DC. Negro Newspapers and Periodicals in the United States, 1943. (August 1944). Negro Statistical Bulletin No. 1.

rising literacy rates. Illiteracy declined from about 30 percent among blacks in 1910 to about 10 percent in the late 1940s and early 1950s, compared to under 8 percent in 1910 and under 3 percent by the early 1950s in the overall US population. From 1910 to 1950, school enrollment of blacks rose from about 45 per 100 persons of school age to 75 per 100. The black population doubled from about 7.5 million in 1890 to 15 million in 1950 (see Tables 2.4, 2.5, and 2.6).

Table 2.4: Percentage of Illiteracy of US Population Fourteen Years and Over by Race, 1910–1952

Year	Overall Population	White	Black and Other Races
1910	7.7	5.0	30.5
1920	6.0	4.0	23.0
1930	4.3	3.0	16.4
1940	2.9	2.0	11.5
1950	3.2	—	—
1952	2.5	1.8	10.2

Note: Ninety-six percent of nonwhites in 1950 were black.

Source: "National Assessment of Adult Literacy: 120 Years of Literacy," 1993, National Center for Education Statistics

Table 2.5: School Enrollment per 100 Persons by Race, 1910–1972

Year	Total Population per 100	White per 100	Black, Other Races per 100
1910	59.2	61.3	44.8
1920	64.3	65.7	53.5
1930	69.9	71.2	60.3
1940	74.8	75.6	68.4
1950	78.7	79.3	74.8
1972	90.0	90.0	90.1

Note: Ninety-six percent of nonwhites in 1950 were black.

Source: National Center for Education Statistics ("National Assessment of Adult Literacy," 1993)

Table 2.6: Black Population Growth, 1890–1950

Year	Population (Millions)	Percent Total	Percent Increase
1890	7.5	11.9	13.8
1900	8.3	11.6	18.0
1910	9.8	10.7	11.2
1920	10.5	9.9	6.5
1930	11.9	9.7	13.6
1940	12.9	9.8	8.2
1950	14.9	9.8	15.1

Source: US Bureau of the Census

Chapter 3

HARNESSING PRESS COVERAGE

CARTER G. WOODSON'S INITIAL APPEARANCE IN THE MEDIA SPOTLIGHT probably occurred at Douglass School in Huntington, West Virginia. He and Trent R. Jenkins were the two students who graduated from Douglass in 1896. The graduation exercise was held at Davis Theater, amid fanfare, including an operetta called "A Trip to Europe" ("Douglass 1892–2003," 2003). Not much information is known about Jenkins, but Woodson graduated after one year at the school, at age twenty, and his star would shortly become ascendant in his adopted home state. Their graduation was reported by the *Huntington Advertiser*, on page 4, May 8, 1896, the earliest date found for his name in any news medium by the present study. Woodson's return to Huntington and Douglass just four years later also was duly noted ("Assignment of Teachers," 1900).

The occasion for Woodson's return to Douglass was his hiring as principal. The article mentioning his hiring in the white-owned *Advertiser* simply stated the school teaching assignments at Douglass. The newspaper did not revisit the circumstances that brought about the vacancy he filled; however, his homecoming was prompted by the firing of the former principal, Woodson's first cousin, Carter H. Barnett, who had been involved in one of the local area's biggest political controversies in 1900 and was covered extensively by the *Advertiser*. It is not known whether the school board was aware of the kinship of the Woodsons and Barnetts.

Carter Barnett, whose mother was the sister of Woodson's father, was fired by the Republican-controlled school board for his political activities outside the classroom, as the defiant editor of the *West Virginia Spokesman*, which supported a breakaway group of independent black Republicans in Huntington politics and advocated dividing black votes among competing political groups at a time when the black population was expected to be loyal to the Republican Party. Woodson's brother Robert was one of the local candidates on the independent black slate ("Barnett Removed as Principal," 1900). Later, as a newspaper columnist, Woodson would express that same independent philosophy, particularly during the 1932 national election, when black support for Republicans began to shift to Franklin D. Roosevelt and the Democrats (Woodson, 1932m).

One of the highlights of Woodson's years as the Douglass principal was establishment of a library ("Douglass 1892–2003," 2003). He became a minor newsmaker, although he was not yet a publicist for any organization or movement. Still, his skills with the media were on display. For instance, following the assassination of President William McKinley in 1901, Woodson conducted a service at Douglass that memorialized the life of the president for a local audience. The *Huntington Advertiser* informed readers that "Principal C. G. Woodson briefly sketched the life of the illustrious dead, and at the close of his talk suggested the singing of 'Nearer My God to Thee'" ("Services at Douglass School," 1901). The *Advertiser* also reported Woodson's commencement address before a graduating class that included his sister Bessie B. Woodson ("Douglass High School Commencement," 1902). After he left Huntington in 1903, Woodson's name was published in a San Francisco newspaper when he sailed to his new job teaching and supervising schools in the Philippines ("Korea's Sailing Delayed," 1903). In the Philippines, his views about improving education were influenced by an education system that taught Filipinos with little attempt to teach them lessons relative to their environment and culture, as blacks were being taught back in the States (Woodson, 1933a).

Huntington had become the foundation for Woodson's early celebrity, which would be enhanced by his graduate degrees from prestigious colleges such as Harvard and the University of Chicago and travels around the world, to far-off places in Asia, Africa, and Europe. He was treated like a celebrity by Black Huntington on his trips home (Scally, 1985). However, the local celebrity he had become in West Virginia provided only a glimpse of the media attention he would attract in Black America following his move to Washington, DC.

His West Virginia fame notwithstanding, Woodson was unknown to African American society and the press corps when he arrived in Washington in 1909 and began research into black history, penniless and laughed at, wearing what he called "hayseed" clothes—as he was attempting to rise above low expectations from those around him (Woodson, 1932c). They did not immediately know Woodson was already a seasoned intellectual who took a backseat to no one. If the move from his birthplace in Virginia to West Virginia had been a "turning point" in his career, as friends said he was fond of saying (Logan, 1973), then Woodson's move to Washington would have to be recognized as a turning point in black history.

Woodson taught French and Spanish in the District of Columbia school system for six years before the press noticed the seriousness of his research. His national breakthrough came in July 1915—less than two months before the launch of ASNLH—with the *New York Times'* appraisal of his book *The Education of the Negro Prior to 1861*, one of three books reviewed that day within a racial context. The other two books reviewed were *America's Greatest Problem: The Negro* by R. W. Shufeldt, M.D., and *The Negro* by W. E. B. Du Bois ("Three Students," 1915).

Woodson's arrival on the national scene cast him in a new role, as the star historian whose work served as a rebuttal to inaccurate, racist scholarship about black history. His supporting cast would include the press, especially black newspapers, which would afford him a national forum for the use of various tactics in a public-education program lasting the remainder of his life, 1915–1950.

Many historians date the beginning of the Modern Black History Movement as the September 1915 date Woodson created the Association for the Study of Negro Life and History. Nearly two months before the start of the movement and the public-education program that followed, the *New York Times*, on July 18, 1915, juxtaposed Woodson's carefully researched book against wild assertions made by Shufeldt, whose historical research and conclusions were the kind Woodson would later rail against. The *Times* reviewed Shufeldt's account with skepticism, as it was not persuaded by his attempts to prove black inferiority and cast doubt on his statement that blacks had no morals to improve ("Three Students," 1915).

On the other hand, the *Times* applauded the works of Du Bois and Woodson, and it was especially complimentary of Woodson's scientific research and dispassionate style ("Three Students," 1915).

Through the years, the *New York Times* published notices of a few of Woodson's speaking engagements around New York, such as when ASNLH met in the city, while mostly ignoring his other activities. The exceptions included occasional book reviews and Woodson's tribute to Booker T. Washington ("Booker Washington," 1932).

White media, for the most part, were segregated and rarely more enlightened on matters of race in the first half of the twentieth century than other

American institutions. However, Logan, Woodson's associate, noted in 1940 that an increasing number of white daily newspapers in the South were capitalizing the word "Negro," a subtle shift toward gaining respectability (Logan, 1940). H. L. Mencken, a widely read writer who frequently commented on issues of race, opposed the capital N movement. He identified Robert R. Moton, the head of Tuskegee Institute, with campaigning for the stylistic change beginning in 1913, with some success among several newspapers and magazines of both races, including the *New York Times*, by 1930 (Mencken, 1944).

Mainstream newspapers usually identified blacks in stories in which race was not an issue until the late 1960s, although several had been moving away from this practice since the 1940s, including the *New York Times*. The *Times'* about-face, announced in an editorial that referenced hatred following a recent lynching of four black people in Georgia, said its new policy would identify people by race only when there is a legitimate purpose. The *Times* knew it was making history and understood the complaints from its black readers, saying, "This may seem a small thing. The Negroes do not think so" ("Race in the News," 1946).

Racial identification was so rampant in the American mainstream press that it seemed uniquely American to Woodson on his first trip to Europe, but more than a quarter-century later, Woodson had claimed in 1933 that European newspapers were adopting this mainstream American journalism routine (Woodson, 1933i).

Classifying black newsmakers by their race was not the only issue. A common complaint in black communities was that white newspapers generally did not hire black journalists or inform most of their readers substantively about news in black neighborhoods. These critics generally disparaged the limited offerings found in the star-editions published by some white newspapers for black customers, as sanitized as they were, never to be seen by white readers who might be offended by black news, unless the stories involved criminal activities (Woodson, 1928b). This treatment of blacks permeated mainstream white news and editorial offerings about African Americans, at least until the new sensibilities brought on by successes of the civil rights movement. The 1968 "Report of the National Advisory Commission on Civil Disorders" was especially critical of the media's—which by the 1960s included television—coverage of black communities ("Report of the National Advisory Commission," 1968).

The limited coverage Woodson received from the white press in the District of Columbia appeared to be an exception. At Armstrong High School in Washington, Woodson made local news when he implemented changes in the curriculum soon after being named principal. He announced new courses in radio, applied electricity, and automobile mechanics and encouraged young men of military draft age to take these courses in order to be better equipped for military service. The school became the center for industrial training for black males in the District ("Preparatory War Work," 1918). After a ten-year career as a teacher and principal in the Washington public schools, Woodson became dean of liberal arts at Howard University in 1919, where he continued his research on African American history and began to make public statements about the education of journalists.

BECOMING A BLACK MEDIA FIGURE

Adelaide Cromwell, a sociologist who knew Woodson and who participated in a tribute to him at the 2006 convention of the Association for the Study of African American Life and History in Atlanta, suggested there were four blacks who reached national recognition between the end of the Civil War and Martin Luther King's civil rights era—Frederick Douglass, Booker T. Washington, W. E. B. Du Bois, and Woodson (ASALH, 2007). Douglass died on February 20, 1895; Washington, on November 14, 1915; Woodson, on April 3, 1950; Du Bois, on August 27, 1963, the day before the March on Washington. Douglass, Washington, Du Bois, Woodson, and King also were adept in the use of the media for publicity in pursuing their causes.

The national recognition Woodson attained was in a segregated America, where he thrived as an important black media figure, largely unnoticed by White America, although his work obviously was known by journalists at several major white newspapers and radio networks. From the beginning, Woodson attempted to enlist newspapers as allies and used his newly discovered celebrity on behalf of the history program. He sought the support of all newspapers, with limited success among white papers, most notably during launch of the scholarly journal and annual observances of Negro History Week. However, Woodson was heavily invested in the black press, both intellectually and culturally, and his acceptance by black newspapers would be central to his success.

The *Chicago Defender* announced two Woodson speaking engagements in 1915, both promoting presentations in support of *The Education of the Negro Prior to 1861*, at the Negro Fellowship League, whose president was Ida B. Wells, the iconic journalist known for crusades against lynching. Wells would become a Woodson supporter, and she noted in her diary on January 13, 1930, that she attended a Negro History club meeting and participated in the reading and discussion of a Woodson book. However, she expressed disappointment that the book, which was not identified, did not mention her antilynching activities (DeCosta-Willis, 1995).

The first of the two brief articles in the *Defender* noted Woodson would be speaking July 25, 1915, and trumpeted his arrival with an introduction that his book was one of "the finest books" on the Negro race ("Negro Fellowship League," 1915). The second item, reporting that Woodson was scheduled to speak August 8, 1915, added an exhortation that the community should not miss "this literary treat" and said a packed audience was anticipated ("Negro Fellowship League," 1915).

After establishing ASNLH in Chicago on September 9, 1915 and incorporating it in Washington, DC, three weeks later (October 2, 1915), Woodson launched the *Journal of Negro History* in January 1916. Baltimore's *Afro-American*'s initial reaction to the first issue of the *Journal* was negative, questioning Woodson's claim that the black race was endangered by misinformation (see chapter 5). However, the *Afro*'s opposition did not presage a battle with the black press. Black press opposition to Woodson was rare. Even the *Afro* joined his team in short order. The barrage of information Woodson was presenting about history had a bandwagon-like effect on the black press. By 1918, the *Afro*'s editorial pages were brimming with enthusiasm for Woodson. The newspaper observed, in an about-face from what it published about him in 1916, that Woodson would tell the truth about blacks without concern for hurt feelings ("Family Skeletons," 1918).

The *Afro-American*'s second verdict on Woodson became, perhaps, his mantra and most enduring public image. From the shaky start with that newspaper, the Woodson image evolved into that of an independent, self-made man in search of truth and justice, unafraid of powerful institutions and powerful men, in defense of a disrespected race. For instance, when Woodson received grants of $25,000 each from the Carnegie and Rockefeller foundations, the *Afro*'s news story featured Woodson as a heroic figure, leading the charge for enlightenment, on page 1 ("$50,000 Gift," 1922). The black press was proud of Woodson's accomplishments, and his success seemed to be interpreted as success for all African Americans.

During the Great Depression, when support from white philanthropy virtually dried up, the black press stood by Woodson as he asserted greater independence and sought financial support from black communities in small donations, including raising money from students and teachers. The *Afro*, for instance, asked readers in an editorial to donate to the association, urging children to give pennies, as it assisted Woodson in finding funds to match a $7,500 gift from a foundation ("Negro History Week," 1933). Wesley used the pennies' theme when he recruited Virginia State College history professor Luther P. Jackson for a larger role in promotions and fund-raising activities for the Association for the Study of Negro Life and History (Wesley, 1936).

Woodson became a newspaper resource. An *Afro-American* feature called "Ask Faith Fallin," which pictured a young woman wearing a veil and answering readers' questions, responded to a thirteen-year-old boy who said he was the only black student in his school and expressed concern that his teacher did not often mention blacks. All the people he read about were white, and the student asked for advice. The student was advised to write to Dr. Woodson ("Ask Faith Fallin," 1932).

Many book reviews published in newspapers examined for this study were similarly favorable to Woodson's research, praising his authorship, scholarship, and work at the *Journal of Negro History*. His research on religion attracted much praise in the 1920s, even in religious publications, before his criticism of black church leaders became a staple of his columns a decade later. Among general-interest publications, the *Chicago Defender* moved strongly into Woodson's camp, applying a positive spin in reviewing *The History of the Negro Church*, commending its "painstaking research" ("The History of the Negro Church," 1922).

The *Norfolk Journal and Guide* went further with its comments in reviewing *A Century of Negro Migration*, saying the book and the *Journal of Negro History* had made inroads among readers from both races interested in black history ("Dr. Woodson Writes on Negro Church," 1921).

BOOK REVIEWS IN THE WHITE PRESS

While black newspapers provided his best coverage, Woodson was also solicitous of the white press, where undoubtedly he could spread his messages to broader audiences, including wealthy white supporters and prospective donors who would be informed of his progress. His collection of papers at the Library of Congress includes many clippings of newspaper articles from the white press about books published and written by him and others whose writings he published through his publishing company, Associated Publishers, many of them sent by the newspapers, friends, and authors acting as clipping services.

Most book reviews by the white newspapers in the Library of Congress collection were generally favorable:

- The *St. Louis Post-Democrat* called *The Rural Negro* a plainly written, comprehensive account ("The Rural Negro," 1930).
- The *Grand Rapids Press* said the book was "an admirable study" ("The Rural Negro," 1930).
- The *Detroit Free Press*, invoking one of the themes that united Woodson and the black journalists—telling the truth—said Woodson had made it interesting ("The Rural Negro," 1930).
- The *State*, of Columbia, South Carolina, took issue with a Woodson assertion in *The Rural Negro* that white planters opposed demonstration agents assisting black farmers because they served in opposition to planters' interests. The newspaper said it would be difficult to confirm such issues while finding the claim incredulous ("Extension Work of Negro Farmers 'Opposed by Planters?'" 1930).
- The *Buffalo Courier* was open to Woodson's discussion of peonage and loss of black rights in the South, while it reported his description was discouraging ("Other Recent Books," 1930).
- The *New York Times*, which launched Woodson's national profile in 1915 with a review of *The Education of the Negro Prior to 1861*, also published a review of *The Negro Professional and the Community*, saying the book's research was presented "fair-mindedly" and made a contribution to knowledge ("Negroes in Professions," 1934).
- In reviewing *The Mis-Education of the Negro*, the *Richmond News Leader* stated Woodson's study was practical and scientific and not the work of a propagandist (Wayland, n.d.).

FORMALIZING THE WOODSON-PRESS PARTNERSHIP

Woodson's Black History Movement was born in Chicago, and his partnership with the black press and his public-education program also began in Chicago.

The oldest Woodson newspaper byline found in the present study was published in 1923, when the *Chicago Defender* serialized, over several weeks, large sections of *The Negro in Our History*. The first installment began with an anecdote inside an editor's note about an Italian in a class of international students in Chicago asking his teacher what the Negro did in the Civil War.

The editor's note claimed the teacher was almost speechless in her response about the glaring omission of African Americans in historical accounts. The newspaper identified Woodson as a noted historian who had dedicated his life to African Americans in history and stated that students would find answers to such questions, as posed by the Italian student, in Woodson's latest book, *The Negro in Our History* ("Editor's Note," 1923). The *Defender* had already lavishly praised the book in a review the previous summer, declaring, "You will find every important phase of history of the Negro has been treated in this volume" (Jackson, 1922).

Before serializing Woodson's book, the *Defender* printed a series of display ads promoting it. The first ad, on December 23, 1922, called *The Negro in Our History* "one of the greatest books ever written" and carried no start date for the series, just promising it would begin soon, as it attempted to build an audience ("Display Ad 47," 1922). It is unclear whether the newspaper or Woodson sponsored the ads.

Support for the movement was building, and Woodson's early success in gaining access to the newspapers—and their readers—would be greatly expanded soon by the black press association itself. Robert L. Vann, editor of the *Pittsburgh Courier*, reported on a February 1927 meeting in Chicago of the National Negro Press Association on page 1. Vann said the group voted unanimous support for Woodson and his black history program (Vann, 1927).

Details of the Negro Press Association meeting were revealed in another article on page 8 of the *Courier*. The article reported that the association urged black religious leaders and the press "to join in being exponents of public opinion." The approval of twelve recommendations was reported, including positions on encouraging better distribution of black doctors who served both rural and urban populations, spreading the migration of blacks across the country more evenly, improving opportunities for blacks to enter business, and securing economic freedom ("Constructive Programme," 1927).

The Pittsburgh article also reported that the press committed itself to encouraging "a complete development and interpretation of Negro history as is typified by the work of Dr. Carter G. Woodson." The press association's statement of values and principles used phrases–prosecution and agitation—that appeared similar to Woodson's prosecution of his war to correct history and advice to Luther P. Jackson and others to keep the protest movement separate from scientific research. In this instance, the press association was committed to a program of moral, spiritual, and intellectual education, without agitation, and it supported "persistent prosecution" of its principles, the newspaper reported ("Constructive Programme," 1927).

The announcement by the *Courier* of the press association's support for Woodson was timely and seemed coordinated, as Woodson was planning ASNLH's 1927 annual meeting in Pittsburgh. Additionally, Woodson announced that on the occasion of the 100th anniversary of *Freedom's Journal*, America's first black newspaper, ASNLH would commemorate the anniversary and honor the black press at that meeting. The press group did not begin observances of black press history itself until more than a decade later—1939 (see chapter 2).

In celebrating the centennial of the newspaper, Woodson deftly combined the history and struggles of the African American press with the history and struggles of all African Americans. The goals of the history movement were similar to those of *Freedom's Journal*, now expressed in an often-quoted statement from *Freedom's Journal*'s first issue about the black editors wanting to plead their own cause instead of continuing to allow others to speak for the black community. Both the historians and the black press wanted to tell correctly the stories of African Americans, and the newspaper industry's commitment to truth made the black press and Woodson natural allies.

Already it should have been apparent to close readers of black newspapers for several years that the black press had been sympathetic to Woodson's program. Now, after the press association's formal embrace of Woodson and his work in 1927, it would be obvious even to casual readers that the black press and the movement were working in tandem. The press meeting in Chicago and the announcements by Woodson and Vann formalized the partnership.

Woodson's announcement about honoring the first black newspaper was more than a simple statement. It was news on its merits—a national conference coming to town and observance of the black press centennial, as well as revelation of Woodson's formal relationship with the press. But it also was a staged publicity moment hyping the event ("Press to Have Place on Programme," 1927).

The *Courier* published other articles about the event in advance of that October 1927 ASNLH annual meeting. The addition of *Freedom's Journal* to the fall program worked both as a history conference event for coverage and as a tactic for press self-promotion, as Woodson was self-promoting his interests. In its coverage, the *Courier* restated Woodson's announcement and provided other details of the program—such as reporting that the upcoming meeting would not only include the centennial observance for the first black newspaper but other aspects of black history, ASNLH, and other issues. The *Courier* combined promotion of the meeting for Woodson's purposes with promotion of its own editor's role on the program and participation by other figures of black journalism ("Ass'n for Study of Negro Life," 1927).

The 1927 ASNLH annual meeting was not the first or last to use newspaper editors as presenters. For example, the tenth annual meeting of the association in 1925 featured Abbott of the *Chicago Defender*, E. Washington Rhodes of the *Philadelphia Tribune*, J. A. Jackson of the *Washington Tribune*, and Vann, who provided insights on development of the black press ("Proceedings," 1925).

ASNLH in 1930 honored African Americans who had served in Congress. W. T. Andrews, editor of the *Herald* and *Commonwealth* of Baltimore, as a program participant evaluated their records in Congress ("Negro History Week Celebration," 1930). The ASNLH meeting in Detroit in 1943 featured an "Editor's Breakfast" and presentations on "The Newspaper as a Source for the Truth," with Louis C. Martin of the *Michigan Chronicle* discussing "The Point of View of the Weekly" and a *Detroit Free Press* journalist arguing that his white daily newspaper was dedicated to truth and fairness ("Proceedings," 1944).

DEFINING WOODSON AS NEWS

Unlike issues involving slavery, lynching, civil rights, and sports, news coverage of history—as events of the past—ordinarily would not be considered newsworthy. Black history was not an easy sell anywhere in the beginning (Franklin, 1957). Few people could make history a hard sell as news in journalistic terms. Woodson had to make history interesting to journalists in order to use them in his movement.

Woodson realized his own communications—the *Journal*, speeches, books, conferences, and pamphlets—had limited audience reach without mass media exposure. He thus incorporated black newspapers into the movement as his partners. The black newspapers supplied the mass audiences of readers and potential converts, and Woodson was generous in his acknowledgment of their support (Woodson, 1938a).

In the newspapers, Woodson was dogmatic and a charismatic salesman. He used the newspapers to sell ideas, and their editors and reporters were willing participants, not mere victims of his promotional efforts. As colleagues in Woodson's program, members of the black press did more than deliver Woodson's messages. For instance, editors of several black newspapers, including the *Norfolk Journal and Guide* and *Afro-American*, took it upon themselves to run Negro History Week promotions (see chapter 5).

Woodson had little reach without the assistance of the newspaper-reading public. For instance, when he died in 1950, Woodson's two history periodicals, according to his ASNLH successor, had combined circulations of only 4,500—about 1,500 for the *Journal of Negro History* and 3,000 for the *Negro History Bulletin* (Logan, 1950). Thus, Woodson's publications alone could not possibly have reached the masses. His school pamphlets, speeches, and books reached thousands, but they, too, needed promotions through newspapers and other vehicles in order for people to know he was making speeches and offering books for sale.

To spread his messages far and wide, Woodson became an opinion journalist for black newspapers and a publicist who developed an alliance that served both his and the journalists' public relations objectives. Woodson gained access to the newspapers' readers, and the newspapers behaved as good corporate citizens and benefited further by receiving from Woodson content reporters and editors would define as news at no charge. In some cases, Woodson was a source of revenue for news organizations when he purchased advertising and other services. ANP owner Claude A. Barnett, who distributed a number of Woodson's columns to various newspapers, for instance, suggested Woodson send him copies of several books as payment for services (Barnett, 1941).

Woodson's handling of the newspapers and their acceptance of him would become pivotal in achieving his goal—preventing African American history from becoming a negligible factor in the world. On numerous occasions, he used the word "negligible" to explain what would happen if African American contributions in history were not preserved and errors corrected in the writing of history ("Race Must Overcome," 1928). His oversight was vertically integrated—from top to bottom, from conducting, sponsoring, and publishing research, to fund-raising, taking trips and making speeches, creating and issuing releases, and lecturing journalists about their business and editorial operations.

Because his mission was based on presenting the truth, correcting the record, and supporting improvements in education, Woodson's values thus appealed directly to the principles of journalism, which are based on truth, accuracy and fairness, and values/factors that determine newsworthiness, including timeliness, impact, the unusual, and conflict. Such values/factors typically influenced news decisions in Woodson's day and since (Mencher, 2008).

Woodson presented his subject in terms journalists could understand, in warlike phrases. His was a movement affecting the future, not just a description of the past. He often used the word "prosecute," expressed in the sense of carrying out a mission involving his black history cause. He used the term like a prosecutor in court or a general on the battlefield carrying out his mission, in pursuit of victories—in this case righting wrongs and correcting historical records—in letters to associates, such as Luther P. Jackson, and in published articles.

Woodson further demonstrated his commitment to correcting the record in the *Negro History Bulletin* when he published a correction involving Benjamin Banneker, the African American mathematician and astronomer. Woodson, Benjamin Brawley, and possibly other writers had relied on the reading of a paper before the Columbian Historical Society of the Capital by a *Washington Evening Star* staff member who incorrectly credited Banneker as the author of an article in Banneker's *Almanac*. The *Bulletin* correction stated, "No historian is thoroughly reliable, and when he discovers his errors he should confess them" ("An Important Correction," 1947).

History was Woodson's primary focus. It was his business and family, as he said himself when explaining why he did not marry. He said he lived on so little and could spare only enough to send to his widowed sister in West Virginia because most of his income was devoted to his cause. The *Chicago Defender* headline referred to this admission in a headline as "The Vow of Poverty" (Woodson, 1933d).

No evidence suggests Woodson was anything but a purest on the subject of historical research. As a mass communicator, however, he often hyped his messages for press attention, calling Jim Crow policies a form of extermination (Woodson, 1933j) and referring to many historians as propagandists ("Chicagoans Hear Dr. Woodson," 1940).

Woodson's use of the press and public relations was a means to an end. Like anyone trying to change public opinion, as his public-education program was designed to do, Woodson found the task difficult. Wesley said Woodson thus "became a popularizer," while maintaining standards of scholarship on the public stage (Wesley, 1951). In fact, in his adherence to the scientific method, Woodson suggested his approach was as objective, if not more so, than other historians, and if he was using Ivy Lee's approach to public relations, which he often did, he was also being objective in presenting the facts to the journalists he was trying to influence (see chapter 5).

The Black History Movement was convenient for newspaper coverage because Woodson's celebrity and values could be defined and transferred as journalistic values and concerns. Without publicity aimed at obtaining press attention and the press association's 1927 endorsement of the movement, stories about history routinely would not have been of interest to journalists of any race, neither in the twentieth century nor in the twenty-first century. A news angle, such as the one provided by blacks recapturing their past from villains, and a face to the movement, supplied by an independent, hard-charging hero (Woodson) doing something about this problem, were both necessary for coverage and in place.

An *Afro-American* editorial stated that Woodson made it possible for blacks to face the future because he took "the cover off the past." Noting how some whites were in denial about black history, the editorial concluded: "Two or three more men like Dr. Woodson and even inaccurate news magazines like 'Time' will cease claiming the Egyptians and Abyssinians for the white race" ("Dr. Carter Woodson," 1930).

This image of Woodson as a hero, which had been expanding since the *Afro-American*'s turnabout and less flattering description of his work initially, seemed made to order for press coverage. Woodson's cultivation of the press also assisted journalists in defining his work as news, and the fact that he understood the news business was advantageous to this task and his cause. His work became both hard news and soft news, available in all sections of the newspapers.

As a general rule, the names of unknown people are not used in headlines or in first paragraphs of hard-news stories—an honor reserved for those with recognizable names. Recognition of the prominence and/or celebrity of prospective newsmakers assists news editors in determining newsworthiness of people, events, and issues, as well as how such coverage should be displayed. The printed names of people known to readers in headlines are believed to attract more readers than unknown names. Even today's articles posted online use key words as tactics to find readers. The same argument usually holds for using familiar names and phrases in the first paragraphs of hard-news stories. Also helping journalists determine newsworthiness are the unusual, as well as conflicts, involving well-known people, as Woodson was keenly aware.

After his newsworthiness was established, Woodson's name was published in headlines and in lead paragraphs, displayed strategically in page layouts as editors signaled Woodson's importance to readers, such as suggested by this headline when Woodson was the commencement speaker in North Carolina in 1932: "C. G. Woodson Speaks Before College Class." The first paragraph of this article also gave Woodson top billing over the college president and the thirty-three North Carolina A&T College students who received degrees ("C. G. Woodson Speaks," 1932). It was not uncommon for newspapers to treat Woodson's presence as more important than the events in which he participated. In so doing, Woodson's became a household name, especially where major black newspapers circulated.

During its early days, virtually any item about the business activity of the association or progress in the history program Woodson disseminated—such as books released and meetings convened, including his plans to celebrate the twentieth anniversary of ASNLH's founding—was reported ("History Association," 1935).

Not all of the news Woodson made, however, was history-related, an indication that he and newspaper editors realized history per se was not news. His commentaries on other issues kept his name and interests before the public on occasions when his program had little news to be reported. Woodson commented on a variety of issues, including international crises involving Ethiopia and Liberia, and he was among celebrities asked to provide Christmas messages to *Afro-American* readers (Woodson, 1931j).

As a celebrity, Woodson attracted press coverage just for being Woodson. The black press treated him like a revered public figure. For example, when his writings were featured in a *New York Amsterdam News* article, the newspaper writer concluded that Woodson "stands out as the only man who has found pleasure in the researches of Negro history" (Oxley, 1927). The *Afro-American* identified him as one of the thirteen most important black people in America in 1930 ("The Thirteen Most Important Negroes," 1930).

An Associated Negro Press reporter spotted Woodson at a Washington train station and dropped a line in his article, declaring Woodson was "always good copy." The article stated that Woodson spent "his spare time sitting in the great waiting room of the Union station here, watching the crowds come and go. Getting material for a new treatise, doc?" (White, 1939). In an earlier column, Woodson had already written that he developed the habit of hanging out at Union Station on his way to the Library of Congress during World War I. "Very soon I found that I was learning much more about life by talking with these people from the South than from any study of books in the national archives," he said (Woodson, 1932r). Woodson's staff were keenly aware of this hangout location (Miles, 1991).

An *Afro-American* writer described in one column the mannerisms of well-known citizens. The columnist noted that Mordecai Johnson, the Howard University president, squinted "through his unrimmed glasses" and spoke "in a modulated voice"; Thomas W. Parks, head of the Washington, DC, Chamber of Commerce, was said to put his hands in his vest pockets and finger his mustache, with his eyebrows slanting upward when he was engaged in serious conversations, "giving his face a pathetic expression." Woodson, Anderson wrote, "continually sulks at the mouth which makes hi[m] rather hard to understand when one first meets him. But he is far from hostile and unsociable." He said Woodson "gestures with a pencil and narrows his eyes when striking a serious pose" (Anderson, 1939).

Stories about meetings, travel, and speaking engagements are staples for news organizations both today and during the first half of the twentieth century. Prominent news sources make news when they meet, travel, and speak, and Woodson's and his association's activities provided ample supplies of such events.

The *New York Amsterdam News* not only reported on an upcoming spring conference of ASNLH to be convened in 1923, but the newspaper predicted success of the event, a step beyond providing publicity: "As the conference is to be held in Baltimore, near which are located so many of our colleges and universities, it is believed that it will be one of the most successful in the history of the association" ("Historical Society," 1923).

Other major black newspapers sometimes provided substantial coverage of the ASNLH meetings, which were usually convened in larger cities— probably because such locations were convenient for transportation and other resources necessary for large black conventions during an era when accommodations were challenging for black travelers. Black newspapers also benefited from the meetings because they helped them serve their reader-ship interests, which in turn provided Woodson access to larger numbers of prospective history movement converts who could not physically attend such meetings.

When Atlanta got its turn as host city, coverage of John Hope, who was president of Atlanta University and ASNLH, magnified the *Atlanta Daily World*'s interest in Woodson and the organization. The *Daily World* covered the conference sessions, including entertainment, as important social and cultural events, as well as meetings for members of the public to learn about history (Jones, 1932).

When he traveled to events, Woodson attracted as much attention as many entertainers and sports figures, but interest in him and his work was dignified, more akin to that involving an elder statesman, or other dignitary, whose life's work was taken seriously. The newspapers often indicated crowd size and response of the public to his visits. Such a response to one of his per-sonal appearances was captured in a *New York Amsterdam News* headline on December 8, 1926: "Many Brave Storm to Hear Lecture of Carter G. Woodson,

Historian: Much of History Read Today Is Propaganda to Perpetuate 'White Supremacy'" ("Many Brave Storm," 1926).

In 1927, Woodson embarked on a grueling ten-city speaking tour through the South—including Birmingham, Selma, and Montgomery in Alabama, and other cities. He was greeted at the conclusion of the tour by this headline: "Dr. Woodson Returns Home." The article informed readers that Woodson would be home until May 15, when he was scheduled to begin another trip, this time to St. Louis and other western cities ("Society," 1927).

Woodson's speeches on these trips were eagerly awaited, the newspapers reported. He often admonished his audiences, as this headline suggested, "Race Must Overcome Inferiority Complex, Dr. Woodson Declares." The speech sounded a consistent theme Woodson was addressing both before and after publication of *The Mis-Education of the Negro*: the black race must feel equal to other races, blacks must learn their past, and position themselves for greatness ahead, or risk "lagging in the progressive march of the times" ("Race Must Overcome," 1928).

In 1931, Woodson had speaking engagements in Baltimore, New York, Cincinnati, St. Louis, Kansas City, and Topeka and had an associate, Lorenzo Greene, fill in for him at other events. He also was commencement speaker at black schools in Ashland, Kentucky; Huntington, West Virginia; Kentucky State Industrial College in Frankfort, Kentucky; Colored Normal and Industrial College in Oklahoma; and Fisk University in Nashville, Tennessee. He reprinted in the *Journal* his standard speech for these occasions, which sounded what would become the familiar themes of his columns and later *The Mis-Education of the Negro*—the necessity of teaching blacks about themselves, creating common-sense schools, and exposing the ironies of teaching blacks to function in a white world that rejected them ("Notes," 1931).

The black press was usually receptive. Following his 1932 speech in Jacksonville, Florida, the *Atlanta Daily World* reported that the Stanton High School audience was "fortunate" in having Woodson as its speaker and that his speech was "very forceful" ("Jacksonville, Fla.," 1932).

Woodson embarked on another such tour in 1934 when he visited New Orleans, Baton Rouge, and Houston, and he wrote columns about this tour and his other travels. The *Louisiana Weekly* promoted the New Orleans visit in three consecutive weekly editions on page 1—on September 22, October 6, and November 17—in addition to covering the speech as an event. Each small item used the same photograph of Woodson in coat and tie, above the fold with a cutline underneath. When newspaper editors print articles and photographs above the fold, the top half of the page that could be seen at newsstands and in the hands of newsboys, they are telling readers what they consider the most important items in the paper, or at least the items the editors expect readers to find most interesting. Such was the case with *Louisiana Weekly* editors, who were also using their publication as an advance PR staff would do for a traveling celebrity or dignitary.

The *Louisiana Weekly* also was under pressure to be the first to inform its readers about upcoming events. In its zeal to break the news of Woodson's upcoming visit, the first photograph and cutline published by the *Louisiana Weekly* proudly announced Woodson would be speaking in New Orleans without specifying a date or place, possibly before it knew such details ("Dr. Carter G. Woodson," 1934a). The second article provided the November 24, 1934, date and location of the speech ("Dr. Carter G. Woodson," 1934b). The third piece was more complete, stating Woodson would stop in New Orleans on his way back from ASNLH's annual meeting in Houston to his Washington home. It reported that Woodson would speak the following Sunday at 4 p.m. at Pythian Temple ("Dr. Carter G. Woodson," 1934c).

As supportive as the *Louisiana Weekly* had been in publicizing Woodson's visit to New Orleans, no newspaper, however, covered Woodson more thoroughly or as vigorously, from 1915 to 1950, than the *Afro-American*—respectfully, but sometimes playfully. For instance, the newspaper teased Woodson about one of his research trips to Europe during the Great Depression, with a photograph and cutline that reported Woodson sailed to Europe on vacation ("Vacationing in Europe," 1932). Woodson took the comments seriously, responding that he was on a research mission and not rich enough to take such a vacation (Woodson, 1932n). However, Woodson did seem to be more relaxed in Paris during the research trips, as noted by associates in chapter 1. The *Afro* just seemed to be having fun with Woodson, as it did when it promoted celebration of Woodson's birthday (see below). Later, it devoted extensive space to his research.

The *Atlanta Daily World*, however, treated the European trip matter-of-factly from the start, reporting that Woodson would be conducting research at the British Museum, conducting interviews and visiting various people, and traveling from Paris to Brussels for other research ("Noted Human Touring," 1932).

Woodson was such an important figure that the black press celebrated his birthday and expressed concerns about the condition of his health as media today would about a president's health. Woodson's health thus became front-page news. Woodson had to issue a statement in 1926 denying he was in poor health, calling a report in the *Afro-American* that he had but a short time to live a "misrepresentation." In a letter published by newspapers, Woodson expressed concern about potential damage to his movement. He admitted a physician had predicted he would kill himself if he did not slow down, but the doctor did not say when he would die. Woodson added, "I am working myself to death for the Negro, but my health is generally good" ("Carter Woodson Refutes Report," 1926).

The *Afro*, however, was not silenced. The newspaper, on the eve of Woodson's birthday on December 19, 1928, published this headline: "YEAR IS OUT; HE'S STILL ALIVE AT 53" ("Year Is Out," 1928). The *Afro* even worked Woodson's health into a story about the annual meeting of ASNLH in New York in 1931, when John Hope, president of Atlanta University and ASNLH, disagreed, politely, with Woodson's criticism of the teaching of history. The *Afro* reported that Hope said he had offered Woodson a job as chairman of the history department at his university two years earlier, but Woodson declined, citing poor health. Hope said, "I think Dr. Woodson enjoys his bad health" ("Hope-Woodson Tilt," 1931).

NEWS: MIS-EDUCATION AND OPINION JOURNALISM

Woodson was not just any celebrity. He had become an opinion journalist whose celebrity made people notice him and his movement. His style attracted the attention of the *Crisis*, the NAACP publication edited by Du Bois. The *Crisis* published an article by Woodson titled "Miseducation* of the Negro" in 1931, after noticing his recent newspaper columns and speeches about black education, which laid out many of his thoughts before publication of *The Mis-Education of the Negro* in book form in 1933. The editor's note to the *Crisis* article stated Woodson was asked to contribute to that issue because he "has recently unsheathed his sword and leapt into the arena of the Negro press and splashed about so vigorously and relentlessly at almost everything in sight that the black world has been gasping each week" (Woodson, 1931d).

Woodson announced plans for releasing *The Mis-Education of the Negro* in a newspaper column (Woodson, 1933c). The book's theme was previewed in Woodson's speeches, and several book passages closely track the texts of newspaper columns he wrote before and after publication of *Mis-Education*. For instance, the bottom half of a column promoting ASNLH's upcoming

---

* Woodson hyphenated mis-education in the book title, but the *Crisis* did not use the hyphen in this article.

convention was a discussion of a polygamous deacon Woodson observed in his youth (Woodson, 1931f), and he retold the story in *The Mis-Education of the Negro*, almost verbatim, pages 71–72. He also repeated a discussion of black newspapers' handling of obituaries in the book, pages 158–159, after using it in a previous column (Woodson, 1932e).

In many of his speeches and articles, Woodson complained well-educated African Americans were mis-educated because they were taught much about whites and other races but little about black history. He also argued that the education system failed everyone, black and white, because it did not teach students how to think for themselves.

The book was met with criticism, too. Howard professor and columnist Kelly Miller greeted news of plans to publish *Mis-Education* by comparing Woodson to Marcus Garvey, (Miller, 1933), who had become a pariah among the black establishment for his willingness to work with the Ku Klux Klan. Miller connected Woodson to Garvey by stating both men supported racial self-respect and self-sufficiency, but Miller considered Garvey a radical and said Woodson's positions were moderated by his having obtained an Anglo-Saxon education and arriving at his efforts to rescue his race late in life. Woodson responded by calling Miller an "Uncle Tom type Negro" and a man of low intellect (Woodson, 1933g).

Lawrence A. Oxley, who headed a black division of public welfare in North Carolina and was later a member of FDR's kitchen cabinet, attacked the book in the white-owned, strongly segregationist *Raleigh News and Observer*. Oxley, whose comments were republished in the *Afro*, complained that Woodson offered no new ideas and dismissed him as "an historian—not an educator" (Oxley, 1933).

NEWS: NEWSPAPER INTERVIEWS, BROADCASTS

The *Afro-American* published a rare 1936 interview with Woodson. The headline called him an "eminent historian," detailed his daily routine, and saluted his decision to choose the low-paying history movement over a career paying a higher salary. Woodson was asked to respond to a Samuel Johnson quotation that writers should only write for money. Woodson responded, "If Johnson is correct, then I am not a writer, because when I write I never think of compensation. I think about the good I can do." In this interview, Woodson revealed he was not paid for his newspaper or magazine articles.

He said, "Only in the case of a few school books have I been able to derive a little profit beyond the cost of production" (Murphy, 1936).

Woodson appeared proud of the fact that he was not being paid to write for the press and used it as ammunition in a disagreement with Luther P. Jackson, who missed a deadline for a project with Woodson. Jackson was being paid for a regular column he wrote for the *Norfolk Journal and Guide* (Jackson, 1945c).

His disclosure about not being paid for the columns probably added to the Woodson mystique, which involved sacrificing economic gain for the greater good. However, it also indicated his understanding of a public relations routine. Public relations professionals usually do not charge newspapers (free media) for using their articles because they expect to be paid by their organizations. In fact, publication of a public relations professional's writings usually serves as proof to clients their messages reached the public.

By the late 1930s, Woodson and others in the history movement were reaping radio airtime from his celebrity status, too, and the radio broadcasts attracted more newspaper coverage. During ASNLH's 1938 meeting, Woodson addressed the nation in a live broadcast from New York, a ten-minute speech highlighting black accomplishments. Several newspapers published stories about the broadcast, including the *Pittsburgh Courier* ("Woodson to Broadcast," 1938) and the *Defender* ("Broadcast Features," 1938). Other papers published stories promoting a broadcast featuring Woodson during Negro History Week the following year, including the *New York Amsterdam News* ("Dr. Woodson to Open Negro History Week," 1939) and the *Cleveland Call and Post* ("'Wings Over Jordan' Program to Feature Carter Woodson," 1939). The *Negro History Bulletin* reported a broadcast supporting Negro History Week over WOC in Davenport, Iowa, by Leon Harris, president of the National Federation of Colored Farmers, and it printed a transcript of the broadcast ("Negro History Week Broadcast," 1939).

Woodson had strong views about what was appropriate for radio, as he had expressed for newspapers. He complained about *Amos 'n Andy* and other shows that stereotyped blacks ("Attacks 'Amos 'n Andy,'" 1930). He also served on an advisory committee for "Freedom's People," which ran on NBC radio (1941–1942), a program produced partly in recognition of black achievements, partly to shore up black support for World War II (Savage, 1999).

NEWS: CONTROVERSY

Woodson frequently was embroiled in controversy, and the newspapers' advocacy of his cause created a stir. For example, the *Afro-American* made Woodson's nonselection in the Who's Who a controversy in 1924. In a page 1 article, the *Afro* said that just 44 of the Who's Who publication's more than 25,000 biographies were sketches of the lives of African Americans. The *Afro* complained that men of far fewer achievements than Woodson's were included ("Who's Who," 1924).

Of course, Woodson himself did not shy away from public disputes, and newspaper coverage of him frequently involved controversies he induced. In a battle against segregation and racism, Woodson had a public falling out with the Chesapeake and Ohio Railroad, a company long associated with his family in Huntington. He thought he was denied a seat on a train from Washington, DC, back to West Virginia on account of his race, and he gave copies of his irate letter to the black press ("Dr. Carter Woodson Flays C&O R.R.," 1932).

Woodson's well-known penchant for challenging conventional wisdom and critiquing positions of colleagues and others with whom he disagreed prompted *Cleveland Call and Post* columnist Floyd Calvin to remark that it was amazing people still respected Woodson, especially educators. Presumably, despite Woodson's temperament and occasional displays of sarcasm, his work was appreciated. "Our point is," Calvin wrote, "Dr. Woodson preaches sound doctrine, whether it is liked or not. We need more Dr. Woodsons to cry aloud in the wilderness" (Calvin, 1937).

Having complained about how the press handled controversies, Woodson was well aware controversies (conflicts) were factors in deciding what to print as news. He clearly understood how to make news. It is not suggested here that all of Woodson's feuds were intended to attract press interest, but events involving controversy attracted news coverage. Woodson earned a reputation among friends both inside and outside the media for speaking his mind and lashing out at foes, as Calvin hinted. Several of the Woodson feuds appeared personal, but even they involved interpretations of history and post-slavery lessons about relationships between the races and control of black institutions and culture—allowing Woodson to position himself as a fighter defending the race—in many disagreements. His heroic adventures and his battles with adversaries, both personal and on behalf of the race, were news.

One of Woodson's most famous rows involved J. Stanley Durkee, the white president of Howard University, where Woodson was serving as dean of liberal arts. He was insubordinate and considered Durkee incompetent and an exploiter of blacks.

Charles H. Wesley, a Woodson confidant, recalled what Woodson told him about a meeting he had with Durkee. During that meeting, Woodson told Durkee he was not worth a continental. Wesley asked whether Durkee understood the reference to continental. Woodson responded he did, although Durkee would have better understood coarser language (Wesley, 1998).

Woodson lost his job in the disagreement with Durkee in 1920, but he remained insolent in his discussions about Durkee for many years. In 1925, the *New York Amsterdam News* and other newspapers reported that Woodson was refusing to speak from the same platform with Durkee. He had accepted a speaking engagement with the Maryland State Teachers' Association, a group of black educators, before he saw the program with Durkee's name. The newspaper reprinted Woodson's letter dated October 31, 1925, to L. S. James. Woodson said he would not appear on the same stage with a person who had "insulted and exploited" blacks as Durkee had done (Woodson, 1925b).

There were other feuds, in the meantime, that the black press followed closely:

- The *Afro* praised the book *Negro Orators and Their Orations*, edited by Woodson in 1925, but the newspaper criticized him for omitting the orations of Kelly Miller and Du Bois, two national figures with whom Woodson occasionally clashed ("Orators," 1925).
- Woodson drew headlines in 1931 when he left the Mu-So-Lit Club in Washington, DC, after the arrival of Perry W. Howard, a black Republican national committeeman in charge of patronage in Mississippi and former assistant to the US attorney general. He accused Howard of calling his friend Mordecai Johnson, a former West Virginia pastor and by then the first black president of Howard University, a Communist. In a letter to the club's directors, the full text of which was reproduced in the *Afro-American*, Woodson urged Howard's exclusion from the membership roster, saying, "I must confess that the presence of this man is so obnoxious to me that when he entered the room of the club where I was a few evenings ago I instinctively walked out" ("MU-So-Lit Club," 1931).
- John Hawkins, president of the Association for the Study of Negro Life and History, resigned in June 1931 after Woodson's attacks

on failures of black leadership. The *Philadelphia Tribune* printed
Hawkins's letter of resignation. The lead paragraph of the article,
distributed by CNS, a news-gathering service, confirmed rumors
about disharmony at ASNLH in hard-news tones and criticized
Woodson for his tirades ("Hawkins Quits," 1931). The newspaper
mistakenly referred to Woodson as publicity director, but it accurately described his role within the organization and history movement ("Hawkins Quits," 1931).

Chapter 4

MAKING NEWS
WITH NEWSPAPER COLUMNS

WOODSON PERSONALIZED THE BLACK HISTORY MOVEMENT BY VOLUN-
teering his personal thoughts about the past, often linking them to various
issues of the day, his family's experiences, and those of his acquaintances
in Washington, DC, West Virginia, and elsewhere. He also highlighted how
uniquely qualified he was to set the record straight in books and articles he
authored, especially in the newspaper columns he distributed for publication
over his final two decades.

No mainstream white news publications are known to have published any
of Woodson's columns, and it cannot be determined how many black newspapers published his work. However, the articles were certainly available in
many urban areas with large black populations, where the major black newspapers circulated—including all of the following newspapers: *Atlanta Daily
World*, *Afro-American*, *Chicago Defender*, *Cleveland Call and Post*, *Louisiana
Weekly* (New Orleans), *Negro World* (New York), *New York Amsterdam News*,
Norfolk Journal and Guide, *Philadelphia Tribune*, and *Pittsburgh Courier*.
The *Atlanta Daily World*, the only black daily newspaper during most of the
period in this study, sometimes published the same column on back-to-back
days, giving him and his thoughts double exposure. The *Louisiana Weekly*
on several occasions published two of his columns in the same edition.

Black newspapers published more than 200 of the Woodson columns
identified for this study, but the exact number he released for publication
remains unknown. Identifying all of the columns is complicated by the fact
that as many as 200 to 300 newspapers had access to the columns at any
given time. The number varied because not all the columns were published

the same week or under the same headlines. Several news agencies were involved in distributing the articles, with most of the papers providing their own headlines and editing and deciding whether to run them in their entirety. Few of the columns have been located in the original forms Woodson released before they were edited in individual newsrooms.

Sister Anthony Scally collected and classified articles and books published by and about Woodson in a bio-bibliography (1985). However, her collection was assembled before many black newspapers were made convenient to researchers in digital databases. She identified 144 columns published in the *Pittsburgh Courier, Chicago Defender*, and *New York Age* from 1931 to 1936. She cited no articles before April 18, 1931, none in 1933, and none after 1936.

Woodson's interest in newspaper writing was expressed as early as the 1920s in correspondence with Marcus Garvey's *Negro World* about writing a review of a book his publishing company was releasing (Fortune, 1923). Editor T. Thomas Fortune indicated interest in publishing such an article, but no such article, if published, was located during the research for this study, which was hampered by the fact that several editions of *Negro World* available on microfilm included unreadable pages. Also, *Negro World* maintained incomplete files of its published editions and missed several issues while it struggled financially and dealt with Garvey's imprisonment for mail fraud and deportation. These circumstances make it difficult to determine how many of the Woodson columns that newspaper published before it folded in 1933.

Woodson's byline was rarely seen in newspapers before 1930. The *Chicago Defender*'s serialization of *The Negro in Our History* in 1923, over several weekly editions, carried the earliest of Woodson's newspaper articles found in this study. Just two other newspaper articles with Woodson's name as the author were located in the 1920s. The first Negro History Week was promoted with a discussion in a column (Woodson, 1926) about black contributions in history, including teaching the world to use iron ore and discovering America. Having established Negro History Week in 1926, Woodson soon began encouraging its observance as an annual national event, as he did in another column (February 2, 1927).

The columns assembled for the present study were published through 1949, but most were published from 1931 to 1937, and more than half of the published pieces were printed before Woodson announced publication of *The Mis-Education of the Negro* in a January 1933 column. The themes of Woodson's columns and speeches before 1933 formed the bulk of that book's content.

Woodson often used the columns to attack the vestiges of slavery (especially segregation) and blacks who were employed in high-profile jobs that aided white segregationists. He often resorted to name-calling, which he did in one column underneath the headline "Reply to Uncle Tom and His Coworkers' Attacks" (Woodson, 1933g).

Many of Woodson's columns supported Negro History Week and provided lessons about slavery, segregation, and the Great Depression, as well as support for ASNLH and its meetings. Woodson also commented on economic independence, international affairs, uplift, politics, the arts, feuds involving foundation executives, and the management of Howard University. An underlying theme in most of his writings involved proposals to reform the education system and black churches, especially during the 1930s, whether it was the main topic of that particular column or not. Woodson did not lose sight of his overall goal to prevent blacks from becoming negligible factors in the world, and invariably he related his commentaries, often lengthy, to educating the public about history through the platforms the newspapers extended him.

On these platforms, Woodson's columns were tactics promoting his campaign. His columns usually did not draw distinctions between journalism and public relations. While it was often clear he was representing the interests of the Association for the Study of Negro Life and History, he rarely disclosed conflicts of interest in promoting his privately held publishing firm, Associated Publishers. Lending support on behalf of his friends and associates was apparent, too, when he urged donations to the Nannie Burroughs boarding school (Woodson, 1932f) and when he occasionally reviewed and/ or commented favorably regarding the books he published as president of Associated Publishers, such as Walter H. Mazyck's *George Washington and the Negro* (Woodson, 1932a); Edwin B. Henderson's *The Negro in Sports* (1939b), which included an editor's note on how readers could purchase Henderson's book; and George W. Brown's *The Economic History of Liberia* (1941a). Two of Woodson's 1941 articles were advances of the ASNLH annual conference, with one previewing Brown's discussion of Liberia at that meeting (1941c, 1941d).

Hyping Mazyck's work, Woodson said that he "has set a fine example of what a trained man can do to discover the truth and uproot propaganda" (Woodson, 1932a). Privately, a decade later, however, Woodson was dismissive of the book in a letter to Luther P. Jackson, dated May 15, 1943. Woodson said the book was not well written, but he hoped it would generate sales (Woodson, 1943b).

Woodson's columns were appealing to newspaper editors: he was an expert on a subject with whom they agreed, and they did not have to pay him for that expertise. He was providing news content, and no evidence was found indicating they considered his articles propaganda. When he went too far in his attacks on enemies, he was simply drawing attention to make news and increase readership.

Woodson did not use the term "columnist" to describe his newspaper work, but the newspapers that published the articles treated them as columns, as does this study. Woodson's photograph was published with many of the articles, which usually read as personal essays and informed, political opinions, making their classification as columns consistent with traditional definitions.

Woodson called his articles and announcements to the newspapers "releases," and the *Afro-American* even teased (promoted) a Woodson column as any newspaper would promote pieces written by syndicated columnists or local writers. "Do not fail to read Dr. Carter G. Woodson's article in the Afro this week," read the lead paragraph. The article told readers about a white southerner on an ocean liner with Woodson who announced in a loud voice he would not eat a meal with a black person ("Looking for Peace or War?" 1932).

References to documents as releases being distributed for publication, whether as news, features, or announcements, were common in the black press during the period of this study. The Associated Negro Press, the distribution service used for many of the articles, for instance, referred to most of the features and news items distributed to newspapers subscribing to its services as releases (articles and other items intended for dissemination). Several of the releases from Woodson were no more than notices about upcoming meetings and program schedules, but often a Woodson byline was affixed to them.

Woodson also used the columns as weapons in his various public feuds. For example, when he had a falling out with Howard University trustee Emmett J. Scott, Woodson complained in a column that Scott and the black Republican leadership exploited the black population. Because Scott's political activities included having made speeches on Herbert Hoover's behalf in the 1928 election, Howard University's independence was threatened by such politics, Woodson reasoned. He said Democrats would be expected to appoint their own employees at the university if they won control of the government (Woodson, 1931c).

Although he complained about politics and accused many politicians of being on the take, Woodson's own public statements often appeared to be political, but not necessarily partisan. A newspaper headline suggested Woodson supported Franklin Roosevelt over Hoover in 1932, but he was actually arguing in that column that blacks should be politically independent. He argued that their alliance with and dependence on the Republican Party following slavery increased racial prejudice and tensions with Democrats, and the GOP showed no loyalty to African Americans when it abandoned them later for a political agenda (Woodson, 1932m).

Woodson cautioned black voters against supporting political machines and advised them to use their votes wisely. He urged independence and warned against getting in the middle of a balance of power struggle between political parties (Woodson, 1932m).

Suspicious of politicians of both parties, Woodson criticized policies of several presidents, especially Herbert Hoover and FDR. He wrote that "the present regime of the oppressor would hang Thomas Jefferson, if he lived today," pointing a finger at FDR (Woodson, 1936c). He also criticized Roosevelt for assigning minor, segregated roles to blacks in his first inauguration (Woodson, 1933f). Of Hoover, Woodson wrote, "I do not think the President knows what he is doing or what he is talking about. Most of what he says on the economic situation reads like any essay of a high school boy" (Woodson, 1932b).

Woodson had a brush with black political independence early in his career in West Virginia. His cousin Carter H. Barnett had been fired in 1900 for promoting an independent black Republican slate as editor of the *West Virginia Spectator*, while holding down the job of principal of Douglass School. Barnett's firing led to Woodson's hiring as principal (see chapter 3).

Woodson respected the presidencies of Abraham Lincoln and George Washington. He even rejected his mother's dislike of Washington and said her low opinion of the first president was based on her view of his statue in Richmond when she was on her way to a slave pen before being auctioned. The statue pointed south, and many slaves interpreted this gesture as a command for blacks to be transported to the southern states to make cotton king, a complaint Woodson said he heard in his parents' home, but rejected as a historian. He commended what Washington did in building a Union that Lincoln saved with the end of slavery. "Had the Union been built upon any other foundation than that on which it was begun," Woodson said, "it would not have endured, and without the preservation of the Union slavery could not have been abolished in 1865" (Woodson, 1936b). Woodson praised US chief justice John Marshall for his nationalism, which he thought the Supreme Court abandoned after Marshall's death and made the government less likely to support black rights (Woodson, 1921).

Woodson frequently made Thomas Jesse Jones, a Phelps Stokes Fund director, a villain and threat to the black community. Jones drew Woodson's indignation because Woodson believed Jones had caused the association to lose support from philanthropists. He also accused Jones of exporting racist notions in the education of American blacks to Africa (Woodson, 1932j). Phelps Stokes also backed the black encyclopedia project that Woodson believed snubbed him.

Woodson expressed disappointment in the African Americans who cooperated on the encyclopedia and challenged their credentials as historians. He had been invited, too, after the group preparing the encyclopedia was organized, but he declined because he thought the invitation was an afterthought and that Jones and his white colleagues were not sincere ("Dr. Carter G. Woodson Scores Noted Negroes!" 1936). Black newspapers stoked the feud. The *Atlanta Daily World* reported that prominent scholar and educator Benjamin Brawley and Woodson were arguing intensely over the black encyclopedia and that W. E. B. Du Bois and other noted blacks were "flayed by eminent historian," in its page 1 article on June 5, 1936. A columnist wrote: "The controversy between Dr. Carter G. Woodson and Benjamin Brawley is about to reach its climax" (Perry, 1936). Woodson followed up with a fiery column, questioning Brawley's scholarship and citing a low estimate of his work published in a *New York Times* review (Woodson, 1936d).

Woodson also criticized the committee planning the celebration of the bicentennial of George Washington's birth, February 22, 1932. He described the committee as a group that only wanted to observe black participation as slaves, unwilling to recognize the many blacks who were part of the nation's founding (Woodson, 1931h, 1931i, 1931j, 1931k, 1931l).

The two most powerful institutions in black communities, it was widely believed, were the churches and newspapers. Woodson criticized the press gently, preferring to educate its members about their responsibilities. However, he waged a long-running battle with black church leaders and frequently attacked what he perceived as their excesses—as problems that needed correcting in order to achieve racial progress—and they resisted his suggested reforms ("Wright Says Woodson Seeks Only Publicity," 1931), often prompting additional coverage beyond the opinion pages, such as Woodson's response to church critics who claimed he only wanted publicity ("Woodson Answers Wright," 1931). The church feud was most pronounced during the 1930s.

Woodson's column-writing style can be compared to that of H. L. Mencken's, whose biting, sarcastic style was a major presence in American journalism during the period of the present study. Mencken also was a harsh critic of black clergy, and his writings were often picked up by black newspapers. At one point, criticism of the black church by Mencken and Woodson, on a day when both of their columns were featured (Woodson, 1931b), was so intense that the editor of the *Philadelphia Tribune* asked a member of the local black clergy to respond and printed a note above Woodson's column ("Editor's Note," 1931).

A response to another Woodson column—that church leaders were enriching themselves and leaving large estates to their families and little or nothing to their congregations after the churchmen died—led to an *Afro-American* investigation of the wills of church bishops, which the newspaper said confirmed Woodson's claim ("Late A.M.E. Prelate," 1931).

While he was criticizing church leaders for leaving large estates to their family members, Woodson was planning to do the opposite, although it was not widely known at that time. Woodson's will, written in 1934, left most of his assets to the Association for the Study of Negro Life and History, with just $500 to each of his surviving siblings. At the time of Woodson's death, one brother and one sister survived him—Robert, who died soon after Woodson, and his sister Bessie, whom he had supported. He had allowed her to live in a home he owned and to rent out rooms for her income in Huntington. That home became the property of ASNLH upon Woodson's death. The association allowed Bessie to take over the home in Huntington, and Nelson and Ancella Bickley, Bessie's grandson and his wife, said they paid off the mortgage (Interview, May 29, 2012). An essay by Willie Leanna Miles, a former Woodson employee, also confirmed the sale and the family's desire to keep the home within the Woodson family (Miles 1991). Woodson could easily have left his estate to family members, especially to the sister he famously stated in a column he was supporting financially (Woodson, 1933d). However, his will's bequeaths helped him avoid being seen as a hypocrite on this issue, unlike the church leaders he criticized.

Woodson's criticism of the church was at its most intense in 1931 with columns such as the one titled "Worthless Pastors Halt the Union of Churches" (Woodson, 1931e). ASNLH scheduled for its 1931 annual meeting a session on black churches—how they had not lived up to their responsibilities.

However, the Rev. R. R. Wright Jr., editor of the *Christian Recorder*, declined an invitation to address ASNLH's November meeting. Instead, he charged Woodson "with being biased and incompetent and describes the program of the meeting to be held by the association . . . as a cheap advertisement of racial weaknesses" ("Wright Says Woodson Seeks Only Publicity," 1931).

Woodson explained his views on organized religion, revealing he was partly influenced by a devout white Episcopalian who boasted about his participation in the brutal lynching of four blacks in Clifton Forge, Virginia, in 1892. Woodson said he met the man at Nuttallburg, West Virginia, during Woodson's six-year apprenticeship in the coal mines. Woodson argued that most blacks had learned religion from men such as the Episcopalian coal miner and slaveholders, who often used religion to support the slavery system. With such a basis for black religion, Woodson questioned its legitimacy (Woodson, 1931f).

Because Woodson often complained about black church leadership, Christian Methodist Episcopal (CME) Church leaders were caught by surprise when the CME's *Christian Index*, the denomination's newsletter, published a Woodson column critical of blacks who assisted racists and profited from segregation. One of the people named was Channing Tobias, a top official of the YMCA's segregated, black division, who would later become chairman of the NAACP in the 1950s. Tobias was an ordained CME minister, and Woodson argued that segregation was un-Christian. Church officials attending a meeting of the Atlanta district passed a resolution condemning the article and the editor, G. C. Parker, for publishing it ("Protest Action," 1932).

Encouraging a streamlining in the number of black churches because he thought there were too many, Woodson also complained about the qualifications of preachers, claiming that "anybody of the lowest type may go into the Negro ministry" (Woodson, 1933h).

Woodson appeared before the African Methodist Episcopal (AME) church board in 1933, declaring, "I am not a preacher fighter, unless that preacher is doing something wrong." He said he was criticizing "our preachers for not saying more about our great men in and out of the church. I find they preach about Alexander and Caesar, both of whom were rascals and brought woe upon us" ("A.M.E.'s Carry On," 1933).

Woodson was active in the Washington, DC, branch of the NAACP, although he tried to avoid mixing what he called race leadership with his history program. He was warning against mixing research and agitation for civil rights until the end of his life. He advised the black historians he knew against "developing into professional race leaders." He said they should be committed to truth, not agitation (Woodson, 1945a).

Woodson wrote columns complaining that communities needed workers committed to their uplift, not leaders who might exploit their plight (Woodson, 1932k), and privately upbraided Luther P. Jackson, the Virginia State College history professor and his leading fund-raiser in Virginia, for his work with the NAACP. Woodson preferred to make his mark as a scientifically trained historian, which he emphasized in correspondence with Jackson.

On several occasions, Woodson openly discussed personal sacrifices in pursuing the history program's goals, offering the sacrifices, in one column, as an explanation for why he did not marry. The newspapers had already made him a sympathetic figure, and the column enlarged his image. A *Chicago Defender* headline called that story "The Vow of Poverty," as Woodson wrote that he returned most of his pay to the association, except for a few dollars he spent on necessities and sent to his widowed sister in Huntington, West Virginia (Woodson, 1933d).

He explained he could not afford a wife under such circumstances, but newspapers remained fascinated by his bachelorhood. A. L. Jackson, head of Chicago's Wabash Avenue YMCA and one of the people who helped Woodson organize ASNLH, said his wife often teased Woodson about being a bachelor. "His reply always was, 'I am married to the Journal'" (Association for the Study of African American Life and History, 1990). Toward the end of his life, he was interviewed about a woman whom he supposedly jilted in the Philippines. He shrugged it off, saying it was more likely he was the jilted one ("Research and Romance," 1947).

Woodson seemed to move effortlessly through the streets of Washington, and he observed urban problems up close. He disclosed in one column that he was robbed at gunpoint of $5. The mugging was at least the second close call for Woodson, who had been caught in downtown Washington in the middle of the 1919 race riot and narrowly escaped with his life (Perl, 1999).

Using strong language condemning the robbers, on the one hand, he also expressed sympathy for their plight and excused their behavior because of the poor state of the economy, on the other. He wanted to find jobs for the perpetrators and, flashing his public relations, goodwill side, managed to plug an ASNLH study in the process. Woodson wrote: "I joined with certain citizens in petitioning employers of labor to provide in some way for the large number of unemployed Negroes, as shown by the recent survey made by the Association for the Study of Negro Life and History" (Woodson, 1933e).

Woodson's newspaper-column writing tapered off after 1937, the year he created the *Negro History Bulletin*. Scally identified fifty-seven Woodson articles that were published in the *Negro History Bulletin*, 1941–1950 (Scally, 1985), a fact suggesting he was no slouch and probably concentrating on building up the content of this magazine (and the *Journal of Negro History*). During the 1940s, Woodson seemed to tone down his language in attacking enemies in the newspaper columns. His revised style used less name-calling, even in speeches, but his passion about history and opposition to racism and segregation did not diminish. However, his career as a newspaper columnist had peaked.

Just 24 of the more than 200 newspaper columns that were located for this study of Woodson and the press were published in his final decade. The black press noted a decline in Woodson's book publishing, too. In an article lamenting an overall drop in the publication of books by African Americans, the *Chicago Defender* singled out Woodson's Associated Publishers for publishing but one book "this Fall season, 'Harriett Tubman,' and that by a white writer, Earl Conrad." While he commended Woodson's work, the newspaper's commentator, Ben Burns, was a white reporter and editor who complained that too many of the books about the black problem were being written by whites (Burns, 1943).

Woodson showed both optimism and pessimism in several of his final columns. He believed African Americans would gain greater access to the political process, but he argued the US government would have to reconcile its mistreatment of blacks with its ambition to lead the free world (Woodson, 1946a), a position that was consistent with the black press's Double-V theme of victory at home and abroad during World War II. Woodson returned to this theme (Woodson, 1946c) when he argued the nation would have difficulty as a world leader because it mistreated nonwhites. He complained about corrupt segregationists and members of Congress who did not know history, while commenting on most presidents through FDR (Woodson, 1946d). He continued to argue, as he had most of his professional life, that the promise of freedom was not delivered following the Civil War (Woodson, 1947a), and he reaffirmed his commitment to Africa (Woodson, 1947b) and truth (Woodson, 1948a). The final column found was a promotion of Negro History Week in 1949 (Woodson, 1949a).

That America would have to improve its treatment of African Americans for reasons involving its international prestige (image and/or public relations) was not just a position held by Woodson and his newspaper supporters. It was argued forcefully by Gunnar Myrdal (1944) and writer Pearl S. Buck (Buck, 1942).

THE KNOWN LIST OF CARTER G. WOODSON COLUMNS

The present study collected writings released by Carter G. Woodson for publication in newspapers from 1926 to 1949. Having stated he was an unpaid newspaper writer, Woodson signaled he was writing to further his program's cause—preventing black history from becoming a negligible force in the world.

While these columns were made available by Woodson to many black newspapers, only one newspaper source is identified below to reduce the possibility of duplicating articles on the list. Woodson was producing about one column a week during the early 1930s, before his production declined. As far as can be determined, no single newspaper published all of the columns found in this study, and each newspaper had the option of editing them and writing distinct headlines, further adding to the difficulty of distinguishing the same article published in different newspapers.

At least two of the newspapers, *Negro World* and *Chicago Defender*, occasionally summarized the columns in news formats, directly quoting and paraphrasing Woodson's statements instead of running the full articles.

On such occasions, the *Defender* and *Negro World* treated Woodson's opinions as news items instead of columns. For example, the *Defender* paraphrased Woodson on such issues as segregated theaters ("Jim Crow Theaters and Our Artists," 1933) and racial unity ("Says Lack of Racial Unity Not Unusual," 1938). In 1940, some newspapers published a Woodson column about plans to discuss the crisis in the West Indies at ASNLH's upcoming Chicago meeting, but the *Defender* summarized it as it would a news release ("Historians to Discuss Plight of West Indies," 1940).

LIST OF COLUMNS IN ORDER OF DATES PUBLISHED

The following is a compilation of more than 200 newspaper columns identified as having been written by Carter G. Woodson and published by one or more general-circulation African American newspapers. The list includes publication dates, headlines, names of the publications, and page numbers.

This list does not include the articles serialized in the *Chicago Defender* from the book *The Negro in Our History* in 1923.

(1926, February 13). Negro was first to discover America, he taught modern world to use iron. *Afro-American*, p. 11.

(1927, February 2). National Negro History Week celebration from February 6 to 13. *New York Amsterdam News*, p. 16.

(1931, January 31). What price education? *Norfolk Journal and Guide*, p. 8.

(1931, February 7). Dr. Woodson answers critics: Defends stand on our school systems. *Chicago Defender*, p. 2.

(1931, February 28). Some suggestions on education. *Norfolk Journal and Guide*, p. 8.

(1931, March 21). Twenty years wasted, says DC historian. *Negro World*, p. 1. (Woodson's byline is not used, as was the case with several columns printed by the *Negro World* and sometimes the *Chicago Defender*. This article is introduced by a statement about Woodson's attack on the higher-education system. Each paragraph begins with a direct quotation of what he said. There is no statement that the quotations are from a speech or taken directly from a column, but the paragraphs read like the cohesive paragraphs of a column.)

(1931, March 21). Bosses or toadies. *Norfolk Journal and Guide*, p. 8.

(1931, March 28). Do highly educated people graduate from the churches of the masses? Noted historian asks. *Norfolk Journal and Guide*, p. 16.

(1931, April 11). Whites plan to exterminate tribes and make Africa white man's country. *Afro-American*, p. 12.

(1931, April 18). Higher education's weaknesses assailed by C. G. Woodson, historian answers criticisms of his accusers. *Norfolk Journal and Guide*, p. 2.

(1931, April 25). Schools and colleges: Legal research at H.U. law school is confined to sniping at Dr. Johnson. *Afro-American*, p. 16.

(1931, May 14). Southern Negroes fall heir to $40,000 bribe money in close presidential elections. *Philadelphia Tribune*, p. 9.

(1931, May 16). Woodson says the business education of the Negro has been a failure. *Norfolk Journal and Guide*, p. 2.

(1931, May 28). Carter Woodson tells why the highly educated clergy preach to benches. *Philadelphia Tribune*, p. 9.

(1931, June 18). The Negro emphasizes "narcotics" of religion: Whites as emotional in field of religion. *Philadelphia Tribune*, p. 9.

(1931, July 2). Sees danger in Howard official playing politics. *Philadelphia Tribune*, p. 9.

(1931, July 29). The inconsistency of students of radicalism. *New York Amsterdam News*, p. 9.

(1931, August 13). Carter G. Woodson earnestly urges union of all Negro churches.... *Philadelphia Tribune*, p. 9.

(1931, August 26). Difficulties now in way of union of Negro churches. *New York Amsterdam News*, p. 9.

(1931, September 2). Some leaders consider church union utopian. *New York Amsterdam News*, p. 9.

(1931, September 5). When the masses learn to think, we will have a united Negro church, says Woodson. *Norfolk Journal and Guide*, p. A7.

(1931, September 8). Radical proposals for united Negro church. *New York Amsterdam News*, p. 9.

(1931, September 16). Church disunion forces preachers into politics. *New York Amsterdam News*, p. 9.

(1931, September 23). Church edifices said to be property in Mortmain. *New York Amsterdam News*, p. 9.

(1931, September 26). Church investments far out of proportion, says Woodson. *Norfolk Journal and Guide*, p. A11.

(1931, September 30). Theology now a factor in disunion of churches. *New York Amsterdam News*, p. 9.

(1931, October 7). Worthless pastors halt the union of churches. *New York Amsterdam News*, p. 9.

(1931, October 10). Churches need enlightened program, says Dr. Woodson: Racketeers of religion are burden, he says. *Norfolk Journal and Guide*, p. 5.

(1931, October 14). Survey shows need for the union of churches. *New York Amsterdam News*, p. 9.

(1931, October 21). To subject Negro church to meeting's acid test. *New York Amsterdam News*, p. 9.

(1931, October 28). Comparison of Negroes in America and West Indies. *New York Amsterdam News*, p. 9.

(1931, October 31). West Indian contribution to U.S. to be studied when historians meet. *Afro-American*, p. 18.

(1931, November 7). West Indian racial purity an advantage in race consciousness: West Indians of pure African type. *Afro-American*, p. 2.

(1931, November 11). An iconoclast expresses his views on the Negro. *New York Amsterdam News*, p. 11.

(1931, November 18). The Negro community finding, working in it. *New York Amsterdam News*, p. 9.

(1931, December 2). Church corruption facts now called "half-baked." *New York Amsterdam News*, p. 8.

(1931, December 9). Vital suggestions on the Washington Bicentennial. *New York Amsterdam News*, p. 8.

(1931, December 10). Negroes' past glorious as other races: In former times 3–4 of all white men in U.S. were slaves. *Philadelphia Tribune*, p. 9.

(1931, December 16). Honoring Washington by traducement. *New York Amsterdam News*, p. 8.

(1931, December 23). Eliminating the Negro from the Bicentennial. *New York Amsterdam News*, p. 8.

(1931, December 30). Bicentennial eliminates Crispus Attucks's day. *New York Amsterdam News*, p. 8.

(1932, January 6). 18th century Negro had more courage than today. *New York Amsterdam News*, p. 8.

(1932, January 13). Mazyck compiles book on George Washington. *New York Amsterdam News*, p. 9.

(1932, January 20). The Negro less outspoken today than a century ago. *New York Amsterdam News*, p. 8.

(1932, January 24). George Washington as he really was. *Atlanta Daily World*, p. 4.

(1932, January 27). Why Negroes do not go in the right direction. *New York Amsterdam News*, p. 8.

(1932, February 4). Incredible work with scant resources done by history association. *Philadelphia Tribune*, p. 9.

(1932, February 7). Dr. Woodson answers critics: Defends stand on our school systems. *Chicago Defender*, p. 2.

(1932, February 13). True dramatization of Negro life needed, belief of Woodson. *Atlanta Daily World*, p. 5.

(1932, February 14). Woodson explains purpose, aims of history week. *Atlanta Daily World*, p. 4.

(1932, February 24). The Depression and its blessings to the Negro. *New York Amsterdam News*, p. 8.

(1932, March 3). "Miseducated, highly educated" Negro does more to keep group in state of turmoil. *Philadelphia Tribune*, p. 9.

(1932, March 5). "Unwise leadership" cause of lack of progress made by Negro race. *Norfolk Journal and Guide*, p. 7.

(1932, March 5). Common sense is vital requisite to advancement. *Pittsburgh Courier*, p. A2.

(1932, March 9). Cooperation hindrances present in Negro race. *New York Amsterdam News*, p. 8.

(1932, March 16). Negro youth now trying to find way in industry. *New York Amsterdam News*, p. 8.

(1932, March 26). O, for the days of $8 suits and return of $10 per month board. *Norfolk Journal and Guide*, p. 7.

(1932, March 30). Poverty from Depression should not be alarming. *New York Amsterdam News*, p. 8.

(1932, April 6). Meager contribution to Washington leadership. *New York Amsterdam News*, p. 8.

(1932, April 7). Knockers make capital graveyard of ambition, proclaims Woodson. *Atlanta Daily World*, p. 2.

(1932, April 9). Auction bridge expertness rated higher than real achievements. *Norfolk Journal and Guide*, p. 7.

(1932, April 13). Some ways of getting out of the bread line. *New York Amsterdam News*, p. 8.

(1932, April 20). Comments on symposium on "higher education." *New York Amsterdam News*, p. 8.

(1932, April 30). Do you study the Negro? Most Negroes do not, claims historian: Tells why race should know itself. *Norfolk Journal and Guide*, p. 7.

(1932, May 14). Carter G. Woodson in fervid plea for Nannie Burroughs. *Pittsburgh Courier*, p. A2.

(1932, May 21). Is educated Negro a liability? Woodson says barber shops are best schools in many cases. *Norfolk Journal and Guide*, p. 7.

(1932, May 21). Negro business man too "individualistic" and too easily becomes a "social lion" to make lasting success of big business enterprises. *Philadelphia Tribune*, p. 9.

(1932, May 28). Vocational guidance. *Chicago Defender*, p. 14.

(1932, June 4). And so Miss Bowles goes the way of Moorland. *Chicago Defender*, p. A2.

(1932, June 8). Exploitation of Negroes can never be education. *New York Amsterdam News*, p. 8.

(1932, June 11). Harpers Ferry president should be forced to leave Storer, Dr. Woodson says. *Afro-American*, p. 9.

(1932, June 18). American Dictionary of Biography another of those things, says Woodson. *Afro-American*, p. 8.

(1932, June 23). Negro has too much hindsight. *Atlanta Daily World*, p. 6A.

(1932, June 28). And the Negro loses his soul. *Atlanta Daily World*, p. 6A.

(1932, June 29). Woodson finds London rife with prejudice. *Atlanta Daily World*, p. 6A.

(1932, July 3). In big fight. *Atlanta Daily World*, p. 1.

(1932, July 6). One most undesirable aspect of segregation. *New York Amsterdam News*, p. 6.

(1932, July 7). White heads of Negro colleges. *Atlanta Daily World*, p. 6.

(1932, July 9). Thomas Jesse Jones termed undesirable; disapproved by Booker T. Washington. *Afro-American*, p. 8.

(1932, July 13). History of segregation and slavery are parallel. *New York Amsterdam News*, p. 6.

(1932, July 20). Illustration of making the most of segregation. *New York Amsterdam News*, p. 6.

(1932, July 23). Races cooperate to take education out of Psalm-Singin' Class–Woodson. *Norfolk Journal and Guide*, p. 7.

(1932, July 30). Are you a segregationist? Let every man examine himself, says Woodson. *Norfolk Journal and Guide*, p. 7.

(1932, August 3). Does segregation solve a problem or make one? *New York Amsterdam News*, p. 6.

(1932, August 6). The majority is not always right, points out Dr. Woodson: Mob wants segregation. *Norfolk Journal and Guide*, p. 7

(1932, August 10). Negro fails to make the most out of segregation. *New York Amsterdam News*, p. 6.

(1932, August 17). Negro can free himself of exploiting leaders. *New York Amsterdam News*, p. 6.

(1932, August 19). Dismal future painted by sage Carter G. Woodson. *Atlanta Daily World*, p. 6.

(1932, August 27). Leadership must be translated into service if the people are to be helped, says Dr. Woodson. *Norfolk Journal and Guide*, p. 7.

(1932, September 3). Political leaders have led rather than forward. *Afro-American*, p. 8.

(1932, September 8). Woodson yearning for Pres. Hoover's defeat. *Atlanta Daily World*, p. 6A.

(1932, September 16). Dr. Woodson urges voters in next election to use ballots discriminately. *Atlanta Daily World*, p. 6.

(1932, September 17). The new Negro in politics is not a politician but a man in the opinion of Dr. Carter G. Woodson. *Norfolk Journal and Guide*, p. 7.

(1932, September 21). The Negro as observed from shores of Europe. *New York Amsterdam News*, p. 6.

(1932, September 22). Principle is the thing in politics, says Woodson. *Atlanta Daily World*, p. A2.

(1932, September 24). Carter Woodson says he is on no vacation; gathering facts on Negro: Finds Africans lack interest. *Norfolk Journal and Guide*, p. 7.

(1932, October 1). "Negro must develop own radicalism"; says historian after survey of conditions in Europe. *Norfolk Journal and Guide*, p. 7.

(1932, October 1). The Black man and Europe. *Chicago Defender*, p. 14.

(1932, October 8). Europe 25 years after. *Chicago Defender*, p. 14.

(1932, October 14). Historians to discuss Jim Crow at meet here Nov. 13. *Atlanta Daily World*, p. 1A.

(1932, October 15). European "Democrats" no more democratic than U.S.; kings ruled better—Woodson. *Norfolk Journal and Guide*, p. 7.

(1932, October 19). Is the Negro any better off today than in 1868? *New York Amsterdam News*, p. 6.

(1932, October 22). History ass'n meets Nov. 13th in far south: Atlanta to be scene of stimulating discussions. *Norfolk Journal and Guide*, p. 3.

(1932, October 29). Carter Woodson ridicules Negroes ashamed of name. *Norfolk Journal and Guide*, p. 3.

(1932, November 2). Europeans plan to honor struggle of Wilberforce. *New York Amsterdam News*, p. 6.

(1932, November 9). Why we should publish truth in self-defense. *New York Amsterdam News*, p. 6A.

(1932, November 17). Negro writers loafing. *Atlanta Daily World*, p. 6A.

(1932, November 19). Woodson objects to debunking "great emancipa-tor": Admits Lincoln used Negroes as game pawns. *Norfolk Journal and Guide*, p. 7.

(1932, December 3). Historian tells what he'd do for Georgia city: Finds that Atlantans have confidence in selves. *Norfolk Journal and Guide*, p. A7.

(1932, December 10). School heads tell why they can or cannot ob-serve Negro history week; some are afraid. *Norfolk Journal and Guide*, p. 7.

(1932, December 17). Males' lack of respect for our womanhood shameful. *Pittsburgh Courier*, p. A2.

(1932, December 17). The melting pot. *Norfolk Journal and Guide*, p. 6.

(1932, December 24). Pictures hung in most schools lack inspiration value, says Dr. Woodson; heroes forgotten. *Norfolk Journal and Guide*, p. 9.

(1932, December 29). Historical black but comely. *Atlanta Daily World*, p. 2A.

(1933, January 7). Dr. Woodson says his salary is less than thirty dollars per week. *Afro-American*, p. 7.

(1933, January 11). "The Mis-Education of the Negro" will be released. *New York Amsterdam News*, p. 6.

(1933, January 18). Has the Negro a sense of social organization? *New York Amsterdam News*, p. 6.

(1933, January 25). Unlucky Friday teaches lessons on thugs. *New York Amsterdam News*, p. 6.

(1933, February 1). Why I disapprove of the March 4 backyard frolic. *New York Amsterdam News*, p. 6.

(1933, February 8). Negro needs consistency in his segregation fight. *New York Amsterdam News*, p. 6.

(1933, February 11). Race leaders lead backwards. *Chicago Defender*, p. 1.

(1933, February 18). A new story of George Washington and the Negro told in novel by J. H. Hill. *Norfolk Journal and Guide*, p. A3.

(1933, February 22, 1933). Reply to Uncle Tom and his coworkers' at-tacks. *New York Amsterdam News*, p. 6.

(1933, February 25). Washington Democrat angling for job as presi-dent of Howard University, asserts Dr. Woodson. *Norfolk Journal and Guide*, p. 2.

(1933, March 4). Jim Crow theaters and our artists. *Chicago Defender*, p. 14 (in news form, paraphrased by the newspaper).

(1933, March 11). Trip through South opens historian's eyes; finds better race relations. *Norfolk Journal and Guide*, p. 16.

(1933, October 14). Sending wrong man to Europe, Woodson writes. *Pittsburgh Courier*, p. A2.

(1933, October 21). Woodson asserts that the race is hurt by "'pimps.'" *Norfolk Journal and Guide*, p. 7.

(1933, October 28). Foreign soil seen as promised land for Negroes with pioneering spirit and proper educational prep. *Norfolk Journal and Guide*, p. A2.

(1933, November 4). Countess De Jumilhac writes with feeling of Abyssinia its peoples, and its customs. *Norfolk Journal and Guide*, p. A7.

(1933, November 11). Revolt in Africa assumes the form of self-assertion of natives thru prophets. *Norfolk Journal and Guide*, p. 7.

(1933, November 18). Modern language teachers to use works of noted European Negro authors. *Norfolk Journal and Guide*, p. A7.

(1933, November 18). Selection of textbooks which treat Negro fairly is made new objective. *Pittsburgh Courier*, p. A2.

(1933, December 2). Opportunity for utilizing all subjects in teaching Negro history pointed out. *Norfolk Journal and Guide*, p. 7.

(1933, December 16). Treatment of Negro due to psychology: Race must rid self of complex to make progress. *Norfolk Journal and Guide*, p. A3.

(1933, December 23). Woodson blasts "scientific investigation"; proving that Negroes copied Negro spirituals. *Norfolk Journal and Guide*, p. A3.

(1933, December 30). Time and foolhardiness have proved B. T. Washington's joke a prophecy. *Norfolk Journal and Guide*, p. A7.

(1934, January 13). What we should learn. *Chicago Defender*, p. 11.

(1934, February 3). All efforts of white social investigators to prove negro inferior have failed. *Pittsburgh Courier*, p. A10.

(1934, February 10). Opposition and indifference to racial history is explained; distinguishing between wheat and chaff is the big problem of the Negro historian. *Norfolk Journal and Guide*, p. 14.

(1934, February 17). Woodson points out virgin territory for those who would add to the present day knowledge of the Negro. *Norfolk Journal and Guide*, p. A15.

(1934, February 24). Carter Woodson lauds "forgotten Negroes" who played major roles in race's march of progress. *Pittsburgh Courier*, p. 4.

(1934, March 3). Race problem is Gordian knot of social difficulties, Woodson finds, but adds his to many panaceas. *Norfolk Journal and Guide*, p. 14.

(1934, March 10). Woodson takes sarcastic poke at Negroes who have had incomes assured by favor of present administration. *Norfolk Journal and Guide*, p. 14.

(1934, March 17). Woodson records forgotten romances from neglected but exciting episodes of history featuring Negro. *Norfolk Journal and Guide*, p. 14.

(1934, March 24). Account of Madison Washington's successful fight for love and freedom is illustrative of literary possibilities in slave experiences. *Norfolk Journal and Guide*, p. 14.

(1934, April 7). Camden, N.J., school music dept. found new reason to bar pupils from opera. *Afro-American*, p. 15.

(1934, April 7). Mutiny led by slave eventually leads to freedom of many who were kidnaped. *Norfolk Journal and Guide*, p. 2.

(1934, April 21). Why some Negroes advocate segregation. *Chicago Defender*, p. 12.

(1934, April 28). Plain speaking: That mischievous advisor on Negro affairs. *Chicago Defender*, p. 12.

(1934, June 2). Miseducation leads Negroes to imitate whites, says Woodson; historian flays segregationists. *Norfolk Journal and Guide*, p. 3.

(1934, August 31). The full dinner-pail and America's Negro citizens. *New York Amsterdam News*, p. 6.

(1935, April 6). $30,000 for the suppressed truth. *Norfolk Journal and Guide*, p. 8.

(1935, August 14). Opposition and indifference to racial history is explained. *Atlanta Daily World*, p. 2.

(1935, September 7). Future task of race history is outlined. *Chicago Defender*, p. 11.

(1935, November 16). Scholar deals with distinguished life of Richard Allen, churchman. *Norfolk Journal and Guide*, p. 9.

(1935, December 14). Noted historian discusses the dramatization of Negro life and history. *Norfolk Journal and Guide*, p. 5.

(1935, December 21). Negro history included in curriculum some places: Woodson gives review of move up to present. *Norfolk Journal and Guide*, p. 5.

(1935, December 28). Carter Woodson debunks propaganda about Ethiopians: Noted historian insists Ethiops are Negroes. *Norfolk Journal and Guide*, p. 3.

(1936, January 4). The horizon: What have we done? Africans more advanced the tenth man not imitators alone. *New York Amsterdam News*, p. 8.

(1936, January 11). The horizon: Wealth with little living within income, rich tastes—poor salary must vie with others. *New York Amsterdam News*, p. 6.

(1936, January 18). The horizon: The African "heathen" should aid Western pagans not by lip service. *New York Amsterdam News*, p. 8.

(1936, February 8). Moral code of Africans higher than ours. *Chicago Defender*, p. 11.

(1936, February 15). Achievements of a race not history, says Dr. Woodson: Proper setting is outlined by noted historian. *Norfolk Journal and Guide*, p. 5.

(1936, February 22). Dr. Woodson makes plea for records of Negro race: Shows need for data on race's achievements. *Norfolk Journal and Guide*, p. 20.

(1936, February 29). George Washington was the most liberal slaveholder—Woodson. *Norfolk Journal and Guide*, p. 19.

(1936, March 7). Carter Woodson raps move to force teachers' oaths of loyalty to government. *Norfolk Journal and Guide*, p. 20.

(1936, March 12). My opinion is . . . *Philadelphia Tribune*, p. 5A.

(1936, March 21). Woodson holds Negro voters have not yet reached political freedom. *Norfolk Journal and Guide*, p. 19.

(1936, May 2). America has always questioned loyalty of Negro, Woodson finds: Lays cause to the unjust treatment. *Norfolk Journal and Guide*, p. 10.

(1936, June 22). Resume "encyclopedia" tiff: Dr. Carter G. Woodson says Brawley guilty of misquotation. *Atlanta Daily World*, p. 1.

(1936, July 25). What Negro do you hate? *Norfolk Journal and Guide*, p. 8.

(1936, October 17). Association on guard. *Norfolk Journal and Guide*, p. 8.

(1937, December 18). Roustabout charge against Attucks evokes anger of Dr. Woodson. *Norfolk Journal and Guide*, p. 5.

(1937, December 25). New approach to observance of History Week urged: Eulogizing of great men not enough. *Norfolk Journal and Guide*, p. 20.

(1938, January 6). Negro history is irrevocably a part of America. *Cleveland Call and Post*, p. 8.

(1938, January 15). The Negro . . . 1865 to 1937; what has race accomplished?: Negro History Week, to be celebrated. *Pittsburgh Courier*, p. 14.

(1938, January 29). Hoosier schoolmarm teaches her pupils to be proud of race: Jane Dabney Shackelford of Terre Haute. *Pittsburgh Courier*, p. 14.

(1938, February 5). Dr. Wesley's new history unmasks the confederacy. *Norfolk Journal and Guide*, p. 9.

(1938, February 6). Says lack of racial unity not unusual. *Chicago Defender*, p. 5.

(1938, February 12). Slave theology must go or church is doomed, warns Dr. Woodson. *Norfolk Journal and Guide*, p. 9.

(1938, February 19). Badly needed: Talented authors to write biographies of race. *Norfolk Journal and Guide*, p. 9.

(1938, February 24). Constructive opposition develops real leadership. *Cleveland Call and Post*, p. 6.

(1938, February 26). Race too mixed to think as one unit—Woodson: Progress must be made in face of opposition. *Norfolk Journal and Guide*, p. 9.

(1938, March 5). Trend to monuments of race leaders lauded. *Norfolk Journal and Guide*, p. 9.

(1938, March 26). Two women make good. *Afro-American*, p. 9.

(1938, March 31). A great crisis in Negro affairs is now imminent. *Cleveland Call and Post*, p. 6.

(1938, April 2). Claims whites learn about Negroes from wrong source: Carter Woodson raps. *Pittsburgh Courier*, p. 6.

(1938, December 15). Urges study of Negro history to further truth in education. *Cleveland Call and Post*, p. 6.

(1939, November 4). Woodson praised book The Negro in Sports. *Norfolk Journal and Guide*, p. 18. (Editor's note tells readers how to purchase the book.)

(1940, January 27). Carter G. Woodson flays white publishers. *Pittsburgh Courier*, p. 12.

(1940, August 24). Fate of 2,199,592 West Indians in doubt: Islanders' destinies hang on outcome of present conflict. *Norfolk Journal and Guide*, p. 11.

(1940, August 31). Could Negro survive in a world in upheaval and ruled by dictators? *Norfolk Journal and Guide*, p. 9.

(1941, July 26). A new voice for Africa. *Norfolk Journal and Guide*, p. 8.

(1941, October 11). Negro history to be main topic at historians' meeting. *Norfolk Journal and Guide*, p. 20.

(1941, October 25). Questions vital to race face discussion at historians meeting. *Norfolk Journal and Guide*, p. 20.

(1942, January 24). Nation turns to observe history week of Negro. *Philadelphia Tribune*, p. 18.

(1942, February 1). The Negro as a factor in World War Number II. *Atlanta Daily World*, p. 4.

(1942, February 7). Why Negro History Week is held in February. *Philadelphia Tribune*, p. 18.

(1943, May 3). The color guard. *Atlanta Daily World*, p. 6.

(1943, June 19). Negroes not united for democracy in America. *Cleveland Call and Post*, p. 8B.

(1943, August 14). Democracy in spite of opposition. *Cleveland Call and Post*, p. 8B.

(1943, October 23). The Negro soldier. *Cleveland Call and Post*, p. 8B.

(1943, November 6). Patriotism. *Cleveland Call and Post*, p. 8B. (Defined patriotism, agreed with those who said patriotism is Negroes loving a country that hates them.)

(1943, November 23). Dangers of political leadership. *Cleveland Call and Post*, p. 4B.

(1943, December 4). Independence. *Cleveland Call and Post*, p. 8B.

(1944, May 6). Tolerance and the Negro. *Cleveland Call and Post*, p. 8B.

(1944, December 30). Development of the Negro community. *Cleveland Call and Post*, p. 8B.

(1945, February 10). Which shall it be? Democracy or empire. *Cleveland Call and Post*, p. 8B.

(1946, January 5). Isolating medievalism. *Cleveland Call and Post*, p. 8B.

(1946, April 6). The deplorable state of the nation. *Cleveland Call and Post*, p. 4.

(1946, May 11). Politics corrupted by selfishness. *Cleveland Call and Post*, p. 4B.

(1946, November 23). Dangers of political leadership. *Cleveland Call and Post*, p. 4B.

(1947, February 15). The unfinished task. *Cleveland Call and Post*, p. 4.

(1947, March 8). Liberia needs help. *Cleveland Call and Post*, p. 4B.

(1948, January 10). The whole truth and nothing but the whole truth. *Philadelphia Tribune*, p. 14.

(1949, January 7). Nation prepares for Negro History Week. *Atlanta Daily World*, p. 3.

Chapter 5

MANAGING PUBLIC RELATIONS

THE PRACTICE OF PUBLIC RELATIONS AT THE START OF THE TWENTIETH century was synonymous with publicity, which evolved into public information and was made famous by Ivy Lee. Broadly speaking, Lee's declaration of principles in 1906, a commitment to facts and accuracy, was an objectivity model similar to journalistic practice. His declaration has been called a pivotal moment in public relations history, but it did not prevent him from being called "Poison Ivy" by Upton Sinclair and criticized by others for supposed errors of fact in representing clients (Russell and Bishop, 2009). Considered the first public relations counselor, Lee ushered in an era of the public-be-informed. Lee's career overlapped with that of Edward Bernays, considered by many to be the "Father of Modern Public Relations." Bernays developed a research-based, two-way communication model with goals of mutual understanding. "Public relations is not a one-way street in which leadership manipulates the public and public opinion," Bernays said. "It is a two-way street in which leadership and the public find integration with each other and in which objectives and goals are predicated on a coincidence of public and private leadership" ("Public Relations: An Overview," 1991).

During its early history, public relations relied on journalists to disseminate information, as did Carter G. Woodson's promotion of black history. In some cases, unscrupulous press agents were known to buy influence for clients needing publicity from reporters (Russell and Bishop, 2009).

Many of the best-known public relations experts began their careers at newspapers, including Lee, a former reporter at several New York newspapers who became one of the profession's iconic figures. George Creel, another former journalist, ran the US publicity office as head of the Committee on Public Information, where he infused elements of propaganda with public relations in support of America's World War I efforts. Creel's work has been called the "greatest public relations effort in history, up to its time" (Baskin, Arnonoff, and Lattimore, 1997). Bernays was a committee staff member, and Emmett J. Scott, a former Booker T. Washington aide and later a member of ASNLH's Executive Council, led the US government's domestic public relations program aimed at African Americans during the war as special assistant to the secretary of war. Following World War I, Woodson promoted Scott's book (*Official History of the American Negro in the World War*) and provided a favorable review in 1919 in support of Scott's agenda to preserve and document black contributions on the military side ("The American Negro," 1919). Scott and Woodson publicly had an up-and-down-relationship, but Scott served as one of the honorary pallbearers at Woodson's funeral.

Several of the early pioneers, not just Lee, were accused of misinformation and propaganda (Ellis, 1991), but such arguments are not being leveled at Woodson. No evidence was found indicating Woodson deliberately misled the media, although he employed many of the tactics the pioneers of public relations were known to employ on behalf of their clients and organizations.

Woodson, in popularizing history, used combinations of the Edward Bernays–Ivy Lee models, as many public relations experts do decades later. He sought to educate and inform, using publicity, a concept especially associated with Lee. A major aspect of Woodson's appeal, too, involved promoting mutual understanding and mutual benefits through his messages to the press and various other publics—Bernays's brand of public relations.

The Public Relations Society of America's study guide for members preparing to take the accreditation examination defines publicity as information from outside sources with news value. Publicity is different from advertising because it is not paid space in the media. It is free and uncontrolled by the sources releasing it; they rely on the media for its placement ("Study Guide," 2010).

Public relations experts often attempt to change public opinion, which is a difficult. Lee, an adviser to the Rockefeller family, submitted articles to newspapers, provided arguments in support of management during the Colorado coal strike and its aftermath in 1913–1914, (Hallohan, 2002), and later helped recast John D. Rockefeller's image ("History of Business Journalism," n.d.) from that of the robber baron to one of the greatest philanthropists of the century, known as much today for funding fights against diseases as for ruthless business practices.

Bernays, a double-nephew of Sigmund Freud, recalled in a public television interview with Bill Moyers in 1984 that one of his clients wanted to combat a taboo against women smoking in public. His solution had a mutual-understanding, even mutual-benefit message: on behalf of his client, the American Tobacco Company, Bernays used his connections to persuade many women participating in the 1929 Easter Day Parade in New York to march, cigarettes in hand, openly defiant of mores—satisfying both the tobacco company's desire to increase market share and the women's aspirations for equal rights (Blumer and Moyers, 1984).

Confronting larger challenges of changing public opinion regarding race rather than selling tobacco products, Woodson's program sought to educate and to recalibrate the opinions of those who thought African Americans had no history worth honoring—which included many blacks with low self-esteem, those who had not been properly educated. The mutual-understanding and/or mutual-benefit theme in Woodson's program was stated clearly and repeatedly: all people would benefit if the truth about black history were known, for there is no black history, just history.

Woodson's use of public relations on behalf of his program sought change among both opinion leaders and the mass public, who could fund his program and change their behavior. Targeted groups for education and re-education included students, teachers, and the media. He condemned the work of his fellow historians, as a group, and attempted to change them, too, with pronouncements that they were wrong and needed correcting, and he often called them propagandists ("Chicagoans Hear Dr. Woodson," 1940). His attacks on the problem were methodical and focused—such as when he penned and published a lengthy open letter in response to a *McNaught's Monthly* article by G. D. Eaton that Woodson said misunderstood slavery and failed to understand that slavery differed from period to period and from nation to nation. Woodson's editor's note introducing the letter said the article "points out the danger resulting from the bias which permeates the so-called histories of our time" (Woodson, 1927c).

In Woodson's day, organizations using public relations frequently relied on the media as gatekeepers, allowing free, uncontrolled media (such as coverage in newspapers) to determine distribution of their external messages. In recent years, the lines have blurred between advertising and public relations, and social media often allow those seeking to influence public opinion to coordinate campaigns with or bypass traditional media. However, in the Woodson era, the Internet did not exist, and television would not reach critical mass until after his death.

When Woodson began his program in 1915, the major media consisted of newspapers and magazines, as was the media landscape, obviously, when Lee and Bernays were just getting started in public relations. Although he purchased some advertising in promotion of books, Woodson mostly used newspapers (publicity) and his speeches, pamphlets, books, the *Journal of Negro History*, and later the *Negro History Bulletin* in delivering messages that promoted his cause. Radio took off in the 1920s, and Woodson's influence would later be heard behind the scenes and in front of microphones in that medium, too (Savage, 1999).

Woodson and Emmett J. Scott were not the only African American leaders known to use public relations. Booker T. Washington often is described as one of the most skilled public figures of his day in the use of public relations, especially in handling publicity and fund-raising. Scott, editor of the *Texas Freeman*, in Houston, was hired as Washington's secretary and to execute "Mr. Washington's publicity ideas and in establishing cordial and effective press relations for his chief" (Holsey, 1948).

Other public relations researchers have focused attention on African Americans who used public relations during the civil rights movement of the 1950s and 1960s. Hon (1997) concluded that African Americans' contributions in public relations generally have been overlooked. Russell and Lamme (2013) found that although protesters pressured businesses for fair treatment along economic lines, they also succeeded out of the business executives' fears about riots and concerns about corporate image.

Martin Luther King Jr. rose to prominence after Woodson's death and provided charismatic leadership of the Southern Christian Leadership Conference (SCLC) and the civil rights movement. King had a staff of public relations people assisting him at the SCLC (Hon, 1997). Woodson, on the other hand, had no dedicated publicity or media relations staff and operated out of a small home-office in Washington, DC. He was known to ask employees engaged in other work to assist him in generating publicity, as he did in a letter addressed to "My dear Coworker" in 1929 when he was preparing for ASNLH's annual meeting in Washington:

> I am enclosing herewith a copy of the program of the annual meeting of the Association, to be held here from the 27th to the 31st of this month. We shall have here representatives of the best thought in this country. Kindly give the conference as much publicity as possible and attend this significant convocation. (Woodson, 1929b)

Woodson's style was textbook public relations, although this study in no way suggests he was a disciple of Bernays (who died in 1995), Lee (who died in 1934), or any of the other public relations pioneers; however, their work was well known to many American opinion leaders during the period of Woodson's program. As a Harvard PhD in history, Woodson was probably aware of his university's links to publicity, which include fund-raising and what many consider the first fund-raising brochure, "New England's First Fruits," in 1643 (Ireland, 2012; Smith, 2008). Woodson was methodical about his program, and his strategic pursuit of goals and tactical use of the press make it possible to conclude he understood modern public relations methods, even if he did not know Bernays and Lee, personally.

Bernays and Woodson, however, shared at least one acquaintance who moved within both of their circles. Bernays was an associate of Arthur Spingarn, one of the founders of the NAACP and whose name is part of the Moorland-Spingarn Research Center at Howard University. Spingarn's brother Joel was a life member of ASNLH who through the years served as a founder, board chair, and president of the NAACP, and Woodson was a life member of the NAACP. In 1920, Arthur Spingarn feared for security at a regional NAACP conference in Atlanta. Bernays, at Arthur Spingarn's request, provided public relations work for the meeting, persuading white segregationists that an NAACP meeting in their city would be good publicity, generating a positive image for Atlanta ("NAACP Conference," n.d.).

While not knowing who borrowed from whom, it is clear the promotion tactics of Woodson and the NAACP were similar. Woodson was a supporter of the Washington office of the NAACP, and he was well aware of many NAACP policies, having spoken at meetings, such as the NAACP's annual conference in Washington, DC, in 1932, when he was a featured speaker at the former home of the late Frederick Douglass ("NAACP Lists Highlights of Meet," 1932). The NAACP's *Crisis* magazine promoted and published an article by Woodson on the "Miseducation of the Negro" two years before Woodson's book by that similar title.

In 1934, during the twenty-fifth anniversary of the NAACP's founding, Associated Negro Press distributed to its customers an article that commemorated the anniversary, highlighting the NAACP's publicity efforts, or, as it reported, "the drive for publicity for Negro problems in the colored, white and foreign newspapers." ANP reported that the NAACP won the first-place prize for its publicity work in 1930. The NAACP publicity program involved the organization's use of annual meetings, books, newspapers, journals,

Table 5.1: Carter G. Woodson's Use of Selected Modern Public Relations Elements	
PR Elements	**Examples Used by Woodson**
Research	ASNLH was a research organization. Although it was not usually engaged in media research, it encouraged the study of black newspapers and supported collecting and maintaining copies for research purposes. Woodson encouraged the public to send documents to his office and the Library of Congress for research.
Media Relations	Woodson agreed to interviews, encouraged journalists to publish articles about his projects, and made coverage of his annual meetings convenient by encouraging speakers to bring summaries of their presentations for use by the press.
Publicity	Woodson routinely disseminated messages through newspapers, magazines, speeches, and pamphlets.
Member Relations	ASNLH maintained communication with members and conducted membership drives.
Fund-raising	Woodson solicited wealthy individuals, teachers, students, and journalists for money to support the movement.
Minority Relations/Multicultural Affairs	This type had not been classified as such in Woodson's day, but he clearly was using it before it was identified as a public relations element. Examples include the public-education program's race relations sub-themes and racial relations strategies.
Special Events and Public Participation	Examples include the annual Negro History Week celebrations and recognition of the centennial of the first African American newspaper in 1927.
Issues Management	In addition to his history agenda, Woodson disclosed ASNLH's financial problems and handled feuds with church and political leaders and the resignation of the association's president.
Sources: Compiled from known Woodson activities and public relations principles.	

lectures, and travels—all the tactics employed by Woodson ("Presenting the Case," 1934).

The Public Relations Society of America has identified fifteen elements of public relations: counseling, research, media relations, publicity, employee/member relations, community relations, public affairs, government affairs, issues management, financial relations, industry relations, development/fund-raising, minority relations/multicultural affairs, special events and public participation, and marketing communications ("Public Relations: An Overview," 1991), and Woodson employed more than half of these elements, often through newspapers, between 1915 and 1950.

Woodson was a consummate promoter. By calling his work the "cause" ("Wanted," 1926) and using the words "popularize" and "prosecute" in describing goals, Woodson was acknowledging that his career was more than the type usually associated with being a historian. As an advocate and the face of a movement, he was the original promoter of African American history and research. Considering the state of black history when he began his campaign, Woodson no doubt created the movement, nurtured it, and popularized it as a trained public relations practitioner would have done. (See Table 5.1 for a comparison of modern public relations elements and Woodson's work.)

WOODSON AS PUBLICIST

Woodson's embrace of public relations began in 1915, just before he founded ASNLH. During the summer of that year, he made appearances in Chicago promoting his first book, *The Education of the Negro Prior to 1861*, and in September he announced formation of the Association for the Study of Negro Life and History to promote and popularize black history.

Publicity per se was not Woodson's objective. Publicity was a tool in disseminating information. The promotional side of the movement, in support of ASNLH, the *Journal of Negro History*, Negro History Week, and the *Negro History Bulletin*, evolved out of the necessity to reach audiences who, potentially, would join the association, collect family records, and study history, thereby improving race relations through recognition of black achievements. The audiences initially targeted by Woodson's *Journal*, mostly scholars and other people of influence, were insufficient for reaching the masses Woodson needed to popularize history. The combined circulation of his magazines was 4,500 by the end of his life (Logan, 1950). Woodson had used larger circulation figures in the annual reports during his tenure, but he acknowledged the limitations of the *Journal*'s reach when he established the *Negro History Bulletin*, for general and school-oriented audiences, in 1937.

One of Woodson's often-stated goals—preventing African Americans from becoming negligible factors in the world—mandated strategies and tactics that would reach mass audiences ("Race Must Overcome," 1928). The newspapers published by blacks and whites circulated widely among general audiences and could provide the access that Woodson coveted.

John Hope Franklin, whom Woodson mentored and whose career as a historian during the second half of the twentieth century is as highly regarded as Woodson's in the first half, recalled the Woodson public relations persona during a 2007 interview. Asked to compare his book *From Slavery to Freedom* with Woodson's earlier work, *The Negro in Our History*, and George Washington Williams's *History of the Negro Race, 1619 to 1880*, published in 1882 and widely considered the first African American history book, Franklin made his assessment of the Woodson book on the basis of Woodson's public relations role. Franklin said his book was more similar to Williams's book because Williams was writing to say what the black experience had been. On the other hand, Franklin said, Woodson's *The Negro in Our History* was largely a work of praise of black achievement (Purnell, 2009).

Franklin's comments, coming from someone classified as one of "Woodson's Boys" even now on the Association for the Study of African American Life and History website ("Our History," n.d.), appear critical of Woodson as publicist and activist for history, but it was an accurate description, and he seemed grateful for Woodson's mentorship. Franklin himself was a self-described activist in assisting legal teams with arguments for *Brown v. Board of Education* and other civil rights cases that played major roles in black history (ASALH, 2007). Indeed, both men were activists for the same cause, only separated by the dictates of their generations. Franklin was born in 1915, the year Woodson began his campaign, which eventually made it possible for Franklin to be known primarily for his scholarship in a discipline (the study of Negro history/black history/African American history) nonexistent before Woodson paved the way and promoted it. Woodson clearly saw his role as one to return black achievements to the history books, which required both research and promotion—steps Woodson performed in lockstep.

The Franklin book was reviewed by Roi Ottley in the *New York Times* on October 12, 1947, and the newspaper observed, "Not since 1922, when Carter G. Woodson completed his monumental 'The Negro in Our History,' has a complete history of the Negro in the United States been written." The review was largely negative, especially critical of what it described as Franklin's brush-off of the black press (Ottley, 1947).

Both Woodson and black newspapers—which joined him as advocates—argued for presentation of all sides of issues. The black press praised Woodson for publicizing the good with the bad ("Family Skeletons," 1918). Woodson praised black newspapers for doing the same in his textbook, *The Negro in Our History* (Woodson, 1922), and he admonished them when he thought they were negligent or their reporting trivial (Woodson, 1948a). In his 1949 director's report to ASNLH, Woodson continued to argue his program did not attempt to hide the truth and he presented "facts in a dispassionate way so that the facts properly set forth may tell their own story" (Woodson, 1949b).

Article II of the Association for the Study of Negro Life and History's amended constitution expressed its purpose in promotional terms: "Its object shall be the collection of sociological and historical documents and the promotion of studies bearing on the Negro." This policy was reflected in ASNLH's publication of the proceedings of the annual meetings and the directors' reports in the *Journal of Negro History*, beginning in 1919.

ASNLH members, according to the organization's reports, discussed plans to attract people from all walks of life (especially teachers, who were targeted for the association's messages). They devoted large portions of their meetings to discussion of achievements of African Americans and presentations from various speakers about how to promote and succeed. For example, John W. Davis, then executive secretary of the YMCA, explained "How to Promote the Study of Negro Life and History." According to the 1920 proceedings, Davis "endeavored to show briefly exactly how there can be constructed the machinery adequate to interesting every individual having pride in the achievements of this large fraction of the population of the country" ("Proceedings," 1919). Davis was hired as president of West Virginia Collegiate Institute in 1919, and hired Woodson as dean there in 1920.

Woodson sent salesmen out into the country to sell books. One salesman, Lorenzo J. Greene, called on editors at many of his stops, and, like Woodson, Greene submitted articles to black newspapers for publication and made speeches on theme. If members of the press were not present at his speaking engagements and other events, Woodson or his staff would send them accounts of what transpired, and often the newspapers used them, as though their journalists had staffed the meetings (Greene, 1989).

Greene's diary recounted details of a research project that included using an *Afro-American* writer to distribute ten questionnaires to newspaper employees and having them mailed to the association's offices for a study Greene and Charles H. Wesley were conducting on the churches. On other occasions, Greene visited the *Afro*'s offices and met with Carl Murphy, the editor, as he did with Claude A. Barnett at ANP offices in Chicago (Greene, 1989).

Working too closely with the media could backfire, as Greene learned after an associate disclosed details about the church study to the *Afro*. He said the entire study was released prematurely to the newspaper (Greene, 1989).

Woodson's other tactics included recruitment of writers and leading figures in journalism—black and white—for membership in the association. Robert Abbott, who founded the *Chicago Defender*, was a life member of ASNLH, as was US senator Joseph Medill McCormick, a member of the family that owned the *Chicago Tribune* and grandson of its founder, Joseph Medill, a nineteenth-century editor who opposed slavery. Oswald Garrison Villard also was a life member of ASNLH and served on the Executive Council. Villard at one point edited and owned the *New York Evening Post* and the *Nation.* He was the grandson of William Lloyd Garrison, editor of the *Liberator,* a major voice against slavery who demanded immediate emancipation. Roscoe Dunjee, editor of the *Black Dispatch* of Oklahoma City, Oklahoma, served on the ASNLH Executive Council, and his newspaper was among the strongest supporters of Negro History Week.

Life members made financial contributions to ASNLH and received certain benefits, including subscriptions to the *Journal of Negro History.* The 1925 annual meeting program indicated regular memberships cost \$3 and life memberships cost \$75. By 1950, life memberships required a one-time payment of \$100. Annual memberships by 1950 cost \$4. Other life members included Mrs. Booker T. Washington and Helen Keller, the blind-deaf author and writer for Industrial Workers of the World (IWW). Life members were routinely listed on the programs for the association's annual meetings.

Woodson also signed up journalists to appear on his programs, and sometimes he used them to help promote his conferences at the local committee level, such as ASNLH's 1945 annual meeting in Columbus, Ohio, whose program listed publicity committee members, including "The Ohio State News" and "Local Newspapers."

Abbott of the *Defender* welcomed the 1,600 attendees at the Chicago annual meeting of ASNLH in 1935. Pearl S. Buck, the Nobel Prize winner in literature, attended ASNLH's twenty-fifth annual meeting in Chicago and was photographed with Woodson, Abbott, and other members at an association dinner. Langston Hughes, the poet and former Woodson assistant, was a *Chicago Defender* columnist and was closely associated with the organization for many years. After Woodson's death, this model of engaging journalists and other writers in the movement was continued when John H. Johnson, the founder of *Jet* and *Ebony* magazines, and Lerone Bennett Jr., an editor at *Jet* and *Ebony,* served on the history organization's Executive Council. As recently as the 2013 Annual Black History Luncheon, the Association for the Study of African American Life and History used Aaron Gilchrist, morning anchorman of NBC 4 in Washington, DC, as master of ceremonies, and recruited A'Lelia Bundles, a former television executive and great-great-granddaughter of Madame C. J. Walker, the black cosmetics entrepreneur, for that role in 2015 and 2016.

Woodson's public-education program went well beyond photo opportunities with celebrities. The annual conferences were packed with results from various research studies. The meetings also included history movement progress statements and an accounting of ASNLH's business operations.

At Woodson's request in 1935, Luther P. Jackson, the Virginia State College history professor, produced a study of the association's first twenty years (and later the first twenty-five years of the *Journal of Negro History* in 1940). Jackson divided the first twenty years into two parts. During the first decade, the association was largely a scholarly association with limited influence on the masses, he said. During the second period, the association reached out to both scholars and the masses. He said the organization sought larger audiences and reached prospective followers through clubs, branches, the annual meetings of the association, speaking engagements by Woodson and his associates, and the promotion of Negro History Week. Jackson said the branches brought out facts about black achievements, and he called the annual meetings "a popularizing force" and Woodson the "chief promoter" (Jackson, 1935). The quest for larger audiences obviously required media access and support.

Woodson did not much deviate from this model. As late as 1948 ASNLH included a discussion at its annual meeting on "Methods for Promoting the Study of the Negro" and a plan for better promoting and "popularizing *The Negro History Bulletin*," which was referred to the Executive Council for further consideration ("Proceedings," 1949).

Having established the public relations function in his organization, Woodson's tactics were emulated by several of his associates and book authors, especially in media relations. Seymour J. Schoenfeld, whose book *The Negro in the Armed Forces* was published by Woodson's Associated Publishers, told Woodson he was "quite certain you are quite familiar with all the possible 'angles' to the publicity that this book requires," but he suggested sending copies of his book to such newspaper columnists and broadcasters as Ernie Pyle, Walter Winchell, Dorothy Parker, and Eleanor Roosevelt (Schoenfeld, 1945). Edwin B. Henderson had similar ideas for promotion of the revised version of his book, *The Negro in Sports*, in 1949. Henderson mailed copies of the book to news organizations, educational institutions, and President Harry Truman (Ayers, 1949). Among the recipients of Henderson's book was Philip Graham, publisher of the *Washington Post*, eliciting this response: "I am hopeful that we can do properly by you." Jackie Robinson was having a historic impact on professional sports and race relations, and Graham added that his children and many other young people did not see Robinson's pigmentation "because they are all so busy cheering him on" (Graham, 1949).

Henderson, a contributor to black newspapers, is considered a pioneer among African Americans in sports. He was already familiar with the *Washington Post*, having collaborated with Eugene Meyer, the newspaper's president, in the 1940s to integrate Washington's professional boxing programs, and Meyer had threatened to withdraw support for local boxing tournaments unless they integrated. The *Washington Post* credited Henderson with introducing basketball to African Americans in the Washington area.

Henderson was probably more like the promoter side of Woodson than any of the historian's other associates, except perhaps Luther P. Jackson. Woodson asked Henderson in 1938 to write about the history of blacks in sports. As a promoter and advocate, Henderson wrote sports articles for such newspapers as the *Washington Star* and claimed more than a dozen newspapers published 3,000 of his letters to editors attacking racial discrimination and supporting African Americans' well-being and dignity (Ungrady, 2013).

INSIDE PUBLIC EDUCATION AND PUBLICITY: THE WOODSON–JACKSON LETTERS

Private letters exchanged between Woodson and Luther P. Jackson, the Virginia State College history professor who assisted the pioneer during the 1930s and 1940s with fund-raising for ASNLH in Virginia, provide vivid details from behind the scenes of the history program's inner workings. The letters covered ASNLH's operations and the specifics of the two collaborators' discussions of publicity, member relations, speeches at annual meetings, newspaper coverage, and fund-raising activities. Their messages provide a roadmap to the planning and execution of Woodson's public-education strategy and publicity tactics, and they further demonstrate Woodson's use of the black press to help him popularize history.

The tone of the letters examined, dating from 1935 to 1950 and covering both men's final years, was usually cordial and businesslike, with Jackson mostly assuming a subservient role as a junior executive would to an omnipotent CEO or gifted graduate student to a learned professor who seemed to rule his universe. Jackson was a well-respected academic, too, but neither he nor Woodson considered Jackson Woodson's equal in their relationship, and he craved Woodson's approval. The rare exceptions to their usual tone involved a few tense exchanges when Woodson feared Jackson was becoming a race leader and expressed concern about associating research with a civil rights agenda, which he labeled agitation. The two men exchanged numerous letters during this period, and Jackson probably received the final letter written and mailed by Woodson, dated April 1, 1950. Woodson died on April 3, 1950, closely followed by Jackson's death on April 20.

Their relationship seemed to develop after Jackson sent Woodson an updated report of his 1934 fund-raising activities in the state of Virginia, dated January 6, 1935. The amount raised was small ($398.43), but important to a financially strapped nonprofit organization such as ASNLH during the Great Depression. Jackson had analyzed the fund-raising landscape in Virginia and reported how "ripe" Virginia was for providing additional support to the association. Significantly, Jackson's letter even used the word "movement" to describe Woodson's program. "Everybody expressed great interest in the movement," he wrote. However, Jackson recommended postponing the $1 sustaining membership program from the fall school year in 1935 to the fall of 1936.

In that same January 6, 1935, letter, Jackson also recommended directing appeals for funds at those in cities and counties that had not contributed during the current period. Among other suggestions for moving forward was one acknowledging Woodson's pull with black newspapers, as Jackson recommended that Woodson provide a report of the program to the black press, saying, "I am especially anxious that you should have an account printed in *The Norfolk Journal & Guide*." He reported only one downside in his fund-raising: a white principal was unhappy after a speech Woodson had delivered some time back at Armstrong High School in Richmond. What Woodson had said to upset the principal was unclear.

Kicking off ASNLH's twenty-first year in 1936, Charles H. Wesley, chair of the Steering Committee, asked Jackson to join the association's nationwide "Sustaining Membership Campaign." Wesley laid out both the strategy behind the new membership drive and the philosophy governing the ongoing public-education program. Large gifts from foundations had dried up during the Great Depression, and Wesley told Jackson ASNLH would be relying more on the generosity of small donors, in a grassroots effort disseminating literature about black history and targeting schools and churches. "The pennies of school children even mount up, when numbers are considered," Wesley stated, adding, "'A penny a child' is not at all a bad slogan" (Wesley, 1936).

Jackson raised thousands of dollars in Virginia for the history program over the years, and many of the letters he and Woodson exchanged involved fund-raising reports from Jackson and thank-yous from Woodson, such as a Woodson letter to Jackson dated February 7, 1936, thanking Jackson for raising $400 and "popularizing the records of the Negro." Jackson also informed Woodson he was promoting history during summer school classes for teachers (Jackson, 1938). Woodson was so impressed with Jackson's fund-raising abilities he informed him that he had distributed a circular for others to learn from Jackson's successful fund-raising technique (Woodson, 1937a). Woodson asked Jackson about "promoting the long neglected study of Negro life and history" (Woodson, 1942), and Jackson wrote to Woodson about an advertising scheme, fund-raising, and detailed promotion ideas (Jackson, 1943).

Publication of the *Journal of Negro History* and the *Negro History Bulletin* was an expensive endeavor and a financial drain on the association, especially during wartime when paper was in short supply, but Woodson was constantly seeking ways to expand his reach among the masses. For example, Woodson planned an upcoming issue of the *Negro History Bulletin* that carried a photograph of the president of Virginia State College and mentioned the institution in several spots. He saw an opportunity to increase circulation sales in nearby communities and asked Jackson whether he had a reliable newsboy or newsstand in Petersburg or Richmond that would be willing to assume the task of selling a few hundred copies of the magazine. He explained he was making this promotional push in order to help increase overall circulation to at least 10,000. "We must do this in order to make it a paying proposition," Woodson said. "At present it is published at a deficit" (Woodson, 1942).

Jackson wrote Woodson on August 2, 1942, that he was unable to commit to writing a book review Woodson had requested because he was wrapped up in other research, including handling a book planned for publication. He closed the letter asking whether Woodson would be available for a meeting with him in Washington, DC, on August 18, 1942, "with respect to some ideas I have about the future promotion of our work in Virginia."

In a correspondence dated October 8, 1942, Woodson thanked Jackson for an annual report on the Negro History Drive, calling it "very illuminating" and adding, "I shall be glad to give publicity to this report about the first of the year when I make an appeal for funds."

In a January 2, 1943, letter, Woodson informed Jackson the organization was "launching the National One-Dollar Sustaining Membership Drive of 1943," and asked Jackson to help form a state committee. "We are urging that the plans be carefully drawn and thoroughly carried out," Woodson wrote.

On January 21, 1943, Jackson wrote Woodson that a teacher at the Carter G. Woodson School in Hopewell, Virginia, and another at Arlington Heights School, also in Hopewell, had requested Negro History Week material. He included his pledge for fund-raising success and thanked Woodson for a favorable review of his book.

Strong interest in the press was often apparent in the Woodson-Jackson correspondence. Jackson reported to Woodson that a Fredericksburg newspaper published his article on the history of Negroes of Fredericksburg and that it ran for two days (Jackson, 1942). That summer he wrote Woodson about rising press interest in his recent research and an editorial about it that was published in a white-owned newspaper, the *Richmond News Leader* (August 2, 1942). Jackson also advised Woodson about a series of articles on the soldiers' project he was running in his weekly column in the *Norfolk Journal and Guide* (Jackson, 1943b) and sent Woodson copies of the article he wrote on black descendants of Revolutionary soldiers (February 19, 1944). Jackson expressed hope that Woodson would produce an article for the press about ASNLH's upcoming 1944 annual meeting in Boston a week or two before it was set to convene. Jackson reminded him that "prior to the war, you used to do this" (Jackson, 1944c).

However, serious tension developed between them over that Boston annual meeting. Woodson had unsuccessfully discouraged Jackson from presenting his research at national NAACP meetings and wondered whether his support of the civil rights organization would prevent Jackson from attending the ASNLH convention in Boston.

As previously noted, Woodson supported the NAACP, but he wanted to keep his research separate from the protest movement, a position he felt was compromised by Jackson's presentation the previous year. Woodson accused Jackson of becoming a race leader, which in Woodson's point of view could do harm to the history movement. Jackson had skipped ASNLH's annual meeting in Detroit in 1943 in order to make a presentation to the NAACP, prompting Woodson to send him a handwritten note at the bottom of a letter promoting a book by a professor of French at Atlanta University, following that Detroit meeting. Woodson continued to berate Jackson, saying, "The annual meeting in Detroit was the most successful meeting in the history of the Assn. You made a mistake in not going. May God help you to repent? You are a historian, not a race leader" (Woodson, 1943a).

Woodson remained angry for months, or longer. In a July 13, 1944, letter to Jackson, Woodson thus wondered whether Jackson planned to participate at ASNLH's 1944 annual meeting: "Do you expect to attend the annual meeting? Will you deliver an address on that occasion or preferably attend a propaganda and political meeting as you did last year? I congratulate you on becoming a race leader."

After Jackson read the lineup on the Boston program in a newspaper, he was concerned Woodson had punished him for missing the previous year's meeting. Jackson registered his complaint with Woodson in an October 15, 1944, letter, saying his name was not on the program. Woodson proclaimed his innocence in an October 17 letter, in which he stated he did not send out a release on that particular meeting: "What you have read came from the Committee in Boston."

Having been scolded, Jackson indeed was included on the Boston program, and in planning the meeting, Woodson asked Jackson to bring four or five copies of his speech for the press. Woodson requested a "digest of 500 or 750 words of your leading thought which you desire to be quoted by the newspapers. This will facilitate publicity" (Woodson, 1944).

Woodson and Jackson also quarreled over an article Woodson published in the *Negro History Bulletin* in May 1944, which complained about "Uncle Toms" meeting with southern whites and leading black communities astray. Jackson, one of his most loyal lieutenants, expressed personal offense in a letter on May 20 because he was one of the organizers of the Southern Regional Council, an interracial group of academics and journalists about which Woodson complained (Jackson, 1944b). Woodson responded with a letter dated May 23, saying he had been unaware Jackson was active in the group, but he did not apologize, saying instead he was suspicious of any group that included several of the whites who participated, including Josephus Daniels, the former secretary of the navy and editor of the *Raleigh News and Observer*, a fervent supporter of segregation.

A year later, on July 21, 1945, Woodson scolded Jackson for missing a deadline for contributing an article to the *Journal of Negro History*, which Jackson also served as assistant editor. Jackson had other projects going, and Woodson used the occasion to remind Jackson of his disapproval of his becoming a race leader, saying, "We realize that you are busy solving the race problem in Virginia and that your duties as a leader of the race in America are arduous, but the insignificant efforts like the Association for the Study of Negro Life and History should not be abandoned altogether" (Woodson, 1945b).

Jackson's response to Woodson on August 8 admitted, "I have been dragged over somewhat into the area which you call race leadership, yet it pays and I have not deserted the cause of historical research." Among the reasons Jackson cited for being busy was his writing of a weekly column in the *Norfolk Journal and Guide*. Jackson said he was paid $100 a quarter for writing the columns, and he needed the money to support his large family (Jackson, 1945c). That statement must have rankled Woodson, who prided himself on not profiting from his newspaper column.

In another letter on September 11 addressing Woodson's complaints, Jackson emphasized how he used his *Norfolk and Journal* column to promote the public-education program and Woodson's book *The Negro in Our History*: "Through my columns in the *Journal and Guide* I have ten or more thousand constant readers each week and often I develop my articles on historical themes and occasionally I write up the association itself. My account of your book is a case in point" (Jackson, 1945d).

On October 4, 1947, when he was making final plans for ASNLH's annual meeting in Oklahoma City, Oklahoma, Woodson passed along a request for Jackson's photograph from Roscoe Dunjee, editor of the *Black Dispatch* in that city, for use as an advance story about Jackson's upcoming presentation, for publicity purposes. Woodson added, "You should bring to the annual meeting several copies of a 400 or 500 word digest of what you will say" (Woodson, 1947).

Despite the tension over Jackson's race leadership, Woodson remained otherwise cordial in their correspondence, repeatedly thanking him for his contributions. To the end of his life, Woodson was seeking ways to promote the association, as he did after Jackson submitted his 1948 annual report. Woodson concluded a letter on October 25 congratulating Jackson by asking him to "reduce this report to literary form that we may give wide publicity to it in the columns of The Negro History Bulletin" (Woodson, 1948b).

In his final letter to Jackson, dated April 1, 1950, Woodson thanked him for a $500 check for fund-raising for ASNLH, which he said arrived during a time of pressing obligations and provided "increasing assurance that we can survive."

EXAMINING PUBLICITY AND TWO WOODSON LEGACIES

Journal of Negro History

Within three months of establishing the Association for the Study of Negro Life and History, Woodson in 1916 founded the *Journal of Negro History* in support of the nascent history organization's research mission. The *Journal* is considered one of Woodson's major successes, along with Negro History Week, and even today in promotions the organization refers to the *Journal* as its "jewel" ("Publications," n.d.). Now called the *Journal of African American History*, the publication achieved respectability despite arriving in dramatic fashion and being pressed into service as a Woodson public relations instrument. In fact, the *Journal* was almost a public relations disaster during its debut, but Woodson claimed it received an overwhelmingly positive reception from the press and other opinion leaders—which, in any event, helped him overcome one of his biggest gambles.

Woodson, in a heavy-handed move, simply sprang the publication on his board. Later, in recounting the association's first decade, he admitted committing ASNLH to publishing the *Journal* when the organization could not afford it. It had nothing in its treasury. A member of ASNLH's Executive Council resigned upon learning of the first issue, and other members threatened to follow. Woodson paid for that first issue and subsidized association deficits of $1,200 to $1,500 each of its first three years with personal funds (Woodson, 1925a).

Having described the association's weak financial condition when the *Journal* was founded, Woodson probably had no detailed business plan or written public relations strategy awaiting execution at the rollout of the *Journal of Negro History*. However, he clearly had a vision in his mind of what he wanted to accomplish and how to do it. The board member's resignation, Woodson's fear that blacks would become a negligible force in the world, and the fact that the entire venture he created desperately needed an infusion of cash at least prompted him to shift into what today would be described as crisis-PR mode at its launch. Later, as the crisis receded, routine elements of a business organization's public relations activities—media relations, member relations, publicity, and fund-raising—were added, and detected in this analysis.

It was apparent from the start that the *Journal of Negro History* was a medium dedicated to scholarship and research. Its promotional role also was evident because Woodson published so many favorable evaluations of the new publication's launch. He was in effect announcing the staging of a public relations coup.

Regardless of the publication's scholarly intentions, the rollout of the *Journal of Negro History* was all public relations—in this instance, attracting the attention of opinion leaders, journalists, and newspaper readers as sources of prospective converts and money. As an editor and businessman, Woodson was not only concerned with printing, content, and readability issues, but he devoted much of his attention to how the *Journal* could be used to promote the sale of subscriptions, ASNLH memberships, and the overall history movement.

In crisis mode, Woodson had no choice but to promote the *Journal* and solicit financial support, something he would continue doing, urgently and without a break, for the remainder of his life. He mailed 200 letters in 1916 to known philanthropists and received a total of $14. Most of the financial support he would receive from philanthropists and grant-making foundations, which sustained his movement in the 1920s, was a decade away (Woodson, 1925a).

One of the 1916 letters eventually attracted the attention of Julius Rosenwald, the head of Sears, Roebuck and Company and a leading philanthropist who helped establish more than 5,000 schools for African Americans in the South. Rosenwald pledged $100 a quarter and continued financial support at least through the first ten years of the *Journal*. He became a member of ASNLH's Executive Council and a life member of the association (Woodson, 1925a). Woodson was said to be so moved by Rosenwald's early support for ASNLH that he kept a photograph of the philanthropist hanging in his Washington office (Miles, 1991). In the meantime, others' initial reaction to the publication was mostly positive, too, despite the organization's internal problems—budget deficits and the Executive Council's trepidation (Woodson, 1925a).

Examination of the first few issues of the *Journal* further reveals Woodson's tactics in promoting the publication and the overall public-education program. From the beginning, Woodson and his organization were sensitive to what the press said about his publication and what journalists thought generally about issues and events, as he had been during his formative years, and that interest carried over to several of the articles he published. For instance, a comment on the new edition of Monroe Work's *Negro Year Book for 1916–17* noted: "The striking new feature of the work, however, is a brief account of what leading thinkers and the press have said about such perplexing problems as the 'Birth of a Nation,' 'Miscegenation,' 'and 'Segregation'" (Scott, 1916).

Many of the respondents to Woodson's solicitation letters reacted so favorably to the first issue of the *Journal* that Woodson converted their accolades into promotional blurbs. As publicity, the blurbs were the kind readers might see today on dust jackets of books or as quotations from movie reviewers that distributors often use in promoting theatrical releases (Woodson, 1925a).

Woodson printed several of the blurbs in the publication's second issue, dated April 1916. Woodson mailed these comments about the *Journal* to opinion leaders of both races, including some of the biggest names in civil rights, history, and newspaper publishing. Joel E. Spingarn, namesake of the NAACP's Spingarn awards for distinguished service, which were then considered the highest honors that could be bestowed on Americans of African descent, and which Woodson would receive in 1926, enclosed a check for a life membership in ASNLH and a year's subscription to the *Journal*; Edward Channing, professor of ancient and modern history at Harvard, enclosed a contribution of $5 to Woodson's research fund; and Oswald Garrison Villard, one of the leading figures in journalism, enclosed $1 in cash for a subscription. W. E. B. Du Bois; Frederick J. Turner, a former president of the American Historical Association; and Charles H. Haskins, dean of the Harvard Graduate School, awarded the work high marks ("How the Public Received *The Journal of Negro History*," 1916).

The list of accolades had not been exhausted. The above individual compliments paralleled strong support from various publications, including Villard's *New York Evening Post* and the *Boston Herald* ("How the Public Received *The Journal of Negro History*," 1916).

Ten years after the founding of the *Journal*, Woodson wrote about the organization's progress and reported additional comments he received but did not publish in 1916 about the publication. The additional comments included support from A. A. Goldenweiser, a Columbia University anthropologist; W. B. Munro, a Harvard University professor of government; Kelly Miller, a Howard University professor, columnist, and one of the people Woodson later identified as predicting Woodson's failure soon after his arrival in Washington; and Frederick L. Hoffman, a statistician of the Prudential Life Insurance Company. Hoffman had previously claimed in a widely read book that blacks were a dying race (Hoffman, 1896), based on what his grandson would later call reliance on racist theories (Rigney, 2002). However, in response to Woodson's academic journal, Hoffman "likened the movement unto the important work started by John R. Green in popularizing the history of England" (Woodson, 1925a).

The picture Woodson painted of the public's reaction to the launch of his journal was not as rosy as he pretended. Aided by Woodson's publicity work, the first issue of the *Journal of Negro History* grabbed the attention of Baltimore's *Afro-American*. An editorial in the newspaper questioned assertions made by Woodson and his colleagues that the well-being of a race was endangered by misinformation. The *Afro-American* hit especially hard at an article that included an African proverb—"Lies however numerous will be caught when truth rises up"—which the newspaper interpreted as Woodson and his associates declaring that truth about black history eventually would prevail (Stafford, 1916). The editorial claimed that proverb contradicted the dire proclamations. The *Afro*'s retort to Woodson and his staff was, "it is difficult to go all the way with the editors when they state with such frankness that the 'whole truth' of the history of a race is in danger of being lost" (*"The Journal of Negro History,"* 1916).

The April 1916 issue of the *Journal of Negro History* that quoted reaction of newspapers and other prominent citizens to the publication's first issue did not cite the *Afro*'s editorial. Woodson also did not mention the newspaper editorial in his article summarizing ten years of the association's progress. Only positive comments were used.

Throughout most of the public-education program, Woodson was known for making bold pronouncements about the state of Black America and the persistence of misinformation in many history books. For example, the *Chicago Defender* reported on a Woodson speech in 1940 at Chicago's Metropolitan Community Church, where 2,000 people turned out to hear Woodson declare that "American history for the most part is propaganda" ("Chicagoans Hear Dr. Woodson," 1940). But his veracity and integrity were rarely challenged by black media. Other critics attacked Woodson and his associates "on a wide front," recalled John Hope Franklin (Franklin, 1957), but rarely did the black press question the quality or importance of Woodson's work.

In its inaugural coverage and commentary about the new history journal, however, the *Afro-American* suggested it at least had caught Woodson in an exaggeration. It was a gotcha-moment, but newspapers historically have been known for attention-grabbing headlines, even sensationalism, to sell their products. Woodson's supposed guilt, if any, in the use of hyperbole probably was no greater than journalists who write edgy headlines to lure readers, or professors who raise their voices to awaken students.

The *New York Amsterdam News*, in a review of Woodson's achievements in historical research that took up much of the page, said of Woodson: "In his books he misses here and there a few correct statements and falls into some misrepresentation, but he is generally well acquainted with the subject and stands best alone in that line." This criticism took up but one sentence in an otherwise laudatory appraisal (Oxley, 1927).

The *Journal of Negro History* often served a secondary purpose as a news release in publicity activities during the period of this study, particularly through publication of a regular feature labeled "Notes." During the early years, "Notes" included a list of recent items of interest, such as notices of new books being published. It even announced the appointment of Woodson to write an article on black education for the *Encyclopedia Americana* ("Notes," 1916). A "Notes" item in 1917 informed readers about speakers and topics at ASNLH's upcoming biennial meeting in Washington, DC (Hart, 1917).

The *Journal* also announced ASNLH's annual meeting, November 18–19, 1920, in Washington, saying the association was "endeavoring to make this meeting one of the most representative ever assembled." It stated the purpose of the meeting would be promoting the collection of sociological and historical documents, stimulating studies in clubs and schools, and bringing about racial harmony. The *Journal* vowed to have reports of accomplishments and listed as prospective speakers A. B. Hart, professor of history at Harvard University; Franz Boas, professor of ethnology at Columbia University, a future member of ASNLH's Executive Council; L. Hollingsworth Wood, president of the Urban League; and Villard, editor of the *Nation*. The *Journal* claimed the "addresses will cover almost every phase of Negro life and history" ("Notes," 1920).

The October issue cited the recent publication of several books by journalists and assured readers that reviews of the books would be included in its next issue. It was announced, too, that Woodson had been appointed dean of the college division at West Virginia Collegiate Institute.

As promised, the January 1921 issue of the *Journal* did include an address by Villard, who discussed "The Economic Bases of the Race Question." Villard's address was described as a "political and sociological treatise based upon facts of history and economics to show the hopelessness of a program to right the wrongs of the Negro" ("Proceedings," 1921).

That January edition of the *Journal of Negro History* also reviewed *The Republic of Liberia* by R. C. F. Maugham, a British foreign service official; *The United States in Our Own Times* by Paul Haworth, a historian; *The American Colonization Society* by Early Lee Fox, a professor of history at Randolph-Macon College; *The Voice of the Negro* by Robert T. Kerlin, a professor of English at the Virginia Military Institute who would lose his job after he spoke out against lynching (Goggin, 1993). The Kerlin work was a compilation of black newspaper coverage of race riots, better known as "Bloody Summer," from July 1 to November 1, 1919. The *Journal* reprinted a November 14, 1920, article published by the *New York World* on the centennial of the historic St. Philip's Episcopal Church, built for black worshippers not wanted at New York's white churches. Kerlin's article and the St. Philip's reprint illustrated how newspaper coverage and preservation of press files could be used to document history—although none of the four books reviewed in the *Journal* was by a journalist, contrary to what had been promoted in the October edition ("Notes," 1921).

The *Norfolk Journal and Guide* was one of the papers that defined the scholarly articles as news when it reported on the release of the January 1921 issue of the *Journal* that featured an article by Woodson ("Fifty Years of Negro Citizenship as Qualified by the United States Supreme Court") lamenting the loss of former chief justice John Marshall's interpretation and enforcement of the Constitution ("Leading Article in Journal of Negro History," 1921).

The April 1921 issue of the *Journal* also had a promotional slant in "Notes." It reported that Woodson's article "Fifty Years of Negro Citizenship as Qualified by the United States Supreme Court" was being used for supplementary reading in a Howard University Law School class, and announced that Woodson's publishing firm, Associated Publishers, would be publishing a Woodson book, *The Negro Church*, a "treatise of the development of religion among the American Negroes," and would soon bring out *The Negro in Our History* ("Notes," 1921).

Use of the *Journal* as a press release and tool for dissemination of information continued through the 1940s. For instance, the January 1941 issue announced ASNLH was distributing literature for the sixteenth annual celebration of Negro History Week—such as posters and circulars—for the week of February 9–16. Another tactic used in promotion of the *Journal* involved prizes that provided cash to authors of the best articles, and several of the awards were promoted through more traditional press releases ("Negro History Study," 1932).

The *Negro History Bulletin*, founded by Woodson in 1937, also was cast in a promotional role and functioned frequently as a Negro History Week pamphlet after its founding. Fewer details about Negro History Week were published in the *Journal* after the *Bulletin* was established, not surprising because the association announced the bulk of History Week information was shifting to the *Bulletin*, whose more general readership was being targeted for the History Week promotions ("Negro History Week," 1941). The *Negro History Bulletin* also was used to announce annual meetings and provide program schedules. For instance, the *Bulletin* announced the October 28–30, 1949, annual meeting, which included a session on "Methods for Promoting the Study of the Negro," at the Theresa Hotel in New York. The announcement stated that "all persons intelligently interested in the Negro are cordially invited to attend" the sessions ("Annual Meeting," 1949).

As a promotional vehicle, the *Journal* came under scrutiny from the US Post Office, which denied a request for a second-class postal rate (used by newspapers and periodicals) for mailing the *Journal of Negro History* at a reduced rate. ASNLH's in-house promotions consumed too much of the content of the January 1931 edition that a postal official examined in determining its eligibility for the special rate. Expressing concerns that the association was not an educational or philanthropic institution, the examiner also found that almost twenty pages of the issue were devoted to advertising the association and Associated Publishers, including eight pages of an index promoting bound copies of previous issues of the *Journal* ("Post Office Department," 1931).

NEGRO HISTORY WEEK

Woodson's promotion of Negro History Week, reliant on his newspaper partners for mass exposure, readily incorporated events suitable for coverage—such as speeches, meetings, interviews, and announcements—and accommodated newspaper formats and schedules. Woodson, for example, often reminded speakers such as Luther P. Jackson to summarize their major points for distribution to the press.

The messages in newspapers, as well as in other communication, often involved what modern public relations professionals generally refer to as calls to action: informing publics of a particular problem and asking them to do something on behalf of the cause, not just telling them about history, but asking them, for example, to send documents, buy books, and attend meetings. As Woodson wrote, "The favorable comment by the leading white and Negro newspapers decidedly stimulated the movement and presented the cause to the public as it has never been before" ("Wanted," 1926).

Although he did not initially call it Negro History Week, Woodson advocated recognition of African American achievements almost from the beginning of his establishment of the Association for the Study of Negro Life and History, as evidenced by his launch of the *Journal of Negro History* so soon after incorporating the organization. He formally launched the Negro History Week observance in 1926, but its celebration had been evolving for several years—with calls to action (see Timeline, Table 5.2).

Woodson had been urging civic organizations to join him since at least 1920. That year, Marcus Garvey's Universal Negro Improvement Association included in its "Declaration of Rights of the Negro Peoples of the World"

Table 5.2: Negro History Week: Constructed Timeline	
Date	Event
September 9, 1915	Association for the Study of Negro Life and History is founded by Carter G. Woodson in Chicago, with James E. Stamps, A. L. Jackson, and George C. Hall.
October 2, 1915	ASNLH is incorporated in Washington, DC, by Woodson, John A. Bigham, and Jesse E. Moorland.
January 10, 1923	The *New York Amsterdam News* reports that during the Omega Psi Phi annual meeting in Philadelphia an official of the NAACP emphasized the "urgent necessity for the study of Negro History." A committee that included Woodson is appointed to develop plans over the next year for "fostering the study of Negro History in the schools and colleges of the country" ("Omega Psi," 1923).
1924	Woodson has been promoting black achievements since founding ASNLH, and his fraternity, Omega Psi Phi, calls its observance Negro Achievement Week in 1924 ("Daryl Michael Scott for ASALH," n. d.).
February 21, 1925	North Carolina A&T begins observing black history in 1924 and the *Norfolk Journal and Guide* covers Woodson as the main speaker at its 1925 observance ("Dr. Carter G. Woodson delivers address at A&T College," 1925).
May 13, 1925	The *Amsterdam News* reports that Woodson gave a stirring speech at Union Baptist Church in Philadelphia to members of Delta Sigma Theta, whose slogan in 1925 was "Invest in Education" ("Delta Sigma Theta sorority notes," 1925).
November 28, 1925	The *Pittsburgh Courier* endorses the 1926 observance in an editorial ("Negro History Week," 1925). Other newspapers also endorse it.
February 7–13, 1926	First national Negro History Week is established by Woodson and observed in many locations. Black newspapers carry a column by Woodson on black achievements (Woodson, 1926).
February 24, 1926	Woodson's Negro History Week speech is excerpted by the *New York Amsterdam News* ("Dangerous lies," 1926).
February 27, 1926	Newspapers announce success of the first observance and Woodson's plans to make it an annual event ("Wanted $20000," 1926).
June 5, 1926	The *Journal and Guide* supports Woodson's fund-raising goal ("Urgent need for funds," 1926).
January 29, 1927	The *Pittsburgh Courier* supports having an annual event ("Editorial," 1927).
February 2, 1927	The *New York Amsterdam News* publishes a Woodson article explaining how to observe history week (Woodson, 1927).
February 6–13, 1927	Woodson acknowledges several newspapers for their support in popularizing Negro History Week: *Charlotte Observer*, *Chicago Daily News*, *Chicago Defender*, *Louisville News*, *New York Times*, *Norfolk Journal and Guide*, *Philadelphia Tribune*, and *Pittsburgh Courier* (Woodson, 1927).
History Week, 1928	Woodson attributes success to "warmhearted support of the press," especially from the *Norfolk Journal and Guide*, *Pittsburgh Courier*, *Philadelphia Tribune* (Woodson, 1928).

History Week, 1929	Woodson praises support from several black newspapers (Woodson, 1929).
History Week, 1930	Woodson celebrates the careers of African Americans who have served in Congress ("Negro History Week Celebration," 1930).
1972	Association for the Study of Negro Life and History changes its name to Association for the Study of African American Lie and History ("ASALH Timeline," n. d.).
February 10, 1976	President Gerald Ford proclaims February Black History Month ("President Gerald R. Ford's Message," 1976).
Sources: Compiled from ASNLH documents and various sources as indicated above	

a demand that black children be taught Negro history in schools ("UNIA," 1920). Woodson also encouraged his fraternity brothers in Omega Psi Phi to begin an observance, which they did in 1924, calling their project Negro Achievement Week (Scott, 2009–2011). North Carolina A&T College also began observing black achievements as early as 1924, and Woodson spoke there at its second commemoration in 1925, a speech that was reported by the *Norfolk Journal and Guide* ("Dr. Carter G. Woodson Delivers Address," 1925).

In the meantime, Charles H. Wesley, the Howard University history professor and Woodson protégé, was encouraging interest in history in high schools. He summarized his monograph, *Negro History in the School Curriculum*, and delivered a speech on the subject at a teachers' institute in Washington, DC. Wesley complained about an "immense amount of ignorance of the facts of history." The *Amsterdam News* reported the speech ("Want Negro History," 1925) and published an adaptation of the speech that October (Wesley, 1925).

These early activities showed promise, but Woodson decided to broaden the celebration and took it national in 1926, beyond just college campuses. He had sounded out the press in 1925. Responses from newspapers were immediately positive, as they usually were to Woodson's initiatives. The *Pittsburgh Courier* was among the newspapers accepting Woodson's call for recognizing black achievements, with an editorial in November 1925. The editorial credited Woodson with publicizing the past of a race that previously had no publicity agents or chroniclers. Adopting the messenger and his message, the newspaper said, Woodson "comes to us with the plea of one deeply concerned. He asks us record our achievements; to leave behind us a history which shall portray truthfully the life of the group. What could be as worthy a cause?" ("Negro History Week," 1925).

Woodson launched the first national observance of Negro History during the second week of February in 1926, a month he chose because of its cultural significance to African Americans and in honor of the births of Abraham Lincoln, Frederick Douglass, and other events. He disseminated pamphlets (stating the purpose of the celebration) to centers, ministers, educators, social workers, and business operators. In response to the promotion, he told *Journal of Negro History* readers, the association received numerous inquiries about the history program, which included exercises about African Americans as explorers, inventors, writers, and artists, and about the press ("Negro History Week," 1926).

Several black newspapers carried a Woodson column promoting Negro History Week in 1926, including one headlined "Negro Was the First to Discover America," in the *Afro-American*. A Negro History Week speech he delivered was excerpted by the *New York Amsterdam News* ("Dangerous Lies on Negro in Books," 1926).

Having achieved success in 1926, Woodson wasted no time in announcing the observance would become an annual national event, and he credited the newspapers' support as a major reason for success that year. "The favorable comment by the leading white and Negro newspapers decidedly stimulated the movement and presented the cause to the public as it has never been before," he said. Announcement of an annual event included declaration of the association's goals: producing a series of historical stories and textbooks depicting black civilizations in Africa and their influence and contributions in America, encouraging schools to adopt the books for use in classrooms, providing adequate reference materials for schools and libraries, and raising $20,000 to finance the movement ("Wanted," 1926).

Drumming up support, the *Norfolk Journal and Guide* was still promoting Woodson's fund-raising goal in June 1926, when it published Woodson's comparison of what he claimed whites were spending ($1 million) to write history to what he was trying to raise—$20,000, or one-fiftieth of what the white population was spending. The newspaper printed Woodson's mailing address where contributions could be sent ("Urgent Need," 1926).

In promoting the 1927 Negro History Week, the *Pittsburgh Courier* announced its support for making the observance an annual event "in order that some definite imprint of the life and achievement of the Negro Group, especially in this country, may be made upon the public mind" ("Negro History Week," 1927).

Just before start of the observance, Woodson distributed a column stating what participants should expect during History Week, February 6 to February

13, 1927 (Woodson, 1927a), and the observance was promoted in the *Journal of Negro History* (Woodson, 1927b). Following that year's events, Woodson proclaimed in the *Journal of Negro History* that the second year's celebration "showed unusual progress toward the desired end of saving and popularizing the records of the race that it may not become a negligible factor in the thought of the world" (Woodson, 1927c).

Woodson also cited the *Norfolk Journal and Guide*'s reports as evidence of the success of Negro History Week:

> *The Journal and Guide* received line upon line of news stories relating the observances of Negro History Week in the schools, colleges, churches, societies and other groups throughout the country, which furnished conclusive evidence that the event was observed on a national scale and with much enthusiasm. (Woodson, 1927c)

Woodson praised other publicity from the press that year, too, including coverage in white daily newspapers: *Charlotte Observer, Chicago Daily News,* and *New York Times.* In addition to the *Norfolk Journal and Guide,* he also cited the work of these other black weeklies—*Philadelphia Tribune, Chicago Defender, St. Louis Argus, Louisville News,* and *Pittsburgh Courier*—for what he called "elaborate editorials." Woodson wrote: "Without the assistance given by these agencies the cause could not have been so well served, and the celebration would not today be pointed to as one of the most significant movements ever started in the interest of the Negro race" (Woodson, 1927c).

The *Pittsburgh Courier* continued supporting Woodson's fund-raising campaign in May 1927 ("Help Wanted," 1927), and he announced an expansion of the public-education program to include home extension courses in black history in October, which was endorsed by the *Courier* ("To Offer Extension Courses," 1927) and other newspapers. The *Norfolk Journal and Guide* added support with a strongly worded editorial highlighting Woodson's "years of painstaking effort to compiling and popularizing the history of the Negro race." It commended plans for the new program and predicted its success ("Extension Courses," 1927).

Before the 1928 observance of Negro History Week, Woodson produced additional materials for promotion and instruction for the celebration, and readers were informed about them in the *Journal of Negro History.* Among several recommendations, Woodson encouraged local communities to establish branches of ASNLH. Members of these affiliates were encouraged to save such records as old newspapers, receipts, manumission papers, deeds, wills, and similar items bearing on the past.

In January 1928, Joseph Boris, editor of *Who's Who in Colored America*, succeeded in having New York's WABC station air a program called "Hour of Negro Achievement " on late-night radio (10:30 to 11:30) on Thursdays. The first program featured W. C. Handy, recognized by many even then as "the Father of the Blues." The second program featured the *Amsterdam News* in a show devoted to achievements of prominent blacks in sports and a discussion of the newspaper's growth in New York ("Who's Who," 1928).

The *Pittsburgh Courier* reported that Philadelphia's mayor would present an award and Woodson would speak at Philadelphia's observance of Negro History Week in 1928. The *Courier* also hyped some of Woodson's successes, with misleading statements, including a claim that the *Journal of Negro History* "now appears in every library of the state and in each university and college in America." Woodson only claimed many such institutions were adopting the books and journals—never all ("Mayor Mackey," 1928).

Woodson, nonetheless, was pleased with the coverage, and said so in his 1928 report in the *Journal of Negro History*: "The unusual success was due in the first place to the warmhearted support of the press. Newspapers gave ample space to the notices of the celebration and published convincing editorials commending the effort" (Woodson, 1928a).

As was his practice in the *Journal of Negro History*, Woodson singled out several of the newspapers for their coverage and publicity (Woodson, 1928a):

- He reprinted a long passage from a February 4, 1928, *Norfolk Journal and Guide* article that provided details of the celebration, praised Woodson's work as "an eminent Negro historian," and accepted the doctrine of his program. The *Journal and Guide* editorial stated, "Let us make the celebration of the third annual Negro History Week the most effective ever attempted."
- Woodson also reprinted text from a *Pittsburgh Courier* editorial in support of his fund-raising activities. The editorial asked readers to purchase books and subscribe to the *Journal of Negro History*.
- He cited the *Philadelphia Tribune* for its expression of support in a similarly strong editorial.

Meanwhile, ASNLH sent a form letter to Abbott, a life member, seeking his support for home extension, as it marketed the program. The letter, attached to an application form, said, "It serves as a foundation for all other courses offered by the Department. Each course costs $20.00. The matriculation fee is $5.00, but it has to be paid only once" (Association for the Study of Negro Life and History, 1929).

In the run-up to the 1929 Negro History Week, the newspapers continued to provide what had become routine support, including coverage of Woodson's speeches and favorable reviews of his books—*African Myths* and *Negro Makers of History*, for example, in the *New York Amsterdam News* ("Book Review," 1929).

Woodson reported a number of supporters used in promoting the 1929 event, but he reserved his most effusive praise in the *Journal of Negro History* for the black newspapers: "The greatest publicity was given the effort by the press," he said, citing such black newspapers as *Philadelphia Tribune, Baltimore Commonwealth, Chicago Defender, Palmetto Leader, Tampa Bulletin, Washington Eagle,* and *Norfolk Journal and Guide.* Woodson said P. B. Young and Robert J. Nelson, editors of the *Journal and Guide,* "undertook in their editorial columns to interpret the significance of the celebration in the development of the youth and also to arouse more interest in a wholehearted public support of the Association" (Woodson, 1929a).

Typical of newspaper support of Negro History Week in 1930 was an editorial in the *Pittsburgh Courier* that promoted reading history books ("Read Negro History," 1930). Woodson also staged a special event in Washington, DC, highlighted by a banquet given in honor of three living black former members of Congress—John R. Lynch of Mississippi, Thomas E. Miller of South Carolina, and H. P. Cheatham of North Carolina—and sitting member Oscar De Priest of Illinois. Journalists were on display at the banquet. Besides Woodson's brother, Robert H. Woodson, of Huntington, West Virginia, the association's report of the meeting in the *Journal of Negro History* said 316 people attended the banquet on February 10, 1930, including George B. Murphy of the *Afro-American.* Another journalist in attendance, W. T. Andrews, editor of the *Herald* and *Commonwealth* of Baltimore, was on the program and evaluated the record of blacks who served in Congress ("Negro History Week," 1930).

While the press continued to support Negro History Week, Woodson's reports do not mention contributions of newspapers during the History Week observances between 1931 and 1936, in contrast to the first five years when the program was getting started. It is not known why Woodson chose not to mention them. However, the most obvious support given the movement by black newspapers during that period was their commitment of space for

Woodson's columns. Many of the columns and other articles published by the newspapers were timed for promoting Negro History Week and ASNLH's annual meetings. For example, a February 7, 1931, Negro History Week promotion carried this headline in the *Negro World*: "Negro History Week! He Fails to Learn His Past Altogether" (see chapter 4 for a list of Woodson's columns).

Promoting the Negro History Week of 1933, one column told of H. W. Peet, a British journalist, who had written admiringly of a history observance he experienced during a visit to Tuskegee Institute (Woodson, 1932q). Another column publicized an annual literary contest on black history (Woodson, 1933g).

The black newspapers had become extensions of Woodson's organization and served as his information medium for black history. For example, in 1934 the *Norfolk Journal and Guide* got the Negro History Week promotion going two months early, asking readers to save papers, diaries, manumission papers, and other records to popularize black history ("People Unwittingly Foil," 1933).

In Atlanta, the *Daily World* listed activities scheduled for the week ("History Week," 1934). Other newspapers' coverage also included advance stories on preparations for the observances, in addition to coverage of the weeklong events each year, such as coverage in the *Cleveland Call and Post* in 1935 ("History Association Makes Preparations to Celebrate 20th Anniversary") and 1936 ("Negro History Week Pamphlet Given Gratis").

The *Norfolk Journal and Guide* reported Woodson's suggestions for the 1937 celebration ("Negro History Week Celebration to Begin This Year February 7, 1937"). The *Cleveland Call and Post* reported increasing demand for ASNLH's sixteen-page illustrated pamphlet for the 1937 observance that was available without charge. The article stated, excitedly, that "so great has been the demand for pamphlets that a new edition of 25,000 had to be printed. In this publication not only the purpose of the celebration is set forth, but the details for exercises are given as helpful suggestions" ("Negro History Week Pamphlet Given Gratis," 1936).

The ASNLH report on Negro History Week in 1937 highlighted the Woodson-newspaper partnership for the first time in several years. The report cited the contributions of Roscoe Dunjee, editor of the *Black Dispatch* in Oklahoma; the editors of educational magazines and periodicals; and several editors of metropolitan dailies. "With these newly interested agencies cooperating with those long thus engaged there was little likelihood that many persons in the country were not reminded in some way of the celebration and its significance," the report in the *Journal* stated ("Negro History Week," 1937).

For 1938's observance, newspapers published two Woodson columns in January previewing History Week activities. One of the columns, published on January 8 by the *Norfolk Journal and Guide*, praised black newspapers for helping to popularize history and urged the reading of black newspapers (Woodson, 1938a). The other column, printed on January 15 by the *Pittsburgh Courier*, involved a promotion in which Woodson provided details about the upcoming observance and asked whether blacks were freer in 1865 (Woodson, 1938b).

The association's report in the *Journal* of the thirteenth year of Negro History Week in 1938 also acknowledged white press support, and a few newspapers, including the *New Orleans Times-Picayune*, provided editorials ("Negro History Week," 1938).

Several black newspapers had begun running their own History Week observances. The *Afro-American* was promoting history in its own fashion with history games ("The Junior Page," 1935) and "Fact Finding Dime Contest," in addition to what Woodson was doing ("Fact Finding," 1939).

Woodson was so pleased with press coverage in Chicago he wrote the editor of the *Chicago Defender* that year, saying its cooperation on the event was significant and that he hoped other newspapers would provide similar support (Woodson, 1939a).

In 1940, a Woodson column published just before History Week attacked racism in the publishing business. He accused white publishing firms of refusing to publish manuscripts regarding black history written by prominent black writers because "they tell the truth." A headline over the column in the *Pittsburgh Courier* presented Woodson in an unusually aggressive tone about this issue (Woodson, 1940b). In Chicago that year, the *Courier* reported, participants paid tribute to Ida B. Wells, the antilynching journalist who died in 1931 ("Life-Work of Ida B. Wells," 1940).

Woodson noted in the *Journal* in 1941 the observance was receiving more and more attention and credited publicity provided by educational journals for increasing the public's interest. However, he expressed concern that the larger educational institutions were just going through the motions (Woodson, 1941b).

Woodson, preparing for the 1942 Negro History Week, distributed three columns about the upcoming observance. In one, published by the *Norfolk Journal and Guide*, Woodson called History Week the most popular activity launched by ASNLH (Woodson, 1942a). After History Week the following month, Woodson commended the work of several Negro History Week supporters in the *Journal*, including support from Oklahoma editor Roscoe Dunjee (Woodson, 1942b).

The *Pittsburgh Courier* reported receiving a letter in 1943 from a Greek American girl who won honorable mention in an ASNLH essay contest. Calling her a "brilliant high school student," the newspaper used the teenager, the daughter of a local doctor, as an example of enlightenment and respect that could be generated if all people were exposed to black history ("Editor's Note," 1943).

The director's report in 1944 again noted progress in getting the cooperation of schools during promotion of Negro History Week and that the annual History Week season generated the most financial support for the cause. Woodson said black donors generated 97 percent of the association's financial support (Woodson, 1944b).

The director's report for 1945 continued to state progress in winning over the public. "Negro History Week still grips the nation as a national celebration," Woodson said. "In the remote parts of the country this observance takes precedence over any other week celebrated in Negro schools and in mixed schools with a considerable Negro enrollment" (Woodson, 1945a).

However, Woodson was concerned about the support of charlatans and exploiters with different agendas. He warned against those in politics who went to mayors and other officials seeking black history proclamations for political points (Woodson, 1945a). He issued similar concerns in 1946 about propaganda organizations exploiting the cause and the tendency of some local groups to deviate from the original intent of the History Week observances (Woodson, 1946e).

The director's report regarding the 1947 celebration continued to complain about the exploiters while declaring the movement's success, which he credited to widespread publicity involving the educational press and other supporters in state departments of education and local superintendents (Woodson, 1947).

The *Chicago Defender* declared that Negro History Week had become "an institution of national scope," and praised Woodson's contributions. The editorial recited many of the historical facts about which Woodson had been writing and speaking. The newspaper concluded: "When the full story is told it will prove to be an epic of tremendous sweep" ("Negro History Week," 1947).

The *Afro-American* observed the 1948 Negro History Week with a special feature package on February 7, including a full-page tribute to history makers

Table 5.3: Woodson's List of the Fifteen Outstanding Events in Negro History in America, 1619–1940
Events
1. Landing of the first Negroes in 1619
2. Slaying of Crispus Attucks at the Boston Massacre, 1770
3. Peter Salem at the Battle of Bunker Hill, 1775
4. Northwest Territory Ordinance, 1787, prohibiting importation of slaves in the Northwest Territory
5. Missouri Compromise
6. Nat Turner's Insurrection, 1831
7. Growth of the Abolitionist Movement
8. Launching of the Underground Railroad
9. Omnibus Bill, 1850
10. Dred Scott Decision
11. Civil War
12. Reconstruction Era
13. First exodus from the South, 1877
14. Booker T. Washington Era
15. The Great Migration
Sources The *Afro-American* (MacKay, 1950); *Ebony* ("The 15 Outstanding Events in Negro History," 1950); and Claude A. Barnett Papers ("Dr. Woodson Lists," 1950)

and a rare lengthy interview with Woodson. The *Afro* explained that by 1948 it was no longer possible to crowd into one week all the accomplishments of African Americans. It noted that more and more schools were offering the study of black history. During the interview, Woodson was still concerned about the lack of sufficient references and documentation for black achievements. The *Afro* concluded its coverage with a list of references suggested for use by students of history. The list was dominated by Woodson's books ("They've Blazed a Trail," 1948). Woodson's report in 1948 expressed satisfaction in winning over international audiences, and, like the newspaper, he was looking forward to the day when the observance of Negro History Week would be yearlong (Woodson, 1948).

Newspaper coverage of Woodson in the late 1940s seemed to sense his looming departure from the scene, with tribute after tribute. The *Chicago Defender*'s national edition, for instance, honored Woodson in its 1949 coverage, referring to him as "the Father of Negro History" and ending its salute with "Hail Woodson" ("Well Done," 1949).

The US Department of Defense began integrating the military in 1948, and the Office of the Secretary of Defense acknowledged Woodson's interest in the history of African Americans in the services. An adviser to the secretary of defense forwarded Woodson a request from Carl Murphy, president of the *Afro-American*, for assistance on a story about the Reserve Officers' Training Corps (ROTC), as well as the adviser's reply in forwarding the request to the department's History Division (Evans, 1948).

Woodson's final annual report to the association on Negro History Week activities was written following the 1949 celebration. It is possible Woodson composed a report on the 1950 observance, but it was not published in the *Journal*. Rayford W. Logan, Woodson's successor at ASNLH, received credit for the next report, with no indication it was prepared from Woodson's notes or other assistance. Woodson's final report in 1949 continued to warn supporters about others' attempts to hijack the movement, as he attempted to refocus attention on the purpose of his movement and how the black history celebrations should be observed (Woodson, 1949b).

In promoting the 1950 observance before Woodson's passing that year, *Ebony* magazine asked Woodson to name the fifteen outstanding events in African American history. This list was distributed by the Associated Negro Press to its newspaper subscribers. He named events, using pictorial reproductions in *Ebony*, ranging from arrival of the first black colonists in 1619 to the black migration through 1940. Publication of Woodson's list (Table 5.3) was indicative of how members of the black press had taken it upon themselves to promote Negro History Week (MacKay, 1950).

ANP provided no details or explanations of the items on the list; however, even casual news readers would have discovered that Woodson's understanding of history included African American contributions since the beginning of the country, purposefully, and his public relations activities in this area were noted. *Ebony* said, "Woodson takes most pride in his role as a promoter—his biggest job being the success of Negro History Week." *Ebony* also included Woodson's defense of a separate black history observance as a temporary response to blacks being left out of most history books ("The 15 Outstanding Events in Negro History," 1950).

The broadcast medium also celebrated Woodson's life during his final Negro History Week in 1950. A radio program, "Destination Freedom," presented a reenactment in a documentary format with actors paying tribute to Woodson's life on a nationwide broadcast and tracing his early interest in correcting history to his accomplishments as a historian (Durham, Betts, and WMAQ, 2000).

During observance of the twenty-fifth anniversary of Negro History Week, the *Afro-American* published a special issue that favorably assessed progress of the observances to date and listed objectives and accomplish-ments over the years. The special section included a message the newspaper stated was from Woodson, in which he hoped the special week would one day be replaced by recognition of black achievements throughout the year. Woodson's public relations instincts seemed present in this message, too, as the newspaper reported that Woodson was "comforted" that "the real history of America has become so widespread that just last week 40 to 50 orders a day [came in] for the Negro History Week kit, a special folder, complete with photos and ideal for classroom use" ("A Special Message from the Daddy of Negro History Week," 1950).

The final edition of the *Negro History Bulletin* under Woodson's editorial direction was the April 1950 issue, which carried an unsigned editorial about support for the fight to liberate African Americans from discrimination and segregation policies, while making a plea for harmony within the black com-munity ("More Strife and Confusion," 1950). That editorial preceded a report on Negro History Week (not signed by Woodson) that defended the desig-nation of a week for observing black contributions in history, as Woodson had done in other media outlets. The report also included an attack on the ABC radio network for indifference to the observance, perpetuation of racial stereotypes, and overall hostility to African American interests (Cartwright, 1950).

Chapter 6

REMEMBERING WOODSON
(and Forgotten Black Press Contributions to His Legacies)

IN HIS FINAL DECADE, WOODSON RESEMBLED LESS THE WARRIOR HE HAD been during the 1920s and 1930s and more of a beloved hero. By 1940, he was making fewer fiery statements that were recorded by the press. His articles still carried punch during the 1940s, however, and Woodson remained active as a scholar and promoter of history. Based on newspaper articles and his reports in the *Journal of Negro History*, he seemed preoccupied with producing a black encyclopedia.

Woodson's accomplishments were feted in black communities across the country, and his celebrity still grabbed headlines in black newspapers when he chose to speak, travel, or accept awards. His partnership with the press remained in force—he just was not required to work as hard for the publicity. Press criticism of Woodson was rare in his final years. Black newspaper articles celebrated his life long before his obituary was set in type.

Woodson's critics, especially Myrdal and others outside Black America, complained that Woodson's movement was propaganda and divisive because his research engendered racial pride in the accomplishments he unearthed. Woodson dismissed Myrdal as lacking informed judgment (Southern, 1987). Myrdal, however, made liberal use of Woodson's research in his study of race in America and grudgingly acknowledged Woodson's work (Myrdal, 1944). In a footnote, Myrdal provided recognition of Woodson's success in the history movement by quoting the curator of the Schomburg Collection of the New York Public Library who declared: "The history of Negro historiography falls into two divisions, before Woodson and after Woodson" (Reddick, 1937).

The black press, Woodson, nine other blacks, and five whites were honored during Negro History Week, February 11–17, 1940, for distinguished achievements in improving race relations. Others being honored included Joe Louis, then First Lady Eleanor Roosevelt, author Richard Wright, and scientist George Washington Carver. The awards were based on a national poll sponsored by the Schomburg Collection and ASNLH. That Woodson would be honored based on a poll cosponsored by his organization was consistent with his use of public relations, and the news story reporting the award did not appear concerned ("First Lady Named," 1940).

Woodson's virtues were extolled following a speech in Charlotte, North Carolina, in May 1940, at the twentieth anniversary of the American Bible Society, at Grace AME Church, apparently without the acrimony he stirred up a decade earlier when he addressed religious groups, accused ministers of corruption, and crusaded for church consolidation. In Charlotte, he was called an "outstanding historian," and his supporters from the Woodsonian History Club of Second Ward High School, named in his honor, were among more than 850 people on hand (Maxwell, 1940).

In September 1940, ASNLH held its twenty-fifth anniversary meeting in Chicago, where it was founded, and Woodson's image as a tireless, underpaid crusader for black history was resurrected and burnished. The anniversary had to compete for press attention with images of Woodson's sacrifices. For instance, the *Atlanta Daily World* divided space between the reelection of officers at the association's business session and discussion by members insisting that Woodson be given a check for his $3,000 annual salary, even though he was returning his pay each year to the organization for its operations (Nelson, 1940).

The parade of newspaper supporters seemed nonstop. The *Cleveland Call and Post*, recapping the major events of 1940, rated Woodson's speech before a Cleveland interracial organization as one of the year's highlights for that community (Loeb, 1941).

The Georgia State Teachers Association convened in Atlanta April 16–17, 1942, and an advance story in the *Atlanta Daily World* predicted attendance of 3,000 teachers, "the largest delegation of teachers ever held in the city," and reported that the main speech Woodson would deliver "is scheduled to be full of information and vital during this period through which we are living" (Bradley, 1942). Following Woodson's speech to the Georgia educators, the *Daily World*'s editorial, calling Woodson "the foremost Negro historian," repeated the familiar themes Woodson had sounded for three decades, but the newspaper restated them more succinctly on this occasion: teach students from within their environment, in a more realistic approach, and keep your heads high "because your face is black and yours is a great heritage" ("Dr. Carter Woodson's Address," 1942).

When President Edwin L. Barclay of Liberia visited Philadelphia in 1943, he was presented with a copy of Woodson's *The Negro in Our History* on behalf of the city's school children (Snead, 1943). Woodson also appeared on Mutual Radio's "My People" during Negro History Week, and newspaper readers were told in an advance story that he would be speaking from Washington, DC. Other guests on the show were Todd Duncan and Etta Moten, stars of *Porgy and Bess*, who appeared from Milwaukee. Moten was the wife of Claude A. Barnett, founder of ANP ("Woodson, Duncan to Appear," 1943).

Woodson remained a symbol of black independence and pride. His efforts were being supported by the people he most wanted to reach. The *Chicago Defender* stated that 95 percent of the financial support for ASNLH and Associated Publishers was derived from black communities (Smith, 1943).

As he accepted praise, Woodson declared success for the movement and expressed optimism about its future in published reports of his speeches. Newspaper coverage in the 1940s appeared to eulogize Woodson and placed him on a pedestal.

Occasionally the coverage of Woodson appeared naive. For example, one story reporting his earnings as $75,000 a year from book publishing failed to challenge the strict separation he supposedly maintained between the not-for-profit ASNLH and for-profit Associated Publishers, his publishing firm. Instead, in a statement that must have kept the Internal Revenue Service off Woodson's back, the *Afro* reported: "The two organizations occupy the same building, but are not interlocked. Not one sheet of paper belonging to one is exchanged with the other. This is to avoid tax obligations" ("Dr. Woodson No Pauper," 1947).

Woodson, ever the press analyst, in old age appeared disillusioned about the mainstream white newspapers. He complained that the leading newspapers were no longer "agents of thought," and were serving the interests of powerful forces pursuing agendas that do not necessarily benefit the people—a point of view in stark contrast to his opinion of the newspapers that had provided him intellectual stimulation as a young man (Woodson, 1946e).

TIME RUNNING OUT

Lawrence D. Reddick, a friend and former Schomburg curator, recalled Woodson's final days: "In the last year of his life, Woodson noticeably mellowed. For the first time he seemed to be more willing to listen than to talk." Reddick said Woodson "appeared to be trying to learn to delegate important tasks, to let others lift some of the load from his individual shoulders" (Reddick, 1953).

Woodson's softer side was illustrated when the *Chicago Defender* argued that his outward toughness and cynicism never fooled his friends. The article also continued the image of Woodson projected by the black press for decades—that of being a superhero who sacrificed personal comforts for a cause important to all of Black America: "He draws no salary for his services to the association and turns back into the business part of that he draws from the prospering publishing concern" (Smith, 1943).

As his time appeared to be running out, praises of Woodson multiplied. During ASNLH's annual meeting in Washington, DC, in 1948, Elmer A. Henderson, a member of the Executive Council and assistant superintendent of Baltimore schools, presided during the Historians' Breakfast session and used the occasion to honor Woodson for his sacrifices "to keep the work of the Association above pecuniary embarrassment and to make it a great force in preventing the race from becoming a negligible factor in the thought of the world" ("Proceedings," 1949).

Although Woodson's health was visibly in decline at the October 1949 ASNLH meeting in New York, the future was not bleak for African Americans, in contrast to when Woodson began promoting history, as demonstrated by the program's lineup. Presentations by stars and rising stars were on the agenda: Langston Hughes, a former Woodson aide and contributor to the Harlem Renaissance, participated in a segment called "An Evening with the Authors"; Robert C. Weaver, of New York University, reported on "Significant Developments in Education with Respect to Negroes," and would be appointed by President Lyndon Johnson to be the first African American to head a US cabinet department (Housing and Urban Development); Thurgood Marshall discussed "The Negro Lawyer in a New Role" and would later successfully argue the *Brown v. Board of Education* cases and become associate justice of the US Supreme Court, the first African American to hold that position, also appointed by President Johnson. Dr. Charles Drew, who developed a process for storing blood plasma at blood banks, discussed "Negro Scholars in Scientific Research." Another Woodson associate, but not on the ASNLH program in 1949, was diplomat Ralph Bunche, a contributor to the *Journal of Negro History* who became the first African American awarded a Nobel Prize in December 1950, just months following Woodson's death.

The movement (and the press) inevitably had to confront a future without Woodson—just as many African Americans had done when Booker T. Washington left the stage in 1915. At the business session during that ASNLH annual meeting in 1949, the association was thrown into a state of turmoil and its future placed in considerable doubt at the mention of a leadership change. Mary McLeod Bethune announced she was resigning from active participation in all organizations, including the presidency of ASNLH, having served in that capacity since 1936. According to the proceedings, her decision surprised the membership because it was already known that Woodson was "far advanced in years and must retire soon." A committee was appointed to consider the association's future and a plan for ASNLH's "perpetuation," and Bethune was persuaded to remain until her successor could be found ("Proceedings," 1950). She was succeeded by Wesley in 1952. Woodson did not make it to retirement. He died about six months after the October 1949 meeting, succeeded by Rayford Logan, whom he mentored, as executive director.

At the time of his death of a heart attack on April 3, 1950, Woodson was one of the most recognizable African Americans—in the world. His death received the kind of news coverage in the black press in 1950 that today would be associated with the passing of a head of state, not unlike the coverage he received lecturing the nation about history.

Most African Americans probably learned of Woodson's death from mainstream media because most black newspapers were published weekly. The *New York Times* reported his death matter-of-factly on April 5, two days after he died, recalling his scholarship, his founding of the *Journal of Negro History*, the *Negro History Bulletin*, and ASNLH, and noting that Theodore Roosevelt Jr. had served on the committee that awarded Woodson the NAACP's Spingarn Award in 1926. The headline, "Dr. C. G. Woodson, Retired Educator," was inaccurate. Woodson never retired. The *Chicago Defender's* national edition and the *Pittsburgh Courier's* Washington edition reported his death in page 1 stories on April 8, 1950, as did the Washington edition of the *Afro-American*.

Praise for Woodson, which had already been high within the black press for three decades, continued in the newspapers immediately after his passing. The *Afro* said, "Few men have contributed so much to generations yet unborn and received so little material reward in return as Dr. Carter G. Woodson, father of Negro History Week, who died last Monday" (Dr. Carter G. Woodson," 1950).

The *Afro*, whose coverage of him was the most complete of any media since his rise, provided full coverage of Woodson's service. His funeral was attended by 500 people at Shiloh Baptist Church in Washington, DC, located a few doors down from Woodson's home-office. Wesley delivered Woodson's eulogy. On numerous occasions, Woodson had requested that his funeral be as brief as possible. "Get it over within fifteen minutes if you can," the *Afro* quoted Woodson. The newspaper said, "Every effort was made to comply with his wish, but it was impossible to pay adequate tribute in less than the hour it took."

The Rev. Jerry Moore, whose Nineteenth Street Baptist Church Woodson often visited, said Woodson told him of a premonition three weeks before dying that he would not live much longer. "I'm just sitting here waiting to die," Moore quoted Woodson ("Thousands Attend," 1950). A sidebar accompanying the main story reported, "Educators from the District and all over the nation have expressed sorrow over the death of Dr. Carter G. Woodson, who died suddenly in his office on Monday" ("Lauded as Leader," 1950).

The *Afro* and other black newspapers divided coverage between Woodson's funeral and services for Dr. Drew, who died in an automobile accident on April 1, 1950, two days before Woodson. The *Afro*'s Woodson salute was respectful—although it committed at least one error of fact for which Woodson the perfectionist probably would have demanded a correction. A cutline identifying Woodson's family and friends leaving the church incorrectly stated that the elderly woman in the photograph being helped down the steps was Woodson's sister Bessie Woodson Yancey. Yancey, however, stated in a letter to ASNLH's treasurer Louis Mehlinger that she had been too ill to attend the funeral. Her grandson Nelson Bickley represented her branch of the family from Huntington (Yancey, 1950).

Woodson's death was a time for the black press to reflect on what his life meant to African Americans and how far the nation had evolved during his movement. Although Woodson had complained about journalistic tendencies to bestow historical significance too quickly, black journalists saw Woodson as an extraordinary figure and recognized his accomplishments immediately.

The *Chicago Defender* declared *The Negro in Our History* and its revised editions as his "crowning achievement" ("Dr. Carter G. Woodson, Historian, Found Dead," 1950).

The *Atlanta Daily World*'s editorial declared Woodson's public-education program a success. It cited the effects of his popularizing of history through his scholarship, including how blacks and whites were regarding black history in a positive light as a result of his work ("Editorial," 1950).

Black newspapers had been accepting of Woodson's periodic pronouncements about success for years, and their reports and editorials already had been reflective of gradual improvements in recognition of black achievements. Upon his death, they seemed to declare a complete victory for his program. The newspapers did not indicate their role in making Woodson's program a success, but they showered him with praise and tended not to claim or share credit for assisting him. Knowledge of their partnership with Woodson largely vanished with the passing of time and in the absence of the newspapers' institutional memory.

THE WOODSON LEGACIES

Carter G. Woodson's advocacy transformed the American way of life. He was not the first black historian. Others before him wrote history, but Woodson and W. E. B. Du Bois were the first scientifically trained African American historians, and Woodson stood alone as one who dedicated his life to his history cause.

Woodson was celebrated before his death as the "Father of Negro History" (a term now updated to "Father of Black History" or "Father of African American History"), recognition for his keeping alive the achievements of Americans of African descent. He created Negro History Week in 1926, and the impact of his leadership on his followers spawned Black History Month in 1976 (Scott, 2009–2011). The name of his organization was changed to Association for the Study of African American Life and History, and his publications became known as the *Journal of African American History* and *Black History Bulletin*. It is not clear what Woodson would have thought of the name changes. He seemed to prefer the name Negro, and he criticized those whom he believed were ashamed of the word. In one column, he argued that it was more important for citizens to be recognized as Americans rather than participate in debates about what to be called (Woodson, 1932p). Black newspapers of Woodson's period reflected a similar theme of wanting blacks to be accepted as Americans.

Just before he died, Woodson was basking in recognition of his achievements, acknowledging that substantial progress had been made in helping to elevate black life and history to a more respectable status. Other victories were on the horizon, although he could not have known that legal segregation was in its final throes.

When he began a program to rewrite the history books that disregarded black achievements, Woodson was not given much of a chance of succeeding. He encountered difficulties trying to persuade many blacks and whites that African Americans had a history worth honoring and that most Americans had been mis-educated because black contributions in history had been largely excluded. And the messenger was the son of former slaves and an outsider, initially, who had no entrée into the world of the educated black elite.

As his crusade matured, Woodson's storytelling illustrated his points about how far his movement had come during his lifetime. In newspapers, he wrote anecdotes about ignorance and how his Washington office was assisting the public with questions about black history. Today, his scholarly *Journal of Negro History* and the historical association he founded are embracing a second century. The weeklong celebrations of black achievements he inaugurated in 1926 now consume a month, with major assistance from news media.

Woodson seemed to sense the challenges of technological change on the horizon, and he was concerned about the ability of the black population to be resourceful, add to progress made by previous generations, and keep pace with other groups and new media. In the Woodson style, he challenged *Negro History Bulletin* readers to step up, but first he educated them about the black past:

> To you then comes the challenge as to what you will do in building upon the foundation which they have laid. These people whose civilization was marked by the kerosene lamp, the wash tub, the hoe, and the ox-cart disappointed the prophets who said they would be exterminated; and on the contrary they enrolled themselves among the great. What will you do in the day of the moving picture, the radio, and the aeroplane? If we do not take hold where they left off and advance further in the service of truth and justice, we are unworthy to claim descent from such a noble people. (Woodson 1940c)

Few people now debate the need to include black achievements in the history books or to teach all students how to think—just how to achieve these goals. The minority who today publicly debate the need for Black History

Month seem uninformed about Woodson's goals and the magnitude of the problem he was fighting—the persistent vestiges of slavery and a segregated society. Woodson's achievements may be taken for granted now because the battles he waged a century ago seem less visible today.

Fully aware his achievements of the past did not guarantee continued success, Woodson had doubts about whether the history movement would survive his death in the form he intended, or whether he would be credited for its success. After all, he left most of his estate to ASNLH, stipulating that he be remembered as founder of the *Journal of Negro History*—as if future generations would not otherwise remember him. ASNLH was not financially secure and had to borrow $2,000 to meet obligations in 1949 (Woodson, 1949b), and other doubts were signaled in his final letter to Luther P. Jackson of Virginia State College.

Woodson struggled in his efforts to balance optimism and pessimism, which were illustrated by penciled-revisions in his 1946 annual report. He said his public pronouncements of research success had been too optimistic and were worse than he had let on. He admitted "the public has been encouraged to believe that the difficulties involved are being rapidly removed." He was especially disturbed about postwar conditions that caused delays in printing and about availability of records in Europe and Africa, many of which had been destroyed (Woodson, 1946).

After his death, the people who remembered and followed Woodson seemed blind to his misgivings. They tended to discuss his commitment to his cause and impact, looking beyond such warnings. They rarely questioned his success. His close friend D .O. W. Holmes, president of Morgan State College when Woodson died, summed up in a newspaper article how Woodson achieved success: "Dr. Woodson was not only the originator, but the enthusiastic promoter" (Holmes, 1950). Woodson's sister Bessie Woodson Yancey, still mourning her brother's death, wrote Louis Mehlinger, the ASNLH treasurer, "Dr. Woodson wore out his tired heart and gave his life for the uplift of his race" (Yancey, 1950).

Goggin, a Woodson biographer, argued that because white historians neglected and/or denigrated black history, Woodson sought to correct the historical record, using census data, marriage registers, birth and death certificates, letters, diaries, and oral histories. She said historians have had to rediscover the methods and works of Woodson and his associates (Goggin, 1983).

Charles H. Wesley, another close associate sometimes referred to as one of "Woodson's Boys," said the history group Woodson founded, and which

Wesley led some years after the founder's death, was the first organized effort of African Americans "to treat the records of the race scientifically and to publish the findings to the world" (Wesley, 1951).

John Hope Franklin, evaluating Woodson's work, argued that "for the first time in the history of the United States, there is a striking resemblance between what historians are writing and what has actually happened in the history of the American Negro" (Franklin, 1957).

In the decades since his death, Woodson's impact on black education and history resonates—most often during annual celebrations of Black History Month—although many members of the public do not know his name. Credits for his achievements have largely disappeared from the popular press. Stories about blacks seeking their cultural identities are often deemed newsworthy, but the leader of the history movement, the grassroots program that generated widespread interest in this area, usually gets ignored. Full-length books and scholarly articles about him and his work also have been few in recent years.

As a historian, Woodson helped people who themselves thought they had no history discover their past. He provided messages of uplift and empowerment to the many suffering from what he diagnosed as low self-esteem and an inferiority complex ("Race Must Overcome," 1928). When he was done, Woodson not only had helped increase notions of race pride, but he had brought about transformation of research and thinking about African American history and culture. He had popularized history, accomplishing this feat at great personal sacrifice.

Woodson advocated an education system that would teach people to think for themselves. His criticisms and proscriptions are manifested throughout *The Mis-Education of the Negro*, and in the newspaper columns on which a great deal of it was based, with arguments for inclusiveness and for making education more practical and relevant to all people (Woodson, 1933a). He was especially proud of a review of *Mis-Education* by Mabel Carney, a Columbia University authority on race and education, and he cited her estimation of the book as evidence of his expertise when he felt snubbed during the height of the black encyclopedia controversy. Carney ordered ten copies of the book and told Woodson she considered it "the most important contribution in its field since the early philosophy and practice worked out by Booker T. Washington" (Woodson, 1936d).

Woodson was a pioneer in education, advocating a system of respect for different cultures and teaching all students about the accomplishments of their own groups as well as the accomplishments of other races (King and

Brown, 2010). His 1946 annual report emphasized his dedication to research in this area, citing his support of a "study of inter-cultural education in the schools of Mexico" (Woodson, 1946).

Woodson's legacies also include mentorship of the next generation of scientifically trained historians* who took up his cause, and he provided leadership of an internationalist perspective on race and economic issues, especially racism, Africa, and war. He included examination of such issues as topics on the dockets of the Association for the Study of Negro Life and History meetings and as content in his publications.

Woodson used the *Journal of Negro History* as a public relations tool, but he did not compromise its research and scholarship goals. An analysis of its 1916–1957 content reported publication of 607 full-length research articles by 381 different contributors, including many historians of both races. It was concluded that during the period covered, "virtually all significant work on Negro history has either appeared in, or been reflected in, the Journal" (Logan, 1959).

Although he was sometimes critical of Woodson's personality, W. E. B. Du Bois was not hesitant in stating the significance of Woodson's founding of the *Journal of Negro History*. Woodson's "service to history was not so much his books as his editorship of the Journal, which brought into print some of the best scholars in this branch of history," Du Bois said (Goggin, 1983).

Woodson receives little attention in America today, and only recently in Huntington, West Virginia, where he and his family migrated for the start of a better life in the late nineteenth century. Many passersby move unknowingly past his statue near the busy intersection of Carter G. Woodson Avenue and Hal Greer Boulevard—across the street from the Auto Zone store, the former site of the first Douglass School, where Woodson made his first impression on local residents and newspapers.

Presidents of the United States have been issuing Black History Month proclamations in various forms since the Ford administration, and they have been known to ignore Woodson's name when proclaiming the observance, such as President Barack Obama's omission in the 2013 proclamation. The president cited other black achievers, but he did not raise Woodson's name, although Obama had recognized Woodson in his 2009 proclamation.

Woodson's achievements never disappeared from popular culture, however—only his name receded from public view. He was advocating a black-is-beautiful theme and the urgency of black business investments in the 1930s in books and newspaper articles, long before their adoption by proponents

---

* Wesley also referred to the historians Woodson mentored as Woodson's "disciples" (Wesley, 1951.)

of Black Power in the late 1960s. However, despite the public's inattention to the subject of Woodson, *The Mis-Education of the Negro* has assumed a life of its own. For example, Black Panther Huey Newton admired Woodson, having discovered his *Mis-Education* in the 1960s (Hughey, 2007). Singer Lauryn Hill sold millions of albums in the 1990s with the title "Mis-Education of Lauryn Hill."

One publisher (Khalifah's Booksellers and Associates, 2006) claimed there are more than 500,000 copies of the book in print, and a letter to the *New York Times* in 2006 from the books editor of *Essence* magazine stated that the work had often held down the top spot on its list of top-selling books (Bass, n.d.). More recently, *Essence* reported *The Mis-Education of the Negro* was number 5 on the list of top nonfiction paperbacks for October 2009, with books by Barack Obama holding down the first three spots ("October 2009 Bestsellers," 2009). It was number 4 in 2012 on the *Essence* list of fifty good books every woman should read ("Black History Month 2013," n.d.).

That Woodson's footprint would be reflected in a twenty-first-century medium is not surprising. The surprise is that his media footprint is so small today, for Woodson was one of the major black public figures of his time, a status he partly attained through black media. The exposure of his messages through the press—then primarily newspapers, magazines, and occasionally radio programming—extended his reach beyond the history group members. Woodson's achievements, even his access to the press, were remarkable, considering the doubts about the significance of African Americans' past and worries about their future when Woodson kicked off the program that eventually popularized their history.

As leader of the Modern Black History Movement, Woodson devoted most of his life to having black history included alongside the histories of other groups—not a separate history for whites and blacks. Almost from the beginning, he was advocating yearlong study of African American history. He and his newspaper supporters settled for a week as an interim solution, because that is all they thought they could get at the time. They celebrated the week and hoped for the year ("How About Negro History Year?" 1942).

Woodson disputed conventional thinking that blacks had no past worth preserving and suggestions that all blacks willingly accepted or at least did not resist slavery. A *New York Times* review of a Woodson book, *The Mind of the Negro as Reflected in Letters during the Crisis, 1800–1860*, provided evidence that his message was getting through to some in the media when the newspaper observed, "what is perhaps the most significant feature of them all, the ardent desire for freedom and opportunity, the longing to struggle in and out of the overwhelming handicaps the white race had forced upon them" ("The Negro Mind," 1926). He pointed to slave uprisings, descriptions of his father defending himself in bondage and freedom, and flaws in the methodology practiced by other researchers. He argued against race superiority, black or white, as did most of the black newspapers in this study ("Proposed Play," 1931).

REMEMBERING THE BLACK PRESS

Woodson's contemporaries in the press and his former associates at ASNLH who could have vouched for their winning partnership have faded from the scene. However, the Woodson-era participants left behind paper trails that Woodson advised them to preserve about their communities, and their clippings help document the role played by that generation of black journalists who cooperated in his public-education program.

In addition to his books and journal articles, much of what the people of Woodson's time knew about him and his issues was delivered by the black press. Following his death, the journalists who covered and remembered Woodson did so using terms that reminisced about his popular movement. For instance, George Murphy Jr., whose family owned the *Afro-American* newspaper, which provided the most sustained, in-depth coverage of him, said Woodson's "most lively monument" was "his founding leadership of Negro History Week" (Association for the Study of African American Life and History, 1990).

For decades, knowledge of the extent of Woodson's collaboration with the newspapers to sell the history of a disrespected people was not widely known, and his status as a media hero was lost. Woodson's biographers and other observers correctly credited his success to combinations of influences from his father, hard work, intelligence, education, personal sacrifice, and the West Virginia coalfields (Franklin, 1957; Goggin, 1993; Dagbovie, 2007; Logan, 1973). But another side to this story exists, as explained in these pages.

One Woodson scholar called him an institution-builder (Daryl Michael Scott, speaker, Marshall University, February 21, 2012). If institution-building merits inclusion among the Woodson legacies, and it should, considering the history association he founded has entered a second century and few black organizations can boast such longevity, then Woodson's advice to and partnership with the press should be classified as institution-building, too. Woodson celebrated the centennial of the black press, one of the black community's oldest and strongest institutions, in 1927, and combined the interests of black history with black press history. When the black press began observance of its own history in the next decade, the industry had Woodson's Black History Week promotions as a model, and many of the black press heroes were blended with black history heroes.

Just two months after his passing, Woodson's newspaper partners conveyed gratitude when the Negro Newspaper Publishers' Association honored President Harry Truman with a Russwurm Award (named for the cofounder of *Freedom's Journal*) and honored Woodson with its Publishers' Award ("Negro Publishers Name Truman," 1950).

Woodson cornered newspaper publicity during the first half of the previous century, although his name is not in the journalism history and public relations books, but it belongs there, as much as it belongs in other history books. The extent of Woodson's use of the press and modern public relations techniques to popularize black history during the first half of the twentieth century has been understated, if not ignored. That he was smart, dedicated, and worked hard, as his biographers have insisted, does not provide a complete explanation for his success.

For most of *their* Black History Movement, Woodson and the black newspapers were inseparable. They were with him to record his first book tour in 1915 and followed him religiously until his death in 1950. Expanded knowledge of their relationship, based on results of the current study, should help elevate the black press as a catalyst and major contributor to Woodson's success. He went from being an unknown scholar from West Virginia to popularizing a subject on which few people would have predicted success. Woodson readily acknowledged the assistance of the black newspapers—especially during Negro History Week, at ASNLH meetings, and in his reports, books, and newspaper columns. As successful as the collaboration proved to be, however, it has gone largely unnoticed in the decades since Woodson's death.

EPILOGUE

DURING A LULL AT THE 2011 ANNUAL MEETING OF THE ASSOCIATION FOR the Study of African American Life and History in Richmond, Virginia, Bob Lewis, then an Associated Press political reporter, a friend, and fellow University of Mississippi alumnus, gave this author a tour of the Virginia Capitol. A polite, elderly white woman (accompanied by her daughter) from Tennessee mistook us (a black man and white man) for security and explained she only wanted to view the statues on the Capitol grounds. She identified herself as a black history researcher and presenter at the ASALH conference, as she examined the statue of Oliver Hill. We identified ourselves as journalists, including the fact that one of us was the Carter G. Woodson Professor, with no authority to run her off. She did not know of Woodson. She was presenting a paper at a conference that prominently displayed his likeness, but she said she did not recognize his name or his work. She was unaware her interest in black history was a testament to his life's work and the embodiment of the war he had waged in popularizing history among *all* people. She was not alone.

The media, not just black, now embrace Woodson's work as their own, but his career is underreported, and one of his major achievements—the annual observance of black history—has been misappropriated and commercialized, echoing fears Woodson sounded before his death. His final report for ASNLH in 1949 warned followers about others' attempts to hijack the movement (Woodson, 1949b) (see chapter 5).

The late John Hope Franklin, one of the critics of commercialization of black history, argued that February is a month used by hucksters to reduce their inventories of trinkets, when publishers sell books by black authors and when scholars collect speaking fees. Franklin said at the first ASNLH convention he attended that he heard Woodson say he looked forward to the time when it would not be necessary to set aside a week for the observance of black history. Out of deference to Woodson's wishes to hurry up that time, Franklin said he accepted invitations to speak only during the other eleven months of the year. "This has been my one-man crusade to hasten the realization of Woodson's dream," he said (Franklin, 1997–1998).

In 1975, a bronze marker was erected in Woodson's memory at his birthplace in Buckingham County, Virginia ("Bronze Marker to Be Placed at Birthplace of Woodson," 1975), in observance of the centennial of his birth. The US Postal Service issued a postage stamp in Woodson's honor during President Ronald Reagan's administration in 1984, and Black History Month was observed in Washington, DC, in 2000, with a special ceremony in recognition of the half-century since Woodson's death (Hartman, 2000). Woodson's former home-office in Washington, DC, was designated a National Historic Landmark in 1976 and is undergoing a restoration that should enable visitors to relive history from a significant vantage point.

Following the civil rights movement, mainstream media seemed more sensitized to black issues and concerns, although there remained disparities in the coverage of blacks and whites. Still some coverage stood out. For example, in 1968, following the assassination of Martin Luther King Jr. and the ensuing riots in major cities, CBS News broadcast a groundbreaking special narrated by actor Bill Cosby on black history that recited lists of black achievements in history that sounded like they could have come from the pages of Woodson's books and articles, but neither Cosby nor his on-camera experts mentioned Woodson ("Black History—Lost, Stolen, or Strayed," 1968). In 1969, ASNLH presented the Negro History Week Award to a white-owned newspaper, the *Nashville Tennessean*, for a series that ran February 9–15, 1969, "covering contributions made to American history by black people, how whites view black history, the Negro church, Black Power, black institutions, Negro History Week in Nashville schools and famous Nashville blacks" ("Current History," 1970).

Evidence of his influence is everywhere, including at the opening ceremonies for the National Museum of African American History and Culture in Washington, DC, on September 24, 2016, when Congressman John Lewis, the civil rights icon, recalled his study of Woodson's work for inspiration as a young man. A *New York Times* article also linked the struggles for respect in black history to Woodson's cause, as well as the contributions of George Washington Williams and John Hope Franklin (Gates, 2016).

What little credit Woodson occasionally receives from the media today comes largely from black-oriented media. For instance, the *Afro-American* has been among the sponsors of the annual observance of Woodson's birthday at Shiloh Baptist Church in Washington, DC, and other black newspapers for a number of years following his death ran editorials and other articles reciting Woodson's work. Black media also have expressed concerns about commercialization in observing Black History Month. For example, the *Atlanta Daily World* printed the headline "Unselling Black History Is a Worthy Goal to Seek" above a column with this advice: "Companies must not use Black History Month solely as a marketing opportunity to peddle their products or tout themselves as good guys in black communities only in black newspaper[s] and magazines" (Hutchinson, 2003).

Black History Month has become a major media event, and some channels on cable television have provided a month of black films and other programming. Information about black history events and corporations professing their interests in diversity proliferates on the Internet and elsewhere.

If black media deserve to share credit for helping make Woodson a success, then mainstream media probably should share the blame for misappropriating black history and ignoring Woodson's lessons about mis-education. The following example from MSNBC's "Morning Joe," during Black History Month in 2012, typifies the news media's missing depth on this subject:

Former Los Angeles Laker Kareem Abdul-Jabbar, author of several books on black history, was interviewed (February 8, 2012) by a panel of distinguished journalists who included Carl Bernstein, a Pulitzer Prize winner who toppled a president. Abdul-Jabbar took advantage of Black History Month to promote his children's book, *What Color Is My World: The Lost History of African-American Inventors*, about blacks whose achievements, presumably, would be lost to the past without Abdul-Jabbar's pioneering research. He recited the names of several inventors, eliciting rhetorical questions by Bernstein about why white Americans do not know about black inventors and what if black history were taught white students. Abdul-Jabbar never mentioned Woodson's name or Woodson's belief that race relations would improve if whites knew more about black history. Abdul-Jabbar's response was mostly that America is a nation of "bad habits" (Kareem Abdul-Jabbar, n.d.).

The fact that Woodson wrote and published books and a magazine for children and teachers (the *Negro History Bulletin*) went unreported on this program. The successful, well-educated journalists, including the one who

brought down President Richard Nixon during Watergate, were—as Woodson might say—mis-educated.

The MSNBC segment demonstrates why it is important to resurrect
Woodson's media image and to rediscover his collaboration with journalists—to prevent his accomplishments from becoming the *negligible* thoughts
he feared black history would become without his intervention.

Young Woodson—Carter G. Woodson portrait, as a young man. Permission granted by Scurlock Collection, Archives Center, National Museum of American History, Smithsonian Institution.

Dinner, 1940—Woodson celebrating the twenty-fifth anniversary of the Association for the Study of Negro Life and History in Chicago, where the association was founded. He is dining with a group that includes Pearl S. Buck (woman in light hat and shawl), winner of the Nobel Prize in literature in 1938, and Robert S. Abbott, owner of the *Chicago Defender*, at Buck's immediate left. Woodson is the fourth person on Buck's right. Permission granted by Association for the Study of African American Life and History.

Woodson in his library, 1948. Permission granted by Scurlock Collection, Archives Center, National Museum of American History, Smithsonian Institution.

Woodson at his desk, late 1940s. Permission granted by Scurlock Collection, Archives Center, National Museum of American History, Smithsonian Institution.

Dedication of the Woodson statue, September 29, 1995—He was rediscovered in Huntington, West Virginia, in the mid-1980s, with the founding of the Carter G. Woodson Memorial Foundation, which raised money for this statue. Standing left of the statue is Newatha Myers, president of the foundation, and Charles Whitehead, former president of Ashland Oil Foundation, immediately to the right. Permission granted by Marshall University and Carter G. Woodson Memorial Foundation.

Statue close-up—Woodson's statue in Huntington, West Virginia, 2016. Permission granted by Charles G. Bailey, Huntington, West Virginia.

Remembering him on his birthday each year in Washington, DC. This photograph was taken at Woodson's 136th birthday celebration, December 19, 2011, at Shiloh Baptist Church, where his funeral took place in 1950. Permission granted by Burnis R. Morris, Huntington, West Virginia.

Restoration—Woodson's former Washington, DC, home and office now under restoration as a National Historic Site. Permission granted by Burnis R. Morris, Huntington, West Virginia.

FATHER OF BLACK HISTORY

In the park—This statue in the Carter G. Woodson Memorial Park was built a block from his former home in Washington, DC. Permission granted by Burnis R. Morris, Huntington, West Virginia.

APPENDIXES

LIBRARIAN OF CONGRESS LETTER TO CARTER G. WOODSON

Letter from Herbert Putnam, Librarian of Congress, dated December 5, 1928, agreeing to accept materials for a Negro collection. The librarian's skepticism about acquiring suitable items should be noted, as well as what is often regarded as a disrespectful reference to black people—the spelling of "Negroes" with a small n (Carter Godwin Woodson Papers, Manuscript Division, Library of Congress, Washington, DC).

LIBRARY OF CONGRESS
WASHINGTON

B
OFFICE OF THE LIBRARIAN

December 5 1928

My dear Mr. Woodson:

I write you to confirm an assurance that I gave you in our conversation day before yesterday. It is, that if, as I understand, the project of your Society for the collection of manuscript family records of negroes in the United States shall result in material of historical interest, we shall be very glad to welcome the custody of each; and be disposed to maintain it as a unit collection of special interest in its bearing upon the history and cultural development of the negro race.

This assumes of course that such material that shall be offered to us shall represent the application of the definition which you gave me, and before final acceptance, come, in our judgment, within the above description.

Very truly yours,

Herbert Putnam

Librarian

Carter G. Woodson Esq. Director
Association for Study of Negro Life and History
1538 - 9th Street N. W.
Washington   D. C.

Woodson October 21, 1929, letter to Association for the Study of Negro Life and History staff requesting assistance in public relations (Carter Godwin Woodson Papers, Manuscript Division, Library of Congress, Washington, DC).

The Association for the Study of Negro Life and History, Incorporated

JOHN R. HAWKINS, President   S. W. RUTHERFORD, Secretary-Treasurer

Executive Council	The Journal of Negro History	Executive Council
JOHN R. HAWKINS, Washington, D. C.		JOHN HOPE, Morehouse College
S. W. RUTHERFORD, Washington, D. C.	CARTER G. WOODSON	WILLIAM E. DODD, University of Chicago
CARTER G. WOODSON, Washington, D. C	DIRECTOR AND EDITOR	BISHOP R. A. CARTER, Chicago, Ill.
JULIUS ROSENWALD, Chicago, Ill.		BISHOP JOHN HURST, Baltimore, Md.
JAMES H. DILLARD, Charlottesville, Va.	1538 NINTH STREET, N. W.	ALEXANDER L. JACKSON, Chicago, Ill.
WILLIAM G. PEARSON, Durham, N. C.		BISHOP R. R. JONES, New Orleans, La.
FRANZ BOAS, Columbia University	Washington, D. C.	T. R. DAVIS, Samuel Huston College
CARL R. FISH, University of Wisconsin		JOHN E. NAIL, New York City
E. A. HOOTON, Harvard University		

October 21, 1929.

My dear Coworker:

I am enclosing herewith a copy of the program of the annual meeting of the Association, to be held here from the 27th to the 31st of this month. We shall have here representatives of the best thought in the country. Kindly give the conference as much publicity as possible and attend this significant convocation.

You are most cordially invited to dine with the visitors at the Whitelaw at 5:30 P. M. on Monday the 28th. This is a Get-Acquainted Dinner when the visitors will be presented to Washington. Each gentleman is requested to pay one dollar for his dinner and an additional dollar for the dinner of one of the visitors. Some public spirited persons have paid more, but this is the minimum. Ladies, however, will not be required to make any such contribution to defray the expenses of entertaining the guests.

Kindly notify us whether or not you will be present at the Dinner that we may not make preparation for those who cannot come. You know how expensive it is to do such a thing under these circumstances.

Thanking you for your cooperation, I am

Very truly yours,

C. G. Woodson,
Director.

Reprinted with permission from the Association for the Study of African American Life and History.

Annual Report of the Director, 1949

The celebration of Negro History Week is scheduled for the seven days beginning February 12. The date is determined by the necessity to cover the birthdays of Lincoln on the 12th and the supposed birthday of Douglass on the 14th. He did not know exactly when he was born; but he requested that he be remembered on Valentine's Day because he was his mother's valentine. The celebration will come later in February 1950 than it did in 1949, and will interfere less with the reorganization work required in schools at the close of the first semester. Teachers still complain, however, that they are handicapped by having to prepare exercises with newly transferred children, with many of whom they do not have time to become acquainted during the few days intervening between the first of the semester and the beginning of the celebration. This cannot be avoided, however, unless we abandon the theme around which the celebration centers. Lincoln was the embodiment of freedom for all men and Douglass was the exponent of the idea of making that freedom count in the attainment of civil rights. The celebration when properly observed is a patriotic manifestation, and all exercises to the contrary are discouraged. Pressure groups, propaganda organizations, and volcanic movements should be discouraged when they try to use this occasion as a means to an end. The work of the Association for the Study of Negro Life and History is educational and scientific, and the organization decries any effort to divert it from this channel. For those organizations otherwise interested, there are fifty-one other weeks in the year, and they should make use of them rather than interfere with the sane program of the Association. The Negro History Week celebration has usually been kept clear of indignation meetings, protesting bodies, and agitation efforts. The Association does not object to such endeavors, but its approach to the solution of the problem confronting the Negro is through the channels of scientific research and education. The Association will not belittle or abuse anyone, however detestable he may be. All persons are welcomed within its circle to hear the whole truth and to promote it as the key to democracy. The celebration of Negro History Week is no occasion for glossing over the tribulations and trials which Negroes have suffered because of man's inhumanity to man, but the desired end is more easily reached by showing the achievements of the Negro in spite of these handicaps. The purpose of all such efforts is not to ignore facts, but to present the facts in a dispassionate way so that facts properly set forth may tell their own story. Men are not won by abuse and vituperation but by bringing men together to hear the truth and to reason.

Possibly Woodson's final letter was dated April 1, 1950, and mailed to Luther P. Jackson, his public relations collaborator and top fund-raiser in Virginia. In this letter, Woodson remained committed to his cause and was concerned about financial problems that threatened ASNLH's future. Woodson died on April 3, 1950, followed by Jackson on April 20, 1950 (Luther Porter Jackson Papers, 1772–1960, Accession #1952-l [35:1003]. Special Collections and Archives, Johnston Memorial Library, Virginia State University, Petersburg).

The Association for the Study of Negro Life and History, Incorporated
FOUNDED SEPTEMBER 9, 1915

MARY McLEOD BETHUNE, President   LOUIS R. MEHLINGER, Secretary-Treasurer

THE JOURNAL OF NEGRO HISTORY

EXECUTIVE COUNCIL
MARY McLEOD BETHUNE, Daytona, Fla.
LOUIS R. MEHLINGER, Washington, D. C.
CARTER G. WOODSON, Washington, D. C.
CHARLES H. WESLEY, Wilberforce, Ohio
EUGENE A. CLARK, Washington, D. C.
F. D. MOON, Oklahoma City, Okla.
LUTHER P. JACKSON, Virginia State College
WILHELMINA M. CROSSON, Boston
W. F. SAVOY, Columbus, Ohio

and
THE NEGRO HISTORY BULLETIN

CARTER G. WOODSON
DIRECTOR AND EDITOR
1538 NINTH STREET, N. W.
WASHINGTON 1, D. C.

EXECUTIVE COUNCIL
HARVEY C. JACKSON, Detroit, Mich.
ELMER A. HENDERSON, Baltimore, Md.
ALEXANDER L. JACKSON, Chicago, Ill.
A. M. SCHLESINGER, Harvard University
BISHOP R. A. CARTER, Chicago, Ill.
A. A. TAYLOR, Fisk University
H. C. TRENHOLM, Alabama State College
LUCY HARTH SMITH, Lexington, Ky.

April 1, 1950

Washington, D. C.

Dr. L.P. Jackson
Virginia State College
Petersburg, Va.

My dear Dr. Jackson:

Thank you very much for your check of $500 which we have deposited for credit to the Association for the Study of Negro Life and History. We are delighted to have this money at the time when we must meet pressing obligations which accumulate rapidly during this season. The unfailing support which we received from Virginia brings us increasing assurance that we can survive. We are emphasizing the fine record of Virginia as an example that other parts should follow. I am sure that those who have improved considerably during the last few years have been very much influenced by this record made under your guidance. You may be interested in knowing that friends in West Virginia are now trying to emulate your example.

Respectfully yours,

C.G. Woodson
Director

df

E. P. Southall sent #33.64 for the Norfolk Division of Virginia State College.

REFERENCES

A.M.E.'s carry on, tho' deficit is $42,308. (1933, April 29). *Afro-American*, p. 19.

Anderson, H. (1939, April 15). Meet your neighbor. *Afro-American*, p. 4.

Annual meeting. (1949, October). *Negro History Bulletin* 13(1): 23.

Aptheker, H. (1969, April). Du Bois as historian. *Negro History Bulletin* 32(4): 6–16.

ASALH. (2007). *Reflections on Carter G. Woodson with Drs. John Hope Franklin and Adelaide M. Cromwell*. DVD. 2006 Annual Meeting of the Association for the Study of African American Life and History, Atlanta.

ASALH Timeline. (n.d.). Association for the Study of African American Life and History. Retrieved from http://www.asalh.org/asalhtimeline.html.

Ask Faith Fallin. (1932, June 25). *Afro-American*, p. 20.

Assignment of teachers. (1900, September 15). *Huntington Advertiser*, p. 6.

Ass'n for Study of Negro Life and History meets here October 24th. (1927, October 15). *Pittsburgh Courier*, p. 12.

Association for the Study of Negro Life and History. (1929, September 20). Letter to Robert S. Abbott. Abbott-Sengstacke Family Papers, Box #4, Folder #15, Vivian G. Harsh Research Collection of Afro-American History and Literature, Chicago Public Library, Chicago.

———. (1990). *75th Anniversary of the Association for the Study of Negro Life and History*. Special Collections, Marshall University Libraries, Huntington, WV.

Attacks Amos 'n Andy radio show for distortion. (1930, May 31). *Afro-American*, p. 3.

Author's birthday. (1934, December 15). *Afro-American*, p. 22.

Ayers, E. (1949, December 23). Letter to Edwin B. Henderson. (Part II, Reel 2, Series 2). Carter Godwin Woodson Papers, Manuscript Division, Library of Congress, Washington, DC.

Barnett, C. (1941, September 23). Letter to Carter G. Woodson. Claude A. Barnett Papers: The Associated Negro Press, 1918–1967, Part I, 1928–1964. Frederick, MD: University Publications of America. Chicago Public Library, Chicago.

———. (1942, March 7). Letter to C. A. Scott. Director, Associated Negro Press, remarks over CBS Radio, transcript, The Negro press in America's war effort. *Atlanta Daily World*

Records (24–26), Manuscript, Archives, and Rare Book Library, Emory University, Atlanta.

Barnett removed as principal. (1900, August 3). *Huntington Advertiser*, p. 1.

Baskin, O., C. Aronoff, and D. Lattimore. (1997). *Public Relations: The Profession and the Practice*. 4th ed. Madison, WI: Brown and Benchmark Publishers.

Bass, P. H. (n.d.). Books. Retrieved from the *New York Times*: http://query.nytimes.com/gst/fullpage.html?res=9C05E4D91F30F93AA35752C0A9609C8B63.

Bayton, J. A., and E. Bell. (1951, Winter). An exploratory study of the role of the Negro press. *Journal of Negro Education* 20(1): 8–15. Retrieved from http://www.jstor.org/stable/2965858.

Berea College Early History. (n.d.). Retrieved from Berea College: https://www.berea.edu/about/history/.

Bickley, A. (2008). Carter G. Woodson: The West Virginia connection. *Appalachian Heritage* 36(3): 59–69.

Bingham, A. (2012, May 12). Five facts about President Obama's mother. Retrieved from http://abcnews.go.com/Politics/OTUS/unordinary-facts-president-obamas-mother/story?id=16330771.

Black history: Lost, stolen, or strayed. (1968). Video (starring Bill Cosby). Retrieved from https://www.youtube.com/watch?v=GbzF1JFLOMI.

Black History Month 2013. (n.d.). Retrieved from *Essence*: http://www.essence.com/2012/11/08/write-or-die-chick-50-good-books-every-black-woman-should-read/.

Blumer, R., and B. Moyers (writers), and D. Grubin (1984). *The Iimage Makers*. In association with WNET/New York and KQED/San Francisco.

Booker Washington honored at shrine: Cabin in Malden, W. Va., where educator spent his boyhood, dedicated as memorial. (1932, June 27). *New York Times*, p. 15.

Book review: A household necessity. [Review of the book *African Myths and Negro Makers of History* by Carter G. Woodson]. (1929, January 30). *New York Amsterdam News*, p. 20.

Book reviews. (1919, October). [Review of the book *The American Negro in the World War* by Emmett J. Scott]. *Journal of Negro History* 4(4): 466–467. Retrieved from DOI: 10.2307/2713450.

Bradley, G. (1942, April 5). Expect 3,000 at teachers' session. *Atlanta Daily World*, p. 1.

Broadcast features meet of life, history group. (1938, November 19). *Chicago Defender*, p. 3.

Bronze marker to be placed at birthplace of Woodson. (1975, December 2). *Atlanta Daily World*, p. 2.

Buck, P. (1942). *American Unity and Asia*. New York: John Day.

Burns, B. (1943, September 25). Books: Wanted: Negro authors. *Chicago Defender*, p. 15.

Calvin, F. (1937, June 3). The digest: Dr. Woodson explodes. *Cleveland Call and Post*, p. 8.

Carter Godwin Woodson. (n.d.). Interview in files of Daryl Michael Scott, Association for the Study of African American Life and History, Washington, DC.

Carter Woodson refutes report about his health. (1926, February 27). *Norfolk Journal and Guide*, p. 1.

Cartwright, M. (1950, April). Negro History Week—1950. *Negro History Bulletin* 13(7): 153.

C. G. Woodson speaks before college class. (1932, June 11). *Chicago Defender*, p. 12. Retrieved from http://ezproxy.marshall.edu:2048/docview/492378844?accountid=12281.

Chicagoans hear Dr. Woodson. (1940, February 7). *Chicago Defender*, p. 12.

Conduct journals in summer schools. (1925, August 15). *Afro-American*, p. 16.

Constructive programme is outlined by press ass'n. (1927, February 26). *Pittsburgh Courier*, p. 8.

Current history. (1970, January). *Negro History Bulletin* 33(1): 19.

Dagbovie, P. (2004). Making black history practical and popular: Carter G. Woodson, the proto Black Studies Movement, and the struggle for black liberation. *Western Journal of Black Studies* 28(2): 372–83.

———. (2007). *The Early Black History Movement, Carter G. Woodson, and Lorenzo Greene.* Urbana: University of Illinois Press.

Dangerous lies on Negro in books: False history ideas pointed out by Carter G. Woodson. (1926, February 24). *New York Amsterdam News*, p. 12.

DeCosta-Willis, M. (1995). *The Memphis Diary of Ida B. Wells.* Boston: Beacon Press.

Delta Sigma Theta sorority notes. (1925, May 13). *New York Amsterdam News*, p. 7.

Display ad 47. (1922, December 23). *Chicago Defender* (*National Edition*). Retrieved from http://ezproxy.marshall.edu:2048/docview/491960722?accountid=12281.

Dolan, M., J. Sonnett, and K. Johnson. (2009, Winter). Katrina coverage in black newspapers critical of government, mainstream media. *Newspaper Research Journal* 30(1): 34–42.

Douglass, F. (1854). *The claims of the Negro, ethnologically considered: An address before the literary societies of Western Reserve College, at commencement, July 12, 1854.* Ithaca, NY: Cornell University.

Douglass 1892–2003 "Wildcats." (2003, August 21–23). Douglass High School Reunion pamphlet.

Douglass High School commencement: Closing exercises of colored school at theatre last night. (1902, May 10). *Huntington Advertiser*, p. 4.

Dr. Carter Woodson. (1930, November 8). *Afro-American*, p. 6.

Dr. Carter G. Woodson. (1934, September 22). *Louisiana Weekly*, p. 1.

Dr. Carter G. Woodson. (1934, October 6). *Louisiana Weekly*, p. 1.

Dr. Carter G. Woodson. (1934, November 17). *Louisiana Weekly*, p. 1.

Dr. Carter G. Woodson. (1950, April 15). *Afro-American*, p. 1 (Reel 1, Series 1). Carter Godwin Woodson Papers, Manuscript Division, Library of Congress, Washington, DC.

Dr. Carter G. Woodson, historian, found dead. (8 April, 1950). *Chicago Defender*, p. 1 (Part II, Reel 1, Series 1). Carter Godwin Woodson Papers, Manuscript Division, Library of Congress, Washington, DC.

Dr. Carter G. Woodson delivers address at A&T College: Speaks at length on the economic developments of the Negro. (1925, February 21). *Norfolk Journal and Guide*, p. 7.

Dr. Carter G. Woodson Founder's Day speaker. (1947, February 15). *Norfolk Journal and Guide*, p. 3.

Dr. Carter G. Woodson scores noted Negroes!: Woodson and Brawley argue over Negro Encyclopedia. (1936, June 5). *Atlanta Daily World*, p. 1.

Dr. Carter Woodson's address. (1942, April 19). *Atlanta Daily World*, p. 4.

Dr. Carter Woodson flays C&O R.R. for K.K.K. policies. (1932, December 10). *Pittsburgh Courier*, p. 2.

Dr. C. G. Woodson, retired educator. (1950, April 5). *New York Times*. (Part II, Reel 2). Carter Godwin Woodson Papers, Manuscript Division, Library of Congress, Washington, DC.

Dr. Woodson lists 15 most outstanding events in Negro history. (1950, January 11). Claude A. Barnett Papers: The Associated Negro Press, 1918–1967, Part I, news releases, 1928–1964. Frederick, MD: University Publications of America. Chicago Public Library, Chicago.

Dr. Woodson no pauper—royalties from books source of income. (1947, February 15). *Afro-American*, p. M12.

Dr. Woodson poses seven queries for history week: Are we freer than in '65. (1938, January 15). *Afro-American*, p. 22.

Dr. Woodson to open Negro History Week on CBS chain. (1939, February 4). *New York Amsterdam News*, p. 4.

Dr. Woodson writes on Negro church. (1921, December 31). *Norfolk Journal and Guide*, p. 6.

Du Bois all wrong in analysis of Woodson says Brewer: Associate of quarter century refutes article by educator. (1950, July 22). *Afro-American*, p. 6.

Durham, R., D. L. Betts, and WMAQ (Radio station: Chicago). (2000). *Destination Freedom: Black Radio Days*. Aurora, CO: No Credit Productions.

Editorial. (1927, January 29). *Pittsburgh Courier*, p. A8.

Editorial. (1950, April 6). *Atlanta Daily World*, p. A6.

Editor's note. (1923, March 17). *Chicago Defender*, p. 14.

Editor's note. (1931, May 28). *Philadelphia Tribune*, p. 6.

Editor's note. (1943, March 6). *Pittsburgh Courier*, p. 19.

Ellis, M. (1991, September). America's black press, 1914–18. *History Today*, pp. 20–27.

Emery, M., E. Emery, and N. L. Roberts. (2000). *The Press and America: An Interpretive History of the Mass Media*. 9th ed. Boston: Allyn and Bacon.

Ethics. (n.d.). Retrieved from PRSA: http://www.prsa.org/aboutprsa/ethics/.

Evans, J. (1948, November 4). Letter to Carter G. Woodson from the Office of the Secretary of Defense. (Part II, Reel 2, Series 2). Carter Godwin Woodson Papers, Manuscript Division, Library of Congress, Washington, DC.

e-WV. (n.d.). Retrieved from The West Virginia Encyclopedia : http://www.wvencyclope dia.org/articles/1824.

Extension courses in Negro history. (1927, October 15). *Norfolk Journal and Guide*, p. 16.

Extension work of Negro farmers 'opposed by planters? [Review of the book *The Rural Negro* by Carter G. Woodson]. (1930, July 11). *The State*, Columbia, SC, (Part II, Reel 2). Carter Godwin Woodson Papers, Manuscript Division, Library of Congress, Washington, DC.

Fact finding dime contest. (1939, February 25). *Afro-American*, p. 20.

Family skeletons. (1918, December 13). *Afro-American*, p. 4.

The 15 outstanding events in Negro history. (1950, January 11). *Ebony* 5(4): 42–46. Retrieved from http://ezproxy.marshall.edu:2111/ehost/detail/detail?sid=532f641b-27ee-4304-bc98 -8eef2d4271c0%40sessionmgr4002&vid=3&hid=4104&bdata=JnNpdGU9ZWhvc3Qtb Gl2ZQ%3d%3d#db=f5h&AN=49010686.

$50,000 gift aids study of Negro life: Carnegie and Rockeffeller interests manifest interest in neglected field. (1922, June 16). *Afro-American*, p. 1.

$50,000 given to promote study of our history. (1922, June 17). *Chicago Defender (National Edition)*. Retrieved from http://ezproxy.marshall.edu:2048/docview/491923395?accountid=12281.

First lady named for aid to Negroes. (1940, February 14). *New York Times*, n.p.

Fisher, K. (1945, April 20). Letter to Carter G. Woodson. (Part II, Reel 2). Carter Godwin Woodson Papers, Manuscript Division, Library of Congress, Washington, DC.

Floyd, C. (1937, June 3). The digest: Judge Davis' turn. *Cleveland Call and Post*, p. 8.

Folkerts, J., and D. Teeter. (2002). *Voices of a Nation*. 4th ed. Boston: Allyn and Bacon.

Fortune, T. (1923, December 21). Letter to Carter G. Woodson. Carter Godwin Woodson Papers, Manuscript Division, Library of Congress, Washington, DC.

Franklin, J. (1957, April). The new Negro history. *Journal of Negro History* 42(2): 89–97. Retrieved from DOI: 10.2307/2715685.

———. (1997–1998). Black History Month: Serious truth telling or a triumph in tokenism? *Journal of Blacks in Higher Education* 18 (Winter): 87–92.

Franklin, V., and B. Collier-Thomas. (2002). Biography, race vindication, and African American intellectuals. *Journal of African American History* 87 (Winter): 160–74. Retrieved from http://www.jstor.org/stable/1562497.

Freedom's Journal, the first U.S. African American–owned newspaper. (1827, March 16). Retrieved from http://www.wisconsinhistory.org/Content.aspx?dsNav=N:4294963828-4294963805&dsRecordDetails=R:CS4415.

The functions of a minority press in war time. (1943, June 12). Letter to C. A. Scott. Transcript, Negro Newspaper Publishers Association, WHAS Louisville, radio broadcast. *Atlanta Daily World* Records (24–26), Manuscript, Archives, and Rare Book Library, Emory University, Atlanta.

Future of *The New York Times*. (2015, June 15). Video (with Jack Rosenthal, Arthur Sulzberger Jr., and Dean Baquet), at Hunter College, New York. Retrieved from http://www.c-span.org/video/?326568-1/future-new-york-times

Gates, H. (2016, September 24). Henry Louis Gates Jr: Restoring black history. *New York Times*. Retrieved from http://www.nytimes.com/2016/09/24/opinion/henry-louis-gates-jr-restoring-black-history.html?smprod=nytcore-ipad&smid=nytcore-ipad-share&_r=0.

Gitlin, T. (1980). *The Whole World Is Watching*. Berkeley: University of California Press.

Goggin, J. (1983, Autumn). Countering white racist scholarship: Carter G. Woodson and *The Journal of Negro History*. *Journal of Negro History* 68(4): 355–75. Retrieved from http://www.jstor.org/stable/2717563.

———. (1993). *Carter G. Woodson: A Life in Black History*. Baton Rouge: Louisiana State University Press.

———. (2014, May 27). Carter G. Woodson (1875–1950). In *Encyclopedia Virginia*. Retrieved from http://www.EncyclopediaVirginia.org/Woodson_Carter_G_1875-1950.

Gould, A. (1985). *West Virgiinia Division of Culture and History*. Retrieved from wvculture.org: http://www.wvculture.org/shpo/nr/pdf/cabell/85003091.pdf.

Graham, P. (1949, December 29). Letter to Edwin B. Henderson. (Part II, Reel 2, Series 2). Carter Godwin Woodson Papers, Manuscript Division, Library of Congress, Washington, DC.

Greene, L. (1989). *Working with Carter G. Woodson, the Father of Black History: A Diary, 1928–1930*. Baton Rouge: Louisiana State University Press.

Hallohan, K. (2002). Ivy Lee and the Rockefellers' response to the 1913–1914 Colorado coal strike. *Journal of Public Relations Research* 14(4): 265–315.

Hancock, G. (1947, March 16). Between the lines: Scholarship. *Atlanta Daily World*, p. 4.

Hart, W. (1917, July). Notes. *Journal of Negro History* 2(3): 331–333. Retrieved from http://www.jstor.org/stable/2713774.

Hartman, C. (2000, February 3). Black history founder is celebrated in DC. *Atlanta Daily World*, p. 7.

Hawkins quits history asso. in indignation: Officials lose heads as Woodson and Hawkins part ways. (1931, June 18). *Philadelphia Tribune*, p. 1.

Help wanted. (1927, May 28). *Pittsburgh Courier*, p. 20.

Henderson, E. (1949, December 30). Letter to Carter G. Woodson. (Part II, Reel 2, Series 2). Carter Godwin Woodson Papers, Manuscript Division, Library of Congress, Washington, DC.

Hendrix, M. (1942, January 12). Letter to C. A. Scott. *Atlanta Daily World* Records (24–26), Manuscript, Archives, and Rare Book Library, Emory University, Atlanta.

Hinton, A. (1947, June 19). Letter to C. A. Scott. Transcript from annual meeting, Negro Newspaper Publishers Association, Gotham Hotel, Detroit. *Atlanta Daily World* Records (24–26), Manuscript, Archives, and Rare Book Library, Emory University, Atlanta.

Historians to discuss plight of West Indies in face of war crisis. *Chicago Defender*, p. 8.

Historical Society to meet April 5–6. (1923, March 7). *New York Amsterdam News*, p. 12.

History. (n.d.). http://www.lincoln.edu/about/history.

History association makes preparations to celebrate twentieth anniversary. (1935, May 4). *Cleveland Call and Post*, p. 8.

History of business journalism. (n.d.). Retrieved from http://bizjournalismhistory.org/main_frame.htm.

A history of the National Newspaper Publishing Association. (2013, June 21). Retrieved from National Newspaper Publishing Association: http://pridepublishinggroup.com/pride/2013/06/21/a-history-of-the-national-newspaper-publishing-association/.

The history of the Negro church. (1922, February 18). *Chicago Defender*, p. 20. Retrieved from http://ezproxy.marshall.edu:2048/docview/491913659?accountid=12281.

History Week will be observed here. (1934, February 12). *Atlanta Daily World*, p. 1.

Hoffman, F. (1896). *Race Traits and Tendencies of the American Negro*. New York: Macmillan.

Holmes, D. (1950, May 13). Carter G. Woodson as I knew him: Spent life bringing about respect for race, heritage. *Afro-American*, p. 13.

Holsey, A. (1948, Summer). Public relations intuitions of Booker T. Washington. *Public Opinion Quarterly* 12(2): 227–35. Retrieved from http://poq.oxfordjournals.org/content/12/2/227.abstract?cited-by=yes;12/2/227.

Hon, L. (1997). To redeem the soul of America: Public relations and the civil rights move-ment. *Journal of Public Relations Research* 9(3): 163–212. Retrieved from http://www .tandfonline.com/doi/abs/10.1207/s1532754xjprr0903_01#.VZwG_4fD_IU.

Hope-Woodson tilt at history association meeting. (1931, November 14). *Afro-American*, p. 13.

How about Negro History Year? (1942, January 24). *Norfolk Journal and Guide*, p. 8.

How the public received *The Journal of Negro History*. (1916, April). *Journal of Negro History* 1(2): 225–32. Retrieved from http://www.jstor.org/stable/3035643.

Hughey, M. (2007, November). The pedagogy of Huey P. Newton: Critical reflections on education in his writings and speeches. *Journal of Black Studies* 38(2): 209–31. Retrieved from http://www.jstor.org/stable/40034976?seq=1#page_scan_tab_contents.

Huntington Advertiser. (1896, May 8). p. 4.

Hutchinson, E. (2003, February 20). Unselling black history is a worthy goal to seek. *Atlanta Daily World*, p. 14.

An important correction. (1947, November). *Negro History Bulletin* 11(2): 26.

Ireland, C. (2012, May 22). Commencements from 1642 onward. *Harvard Gazette*. Retrieved from http://news.harvard.edu/gazette/story/2012/05/commencement-from-1642-onward/.

Jackson, A. (1922, July 22). The bookshelf. *Chicago Defender (National Edition)*. Retrieved from http://ezproxy.marshall.edu:2048/docview/491935424?accountid=12281.

Jackson, L. (1935, January 6). Letter to Carter G. Woodson. Luther Porter Jackson Papers, 1772–1960, Accession #1952-l (35:973). Special Collections and Archives, Johnston Memorial Library, Virginia State University, Petersburg.

———. (1935, October). The work of the Association and the people. *Journal of Negro History* 20(4): 385–396. Retrieved from Association for the Study of African American Life and History, Inc.: http://www.jstor.org/stable/2714255.

———. (1938, July 2). Letter to Carter G. Woodson. Luther Porter Jackson Papers, 1772–1960, Accession #1952-l (35:878). Special Collections and Archives, Johnston Memorial Library, Virginia State University, Petersburg.

———. (1942a, March 1). Letter to Carter G. Woodson. Luther Porter Jackson Papers, 1772–1960, Accession #1952-l (35:983). Special Collections and Archives, Johnston Memorial Library, Virginia State University, Petersburg.

———. (1942b, August 2). Letter to Carter G. Woodson. Luther Porter Jackson Papers, 1772–1960, Accession #1952-l (35:984). Special Collections and Archives, Johnston Memorial Library, Virginia State University, Petersburg.

———. (1942c, August 18). Letter to Carter G. Woodson. Luther Porter Jackson Papers, 1772–1960, Accession #1952-l (35:984). Special Collections and Archives, Johnston Memorial Library, Virginia State University, Petersburg.

———. (1943a, January 21). Letter to Carter G. Woodson. Luther Porter Jackson Papers, 1772–1960, Accession #1952-l (35:988). Special Collections and Archives, Johnston Memorial Library, Virginia State University, Petersburg.

———. (1943b, October 9). Letter to Carter G. Woodson. Luther Porter Jackson Papers, 1772–1960, Accession #1952-l (35:989). Special Collections and Archives, Johnston Memorial Library, Virginia State University, Petersburg.

————. (1944a, February 19). Letter to Carter G. Woodson. Luther Porter Jackson Papers, 1772–1960, Accession #1952-l (35:990). Special Collections and Archives, Johnston Memorial Library, Virginia State University, Petersburg.

————. (1944b, May 20). Letter to Carter G. Woodson. Luther Porter Jackson Papers, 1772–1960, Accession #1952-l (35:990). Special Collections and Archives, Johnston Memorial Library, Virginia State University, Petersburg.

————. (1944c, October 6). Letter to Carter G. Woodson. Luther Porter Jackson Papers, 1772–1960, Accession #1952-l (35:991). Special Collections and Archives, Johnston Memorial Library, Virginia State University, Petersburg.

————. (1944d, October 15). Letter to Carter G. Woodson. Luther Porter Jackson Papers, 1772–1960, Accession #1952-l (35:991). Special Collections and Archives, Johnston Memorial Library, Virginia State University, Petersburg.

————. (1945a, February 22). The Negro newspaper—Indispensable aid for Negro history. Luther Porter Jackson Papers, 1772–1960, Accession #1952-l (65:1626). Special Collections and Archives, Johnston Memorial Library, Virginia State University, Petersburg.

————. (1945b, February 28). The Negro newspaper aid for Negro History. Luther Porter Jackson Papers, 1772–1960, Accession #1952-l (65:1626). Special Collections and Archives, Johnston Memorial Library, Virginia State University, Petersburg.

————. (1945c, August 8). Letter to Carter G. Woodson. Luther Porter Jackson Papers, 1772–1960, Accession #1952-l (35:993). Special Collections and Archives, Johnston Memorial Library, Virginia State University, Petersburg.

————. (1945d, September 11). Letter to Carter G. Woodson. Luther Porter Jackson Papers, 1772–1960, Accession #1952-l (35:993). Special Collections and Archives, Johnston Memorial Library, Virginia State University, Petersburg.

Jacksonville, Fla. (1932, June 1). *Atlanta Daily World*, p. A1.

"Jim Crow" precedes extermination. (1928, April 25). *New York Amsterdam News*, p. 3.

Jim Crow theaters and our artists. (1933, March 4). *Chicago Defender*, p. 14.

Johnson, C. (1928, January). The rise of the Negro magazine. *Journal of Negro History* 13(1): 7–21. Retrieved from http://www.jstor.org/stable/2713910.

Jones, I. (2011). *The Heart of the Race Problem: The Life of Kelly Miller*. Littleton, MA: Tapestry Press.

Jones, L. (1932, November 16). Society slants. *Atlanta Daily World*, p. 3A.

The Journal of Negro History. (1916, March 11). *Afro-American*, p. 4.

The Junior Page: Inner Circle History Games begin this week. (1935, February 23). *Afro-American*, p. 19.

Kareem Abdul-Jabbar. (n.d.). Video: Retrieved from http://kareemabduljabbar.com/?m=201202&paged=2.

Kennedy, R. (n.d.). On this day. Retrieved from http://www.nytimes.com/learning/general/onthisday/harp/1113.html.

King, L., and A. Brown. (2010, September–October). The forgotten legacy of Carter G. Woodson: Contributions to multicultural social studies and African American history. *Social Studies* 101(5): 211–15. Retrieved from http://eric.ed.gov/?id=EJ895121.

Korea's sailing delayed. (1903, November 19). *San Francisco Call*, p. 10.

Late A.M.E. prelate left estate of nearly 50 thousand dollars: Bishop Johnson estate valued at $42,660. (1931, December 12). *Afro-American*, p. 2.

Lauded as leader, scholar: District pays tribute to Dr. Carter Woodson. (1950, April 15). *Afro-American*, p. 7.

Lawson, M. (1945, Summer). The adult education aspects of the Negro press. *Journal of Negro Education* 14(3): 431–36. Retrieved from DOI: 10.2307/2293012.

Leading article in *Journal of Negro History*. (1921, February 26). *Norfolk Journal and Guide*, p. 7.

Len-Rios, M. E., E. Cohen, and C. Caburnay. (2010). Readers use black newspapers for health/cancer information. *Newspaper Research Journal* 31(1): 20–35.

Life-work of Ida B. Wells recalled by Chicagoans: Career paralleled Douglass. (1940, February 24). *Pittsburgh Courier*, p. 8.

Locke, Robinson. (n.d.). Retrieved from Rutherford B. Hayes Presidential Center: http://www.rbhayes.org/hayes/mssfind/487/locker.htm.

Loeb, C. (1941, January 4). Carter G. Woodson, historian, addresses Cleveland interracial group. *Cleveland Call and Post*, p. 6.

Logan, F. (1959, January). An appraisal of forty-one years of the Journal of Negro History, 1916–1957. *Journal of Negro History* 44(1): 26–33. Retrieved from http://www.jstor.org/stable/2716308.

Logan, R. (1940, July). Negro youth and the influence of the press, radio, and cinema. *Journal of Negro Education* 9(3): 425–34. Retrieved from http://www.jstor.org/stable/2292614.

———. (1950, October). Report of the director. *Journal of Negro History* 35(4): 359–67. Retrieved from http://www.jstor.org/stable/2715523.

———. (1973, January). Carter G. Woodson: Mirror and molder of his time, 1875–1950. *Journal of Negro History* 58(1): 1–17. Retrieved from DOI: 10.2307/2717153.

Looking for peace or war? (1932, March 12). *Afro-American*, p. 6.

MacKay, C. (1950, January 14). A quick glimpse over the educational world. *Afro-American*, p. 5.

Many brave storm to hear lecture of Carter G. Woodson, historian: Much of history read today is mere propaganda to perpetuate "white supremacy," he holds. (1926, December 8). *New York Amsterdam News*, p. 9.

Martin, T. (1976). *Race First: The Ideological and Organizational Struggles of Marcus Garvey and the Universal Negro Improvement Association*. Westport, CT: Greenwood.

Maxwell, J. (1940, May 4). Charlotte chatter. *Norfolk Journal and Guide*, p. 12.

Mayor Mackey will make Harmon Award: Gold medal to be presented at mammoth public meeting Sunday. (1928, February 11). *Pittsburgh Courier*, p. 10.

McCombs, M., and D. Shaw. (1993). Twenty-five years in the marketplace of ideas. *Journal of Communications* 43(2): 58–67. Retrieved from DOI: 10.1111/j.1460-2466.1993.tb01262.

Media and Civil Rights Movement. (1998, March 24). Video. John F. Kennedy Presidential Library, Boston.

Meier, A. (1953, January). Booker T. Washington and the Negro press: With special reference to the *Colored American Magazine*. *Journal of Negro History* 38(1): 67–90. Retrieved from DOI: 10.2307/2715814.

Mencher, M. (2008). *Reporting and Writing*. 11th ed. New York: McGraw-Hill.

Mencken, H. (1944). Designations for Colored folk. http://www.virginia.edu/woodson/courses/aas102%20(spring%2001)/articles/names/mencken.htm.

Miles, W. (1991). Dr. Carter Godwin Woodson as I recall him. *Journal of Negro History* 76(1/4): 92–100. Retrieved from http://www.jstor.org/stable/2717413.

Miller, K. (1933, February 11). Carter Woodson is termed new Marcus Garvey. *Afro-American*, p. 22.

More strife and confusion. (1950, April). *Negro History Bulletin* 13(7): 146.

Morris, B. (2009, May 29). A response to Professor Katherine Rodier's study of Bessie Woodson Yancey's letters to the editor of the *Huntington Herald-Advertiser*, 1946–1958, Faces of Appalachia Symposium, Marshall University. Retrieved from Faces of Appalachia: https://ensemble.marshall.edu/Watch/j8D9WtLd.

———. (2012, May 29). Interview, Ancella Bickley and Nelson Bickley, Marshall University Student Center, Huntington, WV.

Murphy, G. (1936, April 25). 17th Woodson book is out: Most eminent historian reveals his own secret. *Afro-American*, p. 1.

MU-So-Lit Club asked to oust Perry Howard. (1931, April 25). *Afro-American*, p. 11.

Myrdal, G. (1944). *An American Dilemma: The Negro Problem and Modern Democracy*. New York: Harper and Row.

NAACP conference in Atlanta: Civil rights action through the media. (n.d.). Museum of Public Relations. Retrieved from http://www.prmuseum.com/bernays/bernays_1920.html.

NAACP lists highlights of meet. (1932, May 12). *Atlanta Daily World*, p. 2.

National assessment of adult literacy: 120 years of literacy. (1993). National Center for Education Statistics. Retrieved from http://nces.ed.gov/NAAL/lit_history.asp#illiteracy.

Nation prepares for Negro History Week. (1949, January 7). *Atlanta Daily World*, p. 3

Negroes in professions. [Review of the book *The Negro Professional Man and the Community* by Carter G. Woodson]. (1934, March 25). *New York Times*. Reviews of Woodson books. (Part II, Box 2, Reel 2). Carter Godwin Woodson Papers, Manuscript Division, Library of Congress, Washington, DC.

Negro Fellowship League. (1915, July 24). *Chicago Defender*. Retrieved from http://ezproxy.marshall.edu:2048/docview/493321238?accountid=12281.

Negro History study association announces prizes for essays. (1932, February 3). *Atlanta Daily World*, p. 4.

Negro History Week. (1925, November 28). *Pittsburgh Courier*, p. 16.

Negro History Week. (1926, April). *Journal of Negro History* 11(2): 238–42. Retrieved from DOI: 10.2307/2714171.

Negro History Week. (1927, January 29). *Pittsburgh Courier*, p. A8.

Negro History Week. (1933, February 4). *Afro-American*, p. 6.

Negro History Week. (1941, January). *Journal of Negro History* 26(1): 135. Retrieved from DOI: 10.2307/2715063.

Negro History Week. (1947, February 8). *Chicago Defender*, p. 14.

Negro History Week begins February 5. (1928, January 23). *New York Amsterdam News*, 10.

Negro History Week broadcast. (1939, March). *Negro History Bulletin* 2(6): 53.

Negro History Week celebration. (1930). *Journal of Negro History* 15(2): 125–33. Retrieved from DOI: 10.2307/2714008.

Negro History Week celebration to begin this year February 7. (1937, January 9). *Norfolk Journal and Guide*, p. A9.

Negro History Week pamphlet given gratis. (1936, December 3). *Cleveland Call and Post*, p. 8.

Negro History Week–the thirteenth year. (1938). *Journal of Negro History* 23(2): 139–41. Retrieved from DOI: 10.2307/2714342.

Negro History Week—the twelfth year. (1937). *Journal of Negro History* 22(2): 141–47. Retrieved from DOI: 10.2307/2714426.

The Negro mind. [Review of the book *The Mind of the Negro as Reflected in Letters during the Crisis, 1800–1860* by Carter G. Woodson]. (1926, October 24). *New York Times*, p. 54. Retrieved from http://timesmachine.nytimes.com/timesmachine/1926/10/24/98400291 .html?pageNumber=54.

Negro Newspapers and Periodicals in the United States: 1943, Negro Statistical Bulletin, No. 1. (1944). Washington, DC: US Department of Commerce, Department of the Census.

Negro publishers name Truman, nine others for Russwurm Award. (1950, July 1). *Chicago Defender*, p. 12.

Nelson, H. (1940, September 19). Reelect history officers: Insist $3,000 salary be paid Dr. Woodson. *Atlanta Daily World*, p. 1.

Newspapers: *The Chicago Defender*. (n.d.). Retrieved from http://www.pbs.org/blackpress/ news_bios/defender.html.

Newspapers, 1775–1860. (n.d.). Retrieved from Bartleby.com: http://www.bartleby.com/226/ 1219.html.

Noted human touring Europe for data. (1932, September 22). *Atlanta Daily World*, p. A6.

Notes. (1916, January). *Journal of Negro History* 1(1): 98. Retrieved from http://www.jstor .org/stable/2713522.

Notes. (1916, April). *Journal of Negro History* 1(2): 223–24. Retrieved from http://www.jstor .org/stable/3035642.

Notes. (1920, October). *Journal of Negro History* 5(4): 492–93. Retrieved from http://www .jstor.org/stable/2713689.

Notes. (1921, January). *Journal of Negro History* 6(1): 123. Retrieved from http://www.jstor .org/stable/2713837.

Notes. (1921, April). *Journal of Negro History* 6(2): 259. Retrieved from http://www.jstor.org/ stable/2713739.

Notes. (1924, October). *Journal of Negro History* 9(4): 578. Retrieved from http://www.jstor .org/stable/2713557.

Notes. (1928, January). *Journal of Negro History* 13(1): 109–19. Retrieved from http://www jstor.org/stable/2713919.

Notes. (1938, July). *Journal of Negro History* 23(3): 403–4. Retrieved from http://www.jstor .org/stable/2714699.

Notes. (1942, April). *Journal of Negro History* 27(2): 238–46. Retrieved from http://www .jstor.org/stable/2714747.

Notes: The director speaks. (1931, July). *Journal of Negro History* 16(3): 344–48. Retrieved from http://www.jstor.org/stable/2713931.

Oak, V. (1942, December 14). Letter to C. A. Scott. The Negro press today *Atlanta Daily World* Records (24–26), Manuscript, Archives, and Rare Book Library, Emory University, Atlanta.

October 2009 bestsellers books list. (n.d.). Retrieved from Essence http://www.essence .com/2009/10/02/october-2009-bestsellers-books-list/.

Omega Psi Phi holds conclave: Colored fraternity to foster study of Negro history. (1923, January 10). *New York Amsterdam News*, p. 7.

Orators. (1925, October 17). *Afro-American*, p. 9.

Other recent books. [Review of the book *The Rural Negro* by Carter G. Woodson]. (1930, August 18). *Buffalo Sunday Courier-Express*. [Reviews of Woodson books]. (Part II, Reel 2). Carter Godwin Woodson Papers, Manuscript Division, Library of Congress, Washington, DC.

Ottley, R. (1947, October 12). [Review of the book *From Slavery to Freedom* by John Hope Franklin]. Genesis of the American Negro. *New York Times*. Retrieved from http://ny times.com.

Our history. (n.d.). Retrieved from http://asalh100.org/our-history/.

Oxley, T. (1927, December 21). The Negro in the world's literature: Carter G. Woodson, editor, historian. *New York Amsterdam News*, p. 5.

Oxley sharply criticizes Woodson's new book. (1933, April 8). *Afro-American*, p. 18.

People unwittingly foil efforts of historians through inability to know worth of documents they possess. (1933, December 16). *Norfolk Journal and Guide*, p. A14.

Perl, P. (1999, March 1). Race riot of 1919 gave glimpse of future struggles. *Washington Post*, p. A 1. Retrieved from the *Washington Post*: http://www.washingtonpost.com/wp-srv/ local/2000/raceriot0301.htm.

Perry, J. (1936, June 8). Society slants: So what! *Atlanta Daily World*, p. 3.

Personalities: Carter G. Woodson. (n.d.). Retrieved from Berea College: http://www.berea .edu/cgwc/personalities/#CarterWoodson.

Persons and achievements to be remembered in October. (1937, October). *Negro History Bulletin* 1(1): 3–4.

Petrova, M. (2011, November). Newspapers and parties: How advertising revenues created an independent press. *American Political Science Review* 105(4): 790–808. Retrieved from http://www.jstor.org/stable/23275353.

Planet/John Mitchell, Jr. (n.d.). Exhibit. Retrieved from the Library of Virginia: http://www .lva.virginia.gov/exhibits/mitchell/.

Post Office Department. (1931, May 12). Letter to C. A. Loescher. (Part II, Reel 2). Carter Godwin Woodson Papers, Manuscript Division, Library of Congress, Washington, DC.

The prayer of twenty millions. (1862, August 20). *New York Tribune*. Retrieved from http:// www.history.com/this-day-in-history/horace-greeleys-the-prayer-of-twenty-millions -is-published.

Preparatory war work at Armstrong school. (1918, September 15). *Washington Sunday Star*, p. 3.

Presenting the case of the Negro to the readers of the *World*. (1934, September 11). *Atlanta Daily World*, p. 6.

President Gerald R. Ford's message on the observance of Black History Month. (1976, February 10). Retrieved from http://www.ford.utexas.edu/library/speeches/760074.htm.

Press to have place on programme. (1927, October 22). *Pittsburgh Courier*, p. 1.

Pride, A. (1950). *A Register and History of Negro Newspapers in the United States, 1827–1950*. Evanston, IL: Northwestern University.

Proceedings of the annual meeting, the celebration of the tenth anniversary of the Association for the Study of Negro Life and History, held in Washington, DC, September 9 and 10, 1925. (1925, October). *Journal of Negro History* 10(4): 583–89. Retrieved from http://www.jstor.org/stable/2714139.

Proceedings of the annual meeting, Washington, D.C., November 18–19, 1920. (1921, January). *Journal of Negro History* 6(1): 126–30. Retrieved from http://www.jstor.org/stable/2713838.

Proceedings of the annual meeting of the Association for the Study of Negro Life and History held in New York City, October 28–30, 1949. (1950, January). *Journal of Negro History* 35(1): 1–8. Retrieved from http://www.jstor.org/stable/2715556.

Proceedings of the second biennial meeting of the Association for the Study of Negro Life and History. (1919, October). *Journal of Negro History* 4(4): 475–82. Retrieved from http://www.jstor.org/stable/2713455.

Proceedings of the thirty-third annual meeting of the Association for the Study of Negro Life and History, held in Washington, D.C., October 29–31, 1948. (1949, January). *Journal of Negro History* 34(1): 1–8. Retrieved from http://www.jstor.org/stable/2715624.

Proceedings of the twenty-fifth annual meeting of the Association for the Study of Negro Life and History, Oct. 29–31, 1943. (1944, January). *Journal of Negro History* 29(1): 1–6. Retrieved from http://www.jstor.org/stable/2714750.

Proposed play for Washington celebration shows poor whites despising Negroes, Woodson says. (1931, December 19). *Norfolk Journal and Guide*, p. 4.

Protest action in letter to editor, church paper. (1932, September 1). *Atlanta Daily World*, p. 1A.

Publications. (n.d.). Retrieved from Association for the Study of African American Life and History: http://asalh.org/mainperiodicals.html.

Public relations: An overview. (1991). *PRSA Foundation Monograph Series* 1 (3): 3–4, 15.

Purnell, B. (2009). Interview with Dr. John Hope Franklin. *Journal of African American History* 94(3): 407–21. Retrieved from http://jstor.org/stable/2563954.

Putnam, H. (1928, December 5). Carter Godwin Woodson Papers, Manuscript Division, Library of Congress, Washington, DC.

Race in the news. (1946, August 11). *New York Times*, p. 80. Retrieved from http://nytimes.com.

Race must overcome inferiority complex, Dr. Woodson declares. (1928, January 21). *Norfolk Journal and Guide*, p. 2.

Read Negro history. (1930, February 15). *Pittsburgh Courier*, p. 10.

Reddick, L. (1937, January). A new interpretation for Negro history. *Journal of Negro History* 22(1): 21. Retrieved from http://www.jstor.org/stable/2714314.

———. (1950). Twenty-Five Negro history weeks. *Negro History Bulletin* 13(6): 8.

———. (1953). As I remember Woodson, in Brief Biographies of Carter G. Woodson, Special Collections, Marshall University Libraries, Huntington, WV.

Report of the National Advisory Commission on Civil Disorders. (1968). US National Advisory Commission on Civil Disorders.

Research and romance: 72-year-old bachelor put study of race ahead of love, but he is no sourpuss. (1947, February 15). *Afro-American*, p. M12.

Rice, C. (2015). Christopher H. Payne. Retrieved from http://www.wvencyclopedia.org/articles/1824.

Rigney, F. J. (2002). Statisticians in history. Retrieved from http://www.amstat.org/about/statisticiansinhistory/index.cfm?fuseaction=biosinfo&BioID=34.

Robert Gordon a successful business man. (1937, November). *Negro History Bulletin* 1(2): 1–3.

Robert Lee Vann. (1941, January). *Journal of Negro History* 26(1): 135–136. Retrieved from http://www.jstor.org/stable/2715064.

Roberts, G., and H. Kilbanoff. (2007). *The Race Beat: The Press, the Civil Rights Struggle, and the Awakening of America*. New York: Knopf.

Robert Sengstacke Abbott. (1940, April). *Journal of Negro History* 25(2): 261–62. Retrieved from http://www.jstor.org/stable/2714613.

Roosevelt favored for return to post: Roosevelt dedicates Mark Twain Bridge. (1936, September 6). *Atlanta Daily World*, p. 1.

The rural Negro. [Review of the book *The Rural Negro* by Carter G. Woodson]. (1930, July 19). *St. Louis Post-Democrat*. [Reviews of Woodson books]. (Part II, Reel 2). Carter Godwin Woodson Papers, Manuscript Division, Library of Congress, Washington, DC.

The rural Negro. [Review of the book *The Rural Negro* by Carter G. Woodson]. (1930, August 2). *Grand Rapids Press*, Grand Rapids, Michigan. (Part II, Reel 2). Carter Godwin Woodson Papers, Manuscript Division, Library of Congress, Washington, DC.

The rural Negro. [Review of the book *The Rural Negro* by Carter G. Woodson]. (1930, September 1). *Detroit Free Press*. (Part II, Reel 2). Carter Godwin Woodson Papers, Manuscript Division, Library of Congress, Washington, DC.

Russell, K., and C. Bishop, C. (2009). Understanding Ivy Lee's declaration of principles: U.S. newspaper and magazine coverage of publicity and press agentry, 1865–1904. *Public Relations Review*, pp. 91–101.

Russell, K., and M. Lamme. (2013, March). Public relations and business responses to the civil rights movement. *Public Relations Review*, pp. 63–73.

R.W.L. (1950, July). Carter Godwin Woodson. *Journal of Negro History* 35(3): 344–48. Retrieved from http://www.jstor.org/stable/2715712.

Savage, B. (1999). *Broadcasting Freedom: Radio, War, and the Politics of Race*. Chapel Hill: University of North Carolina Press.

Says lack of racial unity not unusual. (1938, February 6). *Chicago Defender*, p. 5.

Scally, S. A. (1977, January–February). Woodson and the genesis of ASALH. *Negro History Bulletin* 40(1): 653–54.

——. (1985). *Carter G. Woodson: A Bio-bibliography*. Westport, CT: Greenwood Press.

Schoenfeld, Seymour J. 1945. Letter to Carter G. Woodson. Carter Godwin Woodson Papers, Manuscript Division, Library of Congress, Washington, DC.

Scott, D. (2009–2011). Origins of Black History Month. Retrieved from https://asalh100 .org/origins-of-black-history-month.

——. (2012, February 21). Black History Month Speaker, Marshall University.

Scott, J. (1916, October). Notes. *Journal of Negro History* 1(4): 450–52. Retrieved from http:// www.jstor.org/stable/3035620.

Services at Douglass school. (1901, September 20). *Huntington Advertiser*, p. 4.

Simmons, C. (1998). *The African American Press: With Special Reference to Four Newspapers, 1827–1965*. Jefferson, NC: McFarland.

Simmons, W., and H. Turner. (1887). *Men of Mark: Eminent, Progressive and Rising*. Cleveland: G. M. Rewell.

Smith, A. (1943, August 14). Race funds make study of our history possible. *Chicago Defender*, p. 7.

Smith, R. (2008). Strategic planning for public relations. Retrieved from http://www.rout ledge.com/cw/smith-9780415506762/s1/historypt2/.

Snead, L. (1943, June 12). Liberians find Philadelphia's brotherly love is real thing. *Afro-American*, p. 3.

Society: Dr. Woodson returns home Afro-American. (1927, April 23). *Afro-American*, p. 3.

Southern, D. (1987). *Gunnar Myrdal and Black-White Relations: The Use and Abuse of an American Dilemma, 1944–1969*. Baton Rouge: Louisian State University Press.

A special message from the daddy of Negro History Week. (1950, February 11). *Afro-American*, p. A2.

Stafford, A. (1916, January). The mind of the African Negro as reflected in his proverbs. *Journal of Negro History* 1(1): 42–48. Retrieved from DOI: 10.2307/2713515.

Strother, T. (1978, Autumn). The race-advocacy function of the black press. Black American Literature Forum, St. Louis University, 12(3): 92–99. Retrieved from http://www.jstor .org/stable/3041554.

Study guide for the examination in accreditation in public relations. (2010). Universal Accreditation Board Functioning as part of the Public Relations Society of America, pp. 18, 26–27.

The study of Negro life and history. (1950, March). *Negro History Bulletin* 13(6): 140.

Sullivan, B. L. (2001, June). More than 900 newspapers sponsor NIE programs. *Quill*, pp. 72–73.

Sweeney, A. (1948, February 7). He inaugurated history week. *Afro-American*, p. M3.

They've blazed a trail in history: Annual observance February 8–14. (1948, February 7). *Afro-American*, p. M12.

The thirteen most important Negroes in the United States. (1930, June 28). *Afro-American*, p. 11.

Thousands attend D.C. rites for Drs. Drew, Woodson: Historian held high example. (1950, April 15). *Afro-American*, p. 7.

Three students of the subject view the racial question. (July 18). *New York Times*. Retrieved from http://query.nytimes.com/mem/archivefree/pdf?res-=9A02E6DA1739E233A2575 BC1A9619C946496D6CF.

Togneri, C. (n.d.). Retrieved from http://triblive.com/news/allegheny/3786550-74/smith -black-robinson#axzz3bY87FYZl.

To offer extension courses in Negro life and history. (1927, October 8). *Pittsburgh Courier*, p. 3.

Twelfth Annual Negro Newspaper Week. (1949, March 4). Letter to C. A. Scott. Program, Some significant facts about the Negro press, p. 2. *Atlanta Daily World* Records (24–26), Manuscript, Archives, and Rare Book Library, Emory University, Atlanta.

Ungrady, D. (2013, September 6). E. B. Henderson brought basketball to the District. *Washington Post*. Retrieved from http://washingtonpost.com.

UNIA declaration of rights of the Negro peoples of the World, New York, August 13, 1920. Reprinted in Robert Hill, ed., *The Marcus Garvey and Universal Negro Improvement Papers*, 2 (Berkeley: University of California Press, 1983), 571–80. Retrieved from http:// historymatters.gmu.edu/d/5122.

Urgent need for funds for Negro history writing. (1926, June 5). *Norfolk Journal and Guide*, p. 11.

Vacationing in Europe. (1932, August 6). *Afro-American*, p. 2.

Vann, R. (1927, February 26). The camera: Economic business. *Pittsburgh Courier*, p. 1.

Variety is the spice of life. (1931, February 14). *Negro World*, p. 4.

Virginia breaks tradition. (1963, September 10). Retrieved from the *New York Times*: //query .nytimes.com/mem/archive/pdf?res=F3071EFA39581A7B93C2A81782D85F478685F9.

Wanted $20,000 promote Negro History Week: Dr. Carter G. Woodson announces celebration. (1926, February 27). *Norfolk Journal and Guide*, p. 10.

Want Negro history in public schools. (1925, February 4). *New York Amsterdam News*, p. 8.

Wayland, A. (n.d.). Woodson book filled with practical suggestions. [Review of the book *The Mis-Education of the Negro* by Carter G. Woodson]. *Richmond News Leader*. (Part II, Reel 2). Carter Godwin Woodson Papers, Manuscript Division, Library of Congress, Washington, DC.

Well done. (1949, February 12). *Chicago Defender*, p. 6.

Wesley, C. (1925, October 14). Negro history in school curriculum. *New York Amsterdam News*, p. 16.

———. (1936, January 27). Letter to Luther P. Jackson. Luther Porter Jackson Papers, 1772– 1960, Accession #1952-l (35:974). Special Collections and Archives, Johnston Memorial Library, Virginia State University, Petersburg.

———. (1951, January). Carter G. Woodson—as a scholar. *Journal of Negro History* 36(1): 12–24. Retrieved from DOI: 10.2307/2715774.

———. (1998). Recollections of Carter G. Woodson. *Journal of Negro History* 83(2): 143–49. Retrieved from DOI: 10.2307/2668537.

What Dr. Du Bois said about the late Carter G. Woodson. (1950, July 22). *Afro-American*, p. 6.

White, A. (1939, December 6). Associated Negro Press. *Atlanta Daily World*, p. 6.

Who's Who is latest joke on race. (1924, September 12). *Afro-American*, p. 1.

"Who's Who" sponsors program: W. C. Handy goes on the air tomorrow. (1928, January 25). *New York Amsterdam News*, p. 4.

Wilkerson, D. (1947, Autumn). The Negro press. *Journal of Negro Education* 16(4): 511–21. Retrieved from DOI: 10.2307/2966410.

Williams, G. W. (1888). *Negro Troops in the War of the Rebellion 1861–1865*. New York: Harper and Brothers.

Wilson, J. (1888). *The Black Phalanx: A History of the Negro Soldiers of the United States in the War of 1775–1812, 1861–'65*. Hartford, CT: American Publishing.

"Wings Over Jordan" program to feature Carter Woodson in Negro History Week review. (1939, February 2). *Cleveland Call and Post*, p. 3.

Woodson, C. (1916, January). The Negroes of Cincinnati prior to the Civil War. *Journal of Negro History* 1:1–22. Retrieved from DOI: 10.2307/2713512.

——. (1920, May 14). Journalism in schools. *Howard University Record*, pp. 365–66.

——. (1921, January). Fifty years of Negro citizenship as qualified by the United States Supreme Court. *Journal of Negro History* 6(1): 1–53. Retrieved from http://www.jstor.org/stable/2713827.

——. (1922, January). Early Negro education in West Virginia. *Journal of Negro History* 7(1): 23–63. Retrieved from DOI: 10.2307/2713579.

——. (1922). *The Negro in Our History*. Washington, DC: Associated Publishers.

——. (1924). *The Negro in Our History*. 3rd ed. Washington, DC: Associated Publishers.

——. (1925a, October). Ten years of collecting and publishing the records of the Negro. *Journal of Negro History* 10(4): 598–606. Retrieved from http://www.jstor.org/stable/2714140.

——. (1925b, November 18). Carter Woodson refuses to speak from same platform as Pres. Durkee: "Would not disgrace himself by appearing with man who has exploited race," he wrote. *New York Amsterdam News*, p. 1.

——. (1926, February 13). Negro was first to discover America, he taught modern world to use iron. *Afro-American*, p. 11.

——. (1927a, February 2). National Negro History Week celebration from February 6 to 13. *New York Amsterdam News*, p. 16.

——. (1927b, April). The celebration of Negro History Week, 1927. *Journal of Negro History* 12(2): 103–109. Retrieved from DOI: 10.2307/2714049.

——. (1927c, April). Communications: History made to order. *Journal of Negro History* 12(2): 330–348. Retrieved from http://www.jstor.org/stable/2714058.

——. (1928a, April). Negro History Week—the third year. *Journal of Negro History* 13(2): 121–125. Retrieved from DOI: 10.2307/2713958.

——. (1928b). *Negro Makers of History*. Washington, DC: Associated Publishers.

——. (1929a, April). Negro History Week—the fourth year. *Journal of Negro History* 14(2): 109–15.

———. (1929b, October 21). Letter to coworker. (Reel 1, Series 2). Carter Godwin Woodson Papers, Manuscript Division, Library of Congress, Washington, DC.

———. (1931a, April 18). Higher education's weaknesses assailed by Dr. Carter G. Woodson. *Norfolk Journal and Guide*, p. 2.

———. (1931b, May 28). Carter Woodson tells why the "highly educated" clergy preach to benches as Mencken scores church racketeers. *Philadelphia Tribune*, p. 9.

———. (1931c, July 2). Sees danger in Howard official playing politics. *Philadelphia Tribune*, p. 9.

———. (1931d, August). The miseducation of the Negro. *Crisis*, p. 266.

———. (1931e, October 7). Worthless pastors halt the union of churches. *New York Amsterdam News*, p. 9.

———. (1931f, October 21). To subject Negro church to meeting's acid test. *New York Amsterdam News*, p. 9.

———. (1931g, December 9). Vital suggestions on the Washington Bicentennial. *New York Amsterdam News*, p. 8.

———. (1931h, December 16). Honoring Washington by traducement. *New York Amsterdam News*, p. 8.

———. (1931i, December 23). Eliminating the Negro from the Bicentennial. *New York Amsterdam News*, p. 8.

———. (1931j, December 26). From Dr. Carter G. Woodson. *Afro-American*, p. 8.

———. (1931k, December 31). Calls Crispus Attucks fool. *Philadelphia Tribune*, p. 9.

———. (1931l, December 30). Bicentennial eliminates Crispus Attucks' day. *New York Amsterdam News*, p. 8.

———. (1932a, January 24). George Washington as he really was. *Atlanta Daily World*, p. 4.

———. (1932b, March 24). Hoover writing school boy essays as masses continue living beyond their means. *Philadelphia Tribune*, p. 9.

———. (1932c, April 7). Knockers make capital graveyard of ambition, proclaims Woodson. *Atlanta Daily World*, p. 2.

———. (1932e, May 4). What need is there for "vocational guidance"? *New York Amsterdam News*, p. 8.

———. (1932f, May 14). Carter G. Woodson in fervid plea for Nannie Burroughs. *Pittsburgh Courier*, p. A2.

———. (1932h, June 27). And the Negro loses his soul. *Atlanta Daily World*. Retrieved from http://ezproxy.marshall.edu:2048/docview/490391973?accountid=12281.

———. (1932i, June 23). Negro has too much hindsight. *Atlanta Daily World*, p. 6A.

———. (1932j, July 9). Thomas Jesse Jones termed undesirable; disapproved by Booker T. Washington. *Afro-American*, p. 8.

———. (1932k, August 17). Negro can free himself of exploiting leaders. *New York Amsterdam News*, p. 6.

———. (1932l, September 8). Woodson yearning for Pres. Hoover's defeat. *Atlanta Daily World*, p. 6A.

———. (1932m, September 15). Dr. Woodson urges voters in next election to use ballots discriminately. *Atlanta Daily World*, p. 6A.

———. (1932n, September 24). Carter Woodson says he is on no vacation; gathering facts on Negro: Finds Africans lack interest. *Norfolk Journal and Guide*, p. 7.

———. (1932o, September 24). Observations: The trend of current thought and discussion, looking at the Negro from Europe. *Chicago Defender*, p. 14.

———. (1932p, October 27). Correct name for race not so important. *Philadelphia Tribune*, p. 7.

———. (1932q, December 10). Majority of educators favor History Week celebrations in schools. *Afro-American*, p. 7.

———. (1932r, December 29). Black but comely. *Atlanta Daily World*, p. 2A.

———. (1933a). *The Mis-education of the Negro*. Washington, DC: Associated Publishers.

———. (1933b). Blurb on jacket, *The Mis-education of the Negro*. Drewryville, VA: Khalifah's Booksellers and Associates.

———. (1933c, January 1). The "Mis-Education of the Negro" will be released. *New York Amsterdam News*, p. 6.

———. (1933d, January 7). The vow of poverty. *Chicago Defender*, p. 14.

———. (1933e, January 25). Unlucky Friday teaches lessons on thugs. *New York Amsterdam News*, p. 6.

———. (1933f, February 1). Why I disapprove of the March 4 backyard frolic. *New York Amsterdam News*, p. 6.

———. (1933g, February 22). Reply to Uncle Tom and his coworkers' attacks. *New York Amsterdam News*, p. 6.

———. (1933g, July 8). Annual literary contest of Negro history ass'n. *Pittsburgh Courier*, p. A2.

———. (1933h, October 10). Churches need enlightened programs: Racketeers of religion are burden, he says. *Norfolk Journal and Guide*, p. 5.

———. (1933i, October 21). "Chocolate Dandies" give Paris an eyeful. *Chicago Defender*, p. 1.

———. (1933j, December 30). Holding the Negro between him and the fire. *Louisiana Weekly*, p. 8.

———. (1934, March 10). History lost while emphasizing trifles. *Louisiana Weekly*, p. 8.

———. (1936a, February 15). Achievements of a race not history, Woodson says. *Norfolk Journal and Guide*, p. 5.

———. (1936e, February 22). Dr. Woodson makes plea for records of Negro race: Shows need for data on race's achievements. *Norfolk Journal and Guide*, p. 20.

———. (1936b, February 29). George Washington was the most liberal slaveholder— Woodson. *Norfolk Journal and Guide*, p. 19.

———. (1936c, March 12). My opinion is . . . *Philadelphia Tribune*, p. 5A.

———. (1936d, June 22). Resume "encyclopedia" tiff: Dr. Carter G. Woodson says Brawley guilty of misquotation. *Atlanta Daily World*, p. 1.

———. (1937a, January 21). Letter to Luther P. Jackson. Luther Porter Jackson Papers, 1772–1960, Accession #1952-l (35:975). Special Collections and Archives, Johnston Memorial Library, Virginia State University, Petersburg.

———. (1937b, January). [Review of the book *Horace Greeley and the Tribune in the Civil War* by Ralph Ray Fahrney]. *Journal of Negro History* 22(1): 109–17. Retrieved from http://www.jstor.org/stable/2714325.

———. (1938a, January 8). A few pointers on the observance of History Week given by Woodson: Urges reading newspapers and other publications of race; buy Negro volumes. *Norfolk Journal and Guide*, p. 9.

———. (1938b, January 15). The Negro . . . 1865 to 1937; what has race accomplished?: Negro History Week, to be celebrated. *Pittsburgh Courier*, p. 14.

———. (1938c, February 19). Badly needed: Talented authors to write biographies of race. *Norfolk Journal and Guide*, p. 9.

———. (1939a, February 18). Sets fine example. *Chicago Defender*, p. 16.

———. (1939b, November 4). Woodson praised book *The Negro in Sports*. *Norfolk Journal and Guide*, p. 18.

———. (1940a, January). Notes. *Journal of Negro History* 25(1): 126–38. Retrieved from http://www.jstor.org/stable/2714413.

———. (1940b, January 27). Carter G. Woodson flays white publishers. *Pittsburgh Courier*, p. 12.

———. (1940c, February). The heritage of the Negro. *Negro History Bulletin* 3(5): 78–79.

———. (1940d, August 31). Could Negro survive in a world in upheaval and ruled by dictators. *Norfolk Journal and Guide*, p. 9.

———. (1941a, July 26). A new voice for Africa. *Norfolk Journal and Guide*, p. 8.

———. (1941b, October). Annual report of the director. *Journal of Negro History* 26(4): 413–20. Retrieved from http://www.jstor.org/stable/2715005.

———. (1941c, October 11). Negro history to be main topic at historians' meeting. *Norfolk Journal and Guide*, p. 20.

———. (1941d, October 25). Questions vital to race face discussion at historians meeting. *Norfolk Journal and Guide*, p. 20.

———. (1942, January 2). Letter to Luther P. Jackson. Luther Porter Jackson Papers, 1772–1960, Accession #1952-l (35:984). Special Collections and Archives, Johnston Memorial Library, Virginia State University, Petersburg.

———. (1942, January 3). Letter to Luther P. Jackson. Luther Porter Jackson Papers, 1772–1960, Accession #1952-l (35:984). Special Collections and Archives, Johnston Memorial Library, Virginia State University, Petersburg.

———. (1942, October 8). Letter to Luther P. Jackson. Luther Porter Jackson Papers, 1772–1960, Accession #1952-l (35:987). Special Collections and Archives, Johnston Memorial Library, Virginia State University, Petersburg.

———. (1942, November 2). Letter to Luther P. Jackson. Luther Porter Jackson Papers, 1772–1960, Accession #1952-l (35:987). Special Collections and Archives, Johnston Memorial Library, Virginia State University, Petersburg.

———. (1942a, January 17). Interest grows in Negro History Week observance. *Norfolk Journal and Guide*, p. 8.

———. (1942b, October). Annual report of the director. *Journal of Negro History* 27(4): 371–79. Retrieved from http://www.jstor.org/stable/2715182.

———. (1943a, January 2). Letter to Luther P. Jackson. Luther Porter Jackson Papers, 1772–1960, Accession #1952-l (35:988). Special Collections and Archives, Johnston Memorial Library, Virginia State University, Petersburg.

———. (1943b, May 15). Letter to Luther P. Jackson. Luther Porter Jackson Papers, 1772–1960, Accession #1952-l (35:988). Special Collections and Archives, Johnston Memorial Library, Virginia State University, Petersburg.

———. (1944a, February). My recollections of veterans of the Civil War. *Negro History Bulletin* 7(5): 103–4, 115–18.

———. (1944, May 23). Letter to Luther P. Jackson. Luther Porter Jackson Papers, 1772–1960, Accession #1952-l (35:990). Special Collections and Archives, Johnston Memorial Library, Virginia State University, Petersburg.

———. (1944b, July). Annual report of the director. *Journal of Negro History* 29(3): 251–59. Retrieved from http://www.jstor.org/stable/2714818.

———. (1944, July 13). Letter to Luther P. Jackson. Luther Porter Jackson Papers, 1772–1960, Accession #1952-l (35:990). Special Collections and Archives, Johnston Memorial Library, Virginia State University, Petersburg.

———. (1944, October 17). Letter to Luther P. Jackson. Luther Porter Jackson Papers, 1772–1960, Accession #1952-l (35:991). Special Collections and Archives, Johnston Memorial Library, Virginia State University, Petersburg.

———. (1944, October 23). Letter to Luther P. Jackson. Luther Porter Jackson Papers, 1772–1960, Accession #1952-l (35:991). Special Collections and Archives, Johnston Memorial Library, Virginia State University, Petersburg.

———. (1945a, July). Annual report of the director. *Journal of Negro History* 30(3): 251–59. Retrieved from http://www.jstor.org/stable/2715110.

———. (1945b, July 21). Letter to Luther P. Jackson. Luther Porter Jackson Papers, 1772–1960, Accession #1952-l (35:992). Special Collections and Archives, Johnston Memorial Library, Virginia State University, Petersburg.

———. Annual report. (1946). Association for the Study of Negro Life and History. (Reel 3). Carter Godwin Woodson Papers, Manuscript Division, Library of Congress, Washington, DC.

———. (1946a, January 5). Isolating medievalism. *Cleveland Call and Post*, p. 8B.

———. (1946b, February 23). Letter to Luther P. Jackson. Luther Porter Jackson Papers, 1772–1960, Accession #1952-l (35:994). Special Collections and Archives, Johnston Memorial Library, Virginia State University, Petersburg.

———. (1946c, April 6). The deplorable state of the nation. *Cleveland Call and Post*, p. 4.

———. (1946d, May 11). Politics corrupted by selfishness. *Cleveland Call and Post*, p. 4B.

———. (1946e, November 23). Dangers of political leadership. *Cleveland Call and Post*, p. 4B.

———. (1947, October). Annual report of the director. *Journal of Negro History* 32(4): 407–16. Retrieved from http://www.jstor.org/stable/2714924.

———. (1947, October 4). Letter to Luther P. Jackson. Luther Porter Jackson Papers, 1772–1960, Accession #1952-l (35:998). Special Collections and Archives, Johnston Memorial Library, Virginia State University, Petersburg.

———. (1947a, February 15). The unfinished task. *Cleveland Call and Post*, p. 4.

———. (1947b, March 8). Liberia needs help. *Cleveland Call and Post*, p. 4B.

———. (1948, October). Annual report of the director. *Journal of Negro History* 33(4): 387–94. Retrieved from http://www.jstor.org/stable/2715917.

———. (1948a, January 10). The whole truth and nothing but the truth. *Philadelphia Tribune*, p. 14.

———. (1948b, October 25). Letter to Luther P. Jackson. Luther Porter Jackson Papers, 1772–1960, Accession #1952-l (35:1000). Special Collections and Archives, Johnston Memorial Library, Virginia State University, Petersburg.

———. (1949a, January 7). Nation prepares for Negro History Week. *Atlanta Daily World*, p. 3.

———. (1949b, October). Annual report. *Journal of Negro History* 34(4): 383–390. Retrieved from http://www.jstor.org/stable/2715606.

———. (1950a, January). Oswald Garrison Villard. *Journal of Negro History* 35(1): 105–6. Retrieved from http://www.jstor.org/stable/2715571.

———. (1950b, January). Thomas Jesse Jones. *Journal of Negro History* 35(1): 107–9. Retrieved from http://www.jstor.org/stable/2715572.

———. (1950c, April 1). Letter to Luther P. Jackson. Luther Porter Jackson Papers, 1772–1960, Accession #1952-l (35:1003). Special Collections and Archives, Johnston Memorial Library, Virginia State University, Petersburg.

———. (1969). *The Negro Professional Man and the Community: With Special Emphasis on the Physician and the Lawyer*. New York: Negro Universities Press.

———. (2008). *Carter G. Woodson's Appeal: The Lost Manuscript Edition*. Ed. D. Scott,. Washington, DC.: ASALH Press.

———. (n.d.). Too much "hindsight," insufficient foresight. *New York Amsterdam News*, p. 8.

Woodson, Duncan to appear on "My People." (1943, February 20). *Atlanta Daily World*, p. 1.

Woodson answers Wright: Church politics are flayed. (1931, December 2). *Atlanta Daily World*. Retrieved from http://ezproxy.marshall.edu:2048/docview/490379993?account id=12281.

Woodson to broadcast this week. (1938, November 12). *Pittsburgh Courier*, p. 24.

Woodson will. (1934, November 30). (Part II, Reel 1). Carter Godwin Woodson Papers, Manuscript Division, Library of Congress, Washington, DC.

Wright Says Woodson seeks only publicity. (1931, November 14). *Pittsburgh Courier*, p. A10.

Yancey, B. (1950, June 20). Letter to Louis R. Mehlinger. (Reel 1). Carter Godwin Woodson Papers, Manuscript Division, Library of Congress, Washington, DC.

Year is out; he's still alive at 53. (1928, December 15). *Afro-American*, p. 2.

Yeuell, G. (1928, October). The Negro press as a factor in education. *Journal of Educational Psychology* 2(2): 92–98. Retrieved from DOI: 10.2307/2961865.

Young, T. (1949, May 14). Letter to C. A. Scott. Memo to member publishers, Negro Newspaper Publishers Association, transcript of Newspaper Week broadcast, over NBC network February 26, 1949, "what is the role of the Negro press in our democracy," *Atlanta Daily World* Records, Manuscript, Archives, and Rare Book Library, Emory University, Atlanta.

INDEX

Page numbers in *italics* refer to tables.

CPSIA information can be obtained
at www.ICGtesting.com
Printed in the USA
BVHW03*1339060418
512604BV00003B/57/P